DESIGNING BETTER SCHOOLS FOR CULTURALLY AND LINGUISTICALLY DIVERSE CHILDREN

A Science of Performance Model for Research

Stuart McNaughton

UNIVERSITY OF AUCKLAND

Routledge
Taylor & Francis Group

NEW YORK AND LONDON

First published 2011
by Routledge
711 Third Avenue, New York, NY 10017

Simultaneously published in the UK
by Routledge
2 Park Square, Milton Park, Abingdon, Oxon OX14 4RN

Routledge is an imprint of the Taylor & Francis Group, an informa business

© 2011 Taylor & Francis

The right of Stuart McNaughton to be identified as author of this work
has been asserted by him/her in accordance with sections 77 and 78 of
the Copyright, Designs and Patents Act 1988.

Typeset in Bembo and Stone Sans by
Florence Production Ltd, Stoodleigh, Devon
Printed and bound in the United States of America on acid-free paper by
Walsworth Publishing Company, Marceline, MO

Library of Congress Cataloging in Publication Data
McNaughton, S. (Stuart)
   Designing better schools for culturally and linguistically diverse children:
   a science of performance model for research/by Stuart McNaughton.
      p. cm.
   Includes bibliographical references.
   1. Children of minorities – Education – New Zealand. 2. School
improvement programs – New Zealand. 3. Education – Research.
I. Title.
LC3739.6.M36 2011
371.82900993 – dc22   2010033054

ISBN 13: 978–0–415–88659–8 (hbk)
ISBN 13: 978–0–415–88660–4 (pbk)
ISBN 13: 978–0–203–83582–1 (ebk)

DESIGNING BETTER SCHOOLS FOR CULTURALLY AND LINGUISTICALLY DIVERSE CHILDREN

How can schools be better designed to enable equitable academic outcomes for culturally and linguistically diverse children from communities lacking in economic, political, and social power? McNaughton puts forward a robust 'science of performance' model of school change based on a specified process of research and development in local contexts. Built on assumptions about both teachers (problem solvers and adaptive experts) and teaching, as well as about research, *Designing Better Schools for Culturally and Linguistically Diverse Children*:

- lays out the traditions of optimism and pessimism about effective schooling for students currently at risk in our schools
- reviews the international and national evidence for the effectiveness of schools and school systems in reducing disparities in achievement
- describes the challenges educational research must address to solve the problem of school effectiveness, proposes strict criteria against which effectiveness should be judged, and examines in detail examples where change has been demonstrated
- proposes how researchers, professionals, and policy makers can develop more effective systems.

Bringing together structural and psychological accounts of the nature of schools, and establishing theoretically defensible criteria for judging effectiveness, this book is a critically important contribution to advancing the science of making schools more effective.

Stuart McNaughton is Professor of Education and Director of the Woolf Fisher Research Centre at The University of Auckland.

Dedication

To our grandchildren Nathan, Anahera, Joshua and Kahukura, and their educational futures.

CONTENTS

FIGURES

PREFACE

The question I address in this book is what a science of learning development and teaching needs to do to be more effective in meeting the challenges of designing better schools for culturally and linguistically diverse children.

The book is structured around several themes. Chapters 1–3 provide the initial case for a relatively pessimistic outlook for better designs by presenting the general evidence that schools and school systems appear to make little difference. Chapter 1, "Ongoing optimism, persistent pessimism and their roots," introduces a critical question facing many Western schooling systems: Just how much difference can schools make to the educational achievement of those culturally and linguistically diverse children and their communities who are not economically, socially and politically advantaged in their societies? The roots of relative optimism and pessimism in answers to this question are reviewed. The arguments for a cautious optimism as well as being carefully critical about being able to make substantial differences are outlined. The need to develop a 'science of performance' from which the design of more effective schools can follow is proposed.

Chapter 2, "Weighing up the evidence," introduces the evidence. The evidence, especially in the area of literacy achievement at the level of countries, regions, districts and schools is that strong and enduring associations between achievement and one's background and identity exist. The associations continue to be present even when change over time is examined.

Chapter 3, "Explaining our limitations," outlines six explanations for why we are relatively powerless to equalize the outcomes for children from different groups. (1) schools by default select for and promote certain types of knowledge and practices; (2) schools actively select certain types of knowledge and practices;

(3) schools are differentially resourced thereby limiting their effectiveness; (4) outside of school conditions and limited educational coverage reduce impact; (5) there are yet more discoveries to be made; and (5) a comprehensive 'nested' model of processes is needed.

However, a counter to the generally gloomy picture is provided in Chapter 4, "Optimism in the detail." The variability in achievement outcomes for target groups within the associations and the general experimental evidence for schools making a difference is examined. Variability is examined between countries, within countries, between and within schools; and within groups. Variability as a result of system changes and systematic interventions is also examined. The extent of change possible, given unchanged social and cultural conditions especially in features of relative poverty and the stratification of economic and political power, may be limited. But the evidence is that achievement gaps are not immutable and schools can have a significant role in producing more equitable outcomes.

Given a degree of optimism is indicated, what are the barriers to a more effective science? Chapters 5–9 lay out the substantial problems thrown up by the evidence about trying to change schools. Chapter 5, "Problems for an optimist – Matthew Effects," is about the first of several problems that need to be solved, the pervasive educational phenomenon of 'rich getting richer' effects (where having resources generates further resources and the lack thereof make one susceptible to further limitations). The general explanation is that the more you know or can do that is relevant to an activity or domain, the more sense you can make out of new experiences in that activity or the more accessible new experiences within that domain become. The evidence for how to mitigate the effects shows that effective school changes have to be targeted, developmentally progressive, and early.

Chapter 6, "What is being effective? Accelerating and distributing achievement," introduces several concepts that are partly statistical, and partly to do with defining educational significance. These provide criteria against which interventions to change schools should be judged. They add further challenges if effective changes are to be made. The concepts are *acceleration, matched distributions of achievement*, and *shifting distributions*. The evidence is not strong that these ideal conditions are achieveable currently.

Chapter 7, "Summer Learning," looks at the third of the problems for an optimistic view of schools' effectiveness. It is the case that some children are learning what counts at school over summer and some are not. The explanation for the summer learning effect is related to family social and cultural practices and their access to resources. The case of vocabulary learning is used to illustrate the processes at work. Evidence although limited is presented for two possible solutions: schools working more deliberately with their children and communities to build access to and use of practices over summer; and extending schools themselves, or school like experiences.

Even if these barriers are overcome by research getting the model demonstration of effective change in place is just a first step. Sustaining that change is clearly difficult as shown by the evidence from interventions. In Chapter 8, "Sustaining Change," four meanings of sustainability are described: developmental sustainability, sustaining across changes in cohorts; sustaining school communities; and sustaining these across time. Each of these needs to be addressed if educationally significant changes are to be made. The conditions under which they can be met include conceiving change as a process (and not just the adoption of a new 'programme') and creating partnerships of shared expertise.

Chapter 9 addresses a further problem to be solved: "scaling up" – the planned (and sustained) extension to new sites and new circumstances. Three general approaches to solving are compared – prescriptive programme design with high integrity; exemplary schools such as charter schools; and scaling up a process with high integrity. Each has strengths and limitations especially when judged against the four types of sustainability. Each entails external research partners, although with different roles. The lesson from these approaches is that long-term partnerships are needed for effectiveness. An argument is presented for the overall strength of the third approach.

Chapters 10–12 integrate the preceding ideas, presenting a framework for holding to a more qualified and cautious optimism. Chapter 10, "Understanding the contexts for effective teaching," discusses the accumulating evidence that there are various influences (and levels of influences) that impact on schools being able to make a sustained and generalised impact on enduring disparities. Two models for integrating these contexts and sites to guide the design of better schools are presented. One is a model of nested and coherent systems. A second is a model of teachers as 'adaptive experts.' The features of that adaptive expertise are described.

Chapter 11, "A science of performance: research and development partnerships," proposes a science of performance which is more capable of meeting the challenges described in previous chapters. Several core attributes of this science are outlined: that researchers and educators together recognise and systematise instances of effectiveness; that the shared beliefs about teaching and students focus on the resources, potential and capacities of children; and that there is ingenuity in searching for solutions. The science needs to be based in everyday contexts, it needs to be evidence based; and it needs to be based on effective collaborations.

The proposal for a science of performance is extended in Chapter 12, "Building more effective schools: Notes on a cautious optimism." Designing and scaling up more effective schools for diverse students are long-term commitments. To be fully effective the science requires coherence between what happens within schools and the social, cultural, political and economic contexts within which they function. It requires ongoing collaborations between researchers, practitioners, policy makers and communities. It requires giving teachers the education and resources to be knowledgeable problem solvers and capable of being adaptive and flexible. It requires researchers to rethink the sites in which they work and the rules of their engagement with communities. The book ends with a vignette of one school that exemplifies the basis for my optimism.

ACKNOWLEDGEMENTS

The book owes a great deal to the educators with whom I have worked, the staff in their schools, and the children and families whom their schools serve. The book stresses the need for partnerships to solve educational challenges and it reflects the wealth of knowledge and capability to solve and innovate that exist in our schools.

My thinking in this book reflects collective efforts with a number of colleagues. Many ideas have come from research with colleagues and doctoral students over 12 years at the Woolf Fisher Research Centre. My thanks to Meaola Amituanai-Toloa, Alison Davis, Rebecca Jesson, Mei Kuin Lai, Shelley MacDonald, Thanh-Binh Tran, and Aaron Wilson. Thanks to Colin James for his insightful comments.

My thanks to staff at the Woolf Fisher Research Centre, who have helped in the preparation of this book. They include Jenny Nelson; Sophie Kercher, Selena Hsaio and Angela McNicholl.

The writing of the book has been generously supported by funding made available from the Woolf Fisher Trust. The members of the Trust have through their funding of the Woolf Fisher Research Centre enabled us to conduct research into the crucial question of how to increase the effectiveness of schools, especially those serving communities and their children who have found schools to be 'risky places'. A number of other agencies have provided funding of specific projects through which my ideas have been tested. These include the New Zealand Ministry of Education, Development West Coast, the Teaching and Learning Research Initiative (New Zealand Council for Educational Research).

I appreciate the ongoing support of the University of Auckland for my programme of research.

In previous books I have thanked my family for their love and encouragement. This book is no different from the others. It is also a tribute to the support they constantly give me.

The following Māori proverb (Whakatauki) expresses these acknowledgements and also captures what I want to say in this book about cooperation and sharing of resources:

> *Nā tō rourou, nā taku rourou ka ora ai te iwi.*
>
> With your food basket and my food basket the people will thrive.

1

ONGOING OPTIMISM, PERSISTENT PESSIMISM AND THEIR ROOTS

I am an optimist about educational matters. I realized this by accident. The paper I had given at an Organization for Economic Cooperation and Development conference in New Zealand in 1998 on 'Innovations for Successful Schools' (McNaughton, 1998), followed one that was a critical analysis of schools using concepts from contemporary sociology. Schools were seen to be hegemonic agencies, necessarily reproducing the inequalities we see in society. In my paper I reported experimental demonstrations of how collaborative partnerships between communities and schools can make a difference to the achievement patterns of students from communities traditionally not well served by schools. The rapporteur observed I had much greater optimism about what schools might achieve than some of my sociologist colleagues.

My paper, based on a developmental psychological analysis of teaching and learning, was optimistic about the potential for schools to resist or even modify the predicted stratification. The other paper was more pessimistic. The psychological and the sociological or structural perspectives reflect an enduring tension in applied theories of development and learning and our critical understanding of the role of schooling. We need to understand this tension and clarify the degree of optimism possible, especially so when the disciplinary lines in current research are becoming more blurred. In this book I propose a science of how to understand the effectiveness of schools from which the design of more effective schools can follow. It is a cautiously optimistic approach from a developmental perspective, which specifically recognizes and draws on the insights of critical pessimism.

The tradition of optimism is reflected in how developmentalists in the 1970s saw a natural progression in developmental research. A prescription for developmental psychology was to engage in description, move on to explanation and thence to 'optimization' (Baltes, Reese, & Lipsitt, 1980). This grand vision has some notable success stories. One that has for me a local significance as well as an international history is the noted developmentalist Marie Clay's (1987), design of the Reading Recovery programme for children making low progress after a year at school. The programme is extraordinarily successful. It is a successful intervention programme as attested to by the US Department of Education on its Clearinghouse web site. It really is the "gold standard" against which other early literacy interventions might be compared. A further demonstration of its success is that it has been developed and redeveloped in, at the time of writing this book, educational systems in six countries. It has been adopted, and in the process adapted, in Australia, Barbados, Canada, Denmark, England, the Republic of Ireland, Northern Ireland, the United States and Wales, all of whose local contexts vary in terms of age of entry to school, the types of books used to teach early reading, the qualifications of the teachers and other idiosyncratic aspects of schooling. In 2005, 11,000 New Zealand children were taught the early stages of reading to levels equivalent to peers making normal progress and millions have been so taught worldwide.

As a generic programme of research, the description, explanation and optimization sequence underpinned the development of this highly successful programme. Clay (1987) first studied demonstrably effective teachers to determine the features of their expertise. She next designed and experimentally tested the intervention. She then moved to optimization nationally in New Zealand, working to develop a policy context and an ongoing training regime that would mean the intervention was bedded in across the unique features of both urban and rural schools.

This is a success story. But the move to optimization, in the sense of planned implementation across sites, as Clay (1987) herself learned, is not simple. It is not simple especially in a global context where a balance is required between guaranteeing that the components of the intervention, which are research-based, are put in place with fidelity but flexibily enough to take on board new findings and adapt to local context.

This enthusiasm for optimizing was expressed by theorists early in our traditions. It is captured by John Dewey's (1915) lectures in 1899 to an audience of parents interested in the University of Chicago's own experimental Elementary school.

> Such a school is a laboratory of applied psychology. That is, it has a place for the study of mind as manifested and developed in the child and for the search after materials and agencies that seem most likely to fulfill and further the condition of normal growth.
>
> (Dewey, 1915, p. 88)

A similar enthusiasm was present in England at the same time. William McDougall (1912) writing about child psychology and education, made similar claims to Dewey with a tone that is almost gleeful about the prospects – "Here then is an immense field for research, the extent and importance of which we are now beginning fully to realize. And it is a field for the psychologist" (p. 139).

Despite such examples as Reading Recovery, the initial optimism of developmental psychology has not been widely fulfilled in relationship to substantial educational change and especially for those students and their communities who need educational change the most.

Who are these communities and children? In successive chapters I will refer, where possible, to specific communities, rather than resorting to the often-used labels of 'minority' and 'disadvantaged.' These are too broad and often misleading, inaccurate, or carry connotations that denigrate the cultural and linguistic richness of the communities. The question in this book is the degree of optimism possible about what schools can do for those culturally and linguistically diverse children and their communities who are not economically, socially and politically advantaged in Western developed societies. These are children and their communities in different countries from particular indigenous groups, from particular immigrant groups, from particular working groups, from groups whose historical and current lived experiences have positioned them with less access to and less utilization of the panoply of resources for well-being in their society. Current circumstance may have derived from histories of slavery, subjugation or colonization but may derive also from recent patterns of immigration and asylum seeking. When writing more generically, I will refer to the groups of children for whom schools have traditionally been risky places in which to achieve well.

How optimistic can we be about what schools can change in the relative position these communities and their children have? A spectacular test of the applications of our developmental and educational psychological ideas took place in the United States in the 1960s and 1970s. Across many sites and with many approaches, attempts were made to impact on what was called the 'poverty cycle' in attempts to raise the educational achievement of 'disadvantaged' children.

There have been arguments about the success of these interventions. In essence these attempts were not as successful as they should have been given the promises. 'Head Start' programmes before school had some notable effects but they were limited. 'Follow Through' programmes at school also had some notable successes, but were again limited. Effects on measured intelligence were short lived, and the direct impact on academic achievement was limited (Consortium of Longitudinal Studies, 1983). However, important longer-term benefits have sometimes been detected. In subsequent reevaluations and redevelopment of programmes the scientific community has realized that the optimism needs to be tempered and we need to guard against overselling benefits and to be realistic about what can be accomplished (Zigler, & Styfco, 1994). Importantly, this has led to rethinking basic concepts about development, some of which will be reconsidered in this book (Ramey, & Ramey, 1998).

Developmental and educational psychologists have learned a lot from the Head Start exercise and from other optimization types of research since that time. For example, researchers engaged in the school reform interventions in the US are much more guarded in their optimism than their colleagues in the 1960s and are able to be more precise about what is possible. Their data suggest that trying to change schools so that they are more effective with culturally and linguistically diverse students is not easy (Borman, & Dowling, 2006). Gains are often quite small. It takes a considerable commitment, in current estimates about five years of research and development with a school, to meet criteria for being effective, such as accelerated achievement. I will describe these criteria in later chapters.

But the optimism is still there. There is a new set of strong voices that celebrate the potential of an applied developmental science to solve real world problems. The optimists have more humility, greater caution and are better informed than their predecessors, but they remain optimistic.

Others have commented on the optimism of developmental psychology and in its extreme formulations have called it naive. The theoretical psychologist William Kessen (1979) developed this idea in a brilliant essay in his classic "The American child and other cultural inventions." In that essay he argued that at the birth of modern psychology there were several parents in terms of philosophical traditions. These were buttressed in the United States by three strong themes each positive and inherently optimistic. And each led to a naive view of what is possible.

One was a commitment to science and technology and what they can achieve. There was a belief that we can find the truths, and if only we can provide the right guidance based on these truths to parents and teachers, appropriate development will be assured. Kessen (1979) argues this theme is associated with an underlying 'Salvationist' view, captured in the old adage that the 'child is father to the man.' But, he argued, the truths are often relative, often legitimizing after the fact of changes that have already occurred, often dependent on other economic and political changes and often appropriate to historical times and places. Without understanding these relativities the guidance is at best naive and likely to be of limited lasting value.

A second was a belief in caregivers and caregiving, in the first instance in mothers and the need for early experience with them. Underlying this theme is a fraught assumption that someone is responsible for development, for good or for ill. The naivety here is in placing the blame for developmental problems at some one person's (or group's) door.

The third was a belief in the individual and self-contained children. This implied that the appropriate unit of analysis is the child, and the child and his or her development must be studied in isolation from wider social and cultural forces to discover fundamental principles. It follows too that the individual child should be the focus of our attempts to optimize. Kessen (1979) saw this as conceptually weak because children's development is embedded in contexts and derives from sources of interaction and patterns of constraints and affordances in those contexts. The former view means a limited focus on where to look for optimizing.

The iconic image of the child as the single unit of analysis is captured in the 'Skinner box' for studying behaviour that used rats and pigeons. The box was designed to reduce extraneous factors such as fluctuations in food, temperature, and access to gratification and light; keeping these to a minimum in a controlled environment. The true and basic processes of behaviour and learning then could be studied without contamination. Context was a problem (technically a source of error variance) if it wasn't controlled and the Skinner box did a superb job of reducing the seemingly extraneous variables. In a science that can explain achievement patterns in schools and develop principles for the design of more effective schools, the unit of analysis has to be context enriched. Indeed, a multifaceted context, including those dimensions that are economic and political, need to be central to the analysis.

Like Kessen (1979), the arguments in this book challenge these beliefs. Collectively the earlier beliefs have supported a scientific approach based on a simplistic view of the physical sciences. We attempted to discover abiding laws that are context free, and then have layed blame on parents, families, and communities (or schools) for their children's low achievement at school.

Kessen (1979) contributed to a sea change in thinking that led to the idea that children and families are located in cultural and social systems. Children develop within and are a reflection of social, cultural, physical, economic, and political forces that create contexts for development. Even more threatening to developmental science, his central claim was the idea that not only are children cultural inventions, developmental psychology is itself a cultural invention, and we developmentalists, by contributing rationales or even modifications to the practices of childhood and development, conspire in that invention.

This postmodern psychological view does not fatally undermine the optimism in my view. But it radically tempers how optimistic we can be and provides a basis for integrating psychological approaches to the design of schools with the critical structural analysis. In its new forms the developmental psychology of change has found new names. For example, some developmentalists have proposed establishing an 'applied developmental science' to recapture the optimization of the earlier definition (Lerner, Fisher, & Weinberg, 2000). The science would recognize the grounded and contextualized nature of children's development. With interdisciplinary help and better-designed research strategies we would be able to study how historical and contemporary forces, including social and economic policy contexts, create conditions for development. Having studied these we can contribute to the design of new systems.

This book builds on the idea of an applied developmental science summarizing the approach using the concept of a "science of performance". Atal Gawande (2007) used this term to describe how medical researchers solve real world problems in health to make medical practice more effective. I propose that in addition to having multifaceted models of contexts, we need to understand how development and learning take place, we need to understand also why they vary in the complicated and messy everyday sites of schools, families, and community settings. We need better evidence from the systematic study of effectiveness to design generalizable practices. Our research needs to involve ideas and evidence that are shared between researchers, professionals, community members and policy makers to enable collaboration in the design and implementation of change.

So there is a long history of optimism about how psychology in general, and developmental psychology in particular, might contribute to child rearing and education. The optimism in Western thinking about education can be traced back earlier than the advent of modern psychology. Steven Shapin (1995) in *A social history of truth: Civility and science in seventeenth century England*, describes the founding of the Royal Society in the seventeenth century. The scientists such as Bacon, Boyle, and Newton who established that esteemed society were passionate advocates of discipline-based debate and discussion. Their view was that through scientific conversation, truth seeking, and truth telling, truths could be established. Science could lay the foundation for better education and better societies could be created.

There is an even earlier history leading to this enlightened thinking which can be traced from before the empiricist philosophers and their scientific colleagues back to debates by the Greek philosophers over the nature of permanence and impermanence and the function of education for individual freedom or for political position (Plato, trans. 1984).

This is the optimist part; from where did the more pessimistic view of what schools can achieve come? There are several roots to the view of schools as filtering devices that are iconoclastic and largely impermeable to anyone who is not part of the controlling and powerful communities whose institutions they reflect. One can find the recognition of the significance of social stratification in Plato's (trans. 1974) arguments about the need to create and control strata for a productive and orderly society. Interestingly, in Plato's plan (trans. 1974) educational assessment would play a central part in consigning people to their appropriate strata. This becomes in Hobbes' (1651/1962) view the problem of man's brutish nature and the need to manage that by solving the problem of a good order. Through Hegel (as cited in Popper, 1952) and his view of the war of nations comes the war of classes, that there is an inevitability about needing to keep order using institutions that control.

Modern writers do not necessarily share the early views of the need to control but there is a basic recognition that that is what schools do. The eminent language and educational theorist Basil Bernstein (2003) wrote about de facto and deliberate stratification through the processes of schooling. The process is inherent in how language signals identity and creates ways of knowing, and classroom teaching filters and selects at least partly on this basis. The French philosopher Bourdieu (1996) uses the powerful concept of 'cultural capital.'

Children's knowledge and skills develop through the socialization processes provided by communities and families. Those skills and that knowledge are of various sorts. Some are reflected in and are recognized by schools because they are valued and promoted in schools. That means they have capital, they can be cashed in at school.

The development of the concept of 'cultural capital' signals another root, one in Marxist theorizing. Perhaps this is also where the clash with psychological views of the promise of schools was fueled. Marx opposed what he denigrated as psychologism captured in the epigram "It is not the consciousness of man that determines his existence – rather it is his social existence that determines his consciousness" (as cited in Popper, 1952, p. 89). Marx's influence on educators' pessimism comes through his ideas about determinism; what Karl Popper (1952) calls 'historicist prophecy' (p. 87). This was the idea that capitalism creates forms of existence that determine forms of consciousness. This is what has led educators in capitalist societies to a more pessimistic view, expressed by Gintis and Bowles (1988) thus:

> The transformation of schools cannot proceed without parallel development at the site of capitalist production. Demands for the democritisation of the social relations of education therefore are likely to be effective only in the context of workers demands for the democratisation of the production process – in short the full development of workers' control.
>
> (Gintis, & Bowles, 1988, p. 30)

But, curiously, the Marxist root is both pessimistic and optimistic at the same time and only partly deterministic. The original position claims that social existence determines consciousness. But it also proposes that it is possible for workers' consciousness to change, which could enable the structural changes. Marx's view includes the promise that collectively individuals can act effectively to overcome structures. This resonates for educators with an emancipatory concern, a concern for equity. From where does the change in individual consciousness come; could schools have a role in changing consciousness? This is another way of expressing the tension – in what direction is change possible? Can one change schools to change structures? Or is it necessary to change structures so that schools can change and in doing so create new forms of cultural capital?

As a footnote to this history, Marx's critique of psychology would now be wide of the mark as more recent psychological views of the nature of learning and development have been profoundly influenced by Russian psychological theorizing, seeing both individual and social and cultural processes as mutually constructive. The proposals in this book are based on this later history of socio-cultural or co-constructivist theorizing about development, learning and teaching that have drawn on the Russian traditions (McNaughton, 1995; Rogoff, 2003; Valsiner, 1994).

Tracing the development of competing ideas and the roots of the tension around being relatively optimistic or pessimistic is an interesting historical exercise. More detailed analysis than can be provided here is needed to elaborate the complexities. For example, the brief references above are all to 'Western' ideas and their roots. Robert Watson (1960), who researched the history of psychology, pointedly noted almost 50 years ago a provincialism in the accounts of psychology. Islamic scholars who were intellectual leaders in the late medieval period and who were influential in forming the views and basic assumptions of psychological science were excluded from histories of psychology. It would be an important exercise to examine the roots of optimism and pessimism about individuals, societies and the role of educational institutions through writings from these other traditions.

This book aims to develop a reasonable view of how optimistic we can be about what schools can achieve. Why? Because it is imperative that we integrate these ideas so that we can create more equitable and just societies. The society in which I live and work is committed through its education system to provide educational outcomes that are not limited by ethnicity, by social identity or cultural identity. Yet we are not as effective as we should be given this ideal. Our educational limitations in effectiveness, particularly for Māori children (from the indigenous community) and Pasifika children (from new and well-established communities from the Pacific Islands) and those in communities who have limited economic and political resources occur across curriculum areas and throughout the educational system.

There is a bleaker view that suggests that extra targeted resourcing for schools, and expending a lot of research energy on looking for better instruction, is wasted. This more cynical view is that such work helps prop up the inequalities either by designing trivial differences or by obfuscation of these problems. This view suggests that more equitable schooling for the communities with little economic and political power can only follow structural change.

But if some optimism is justified, then with humility and caution more research and development work with schools and school systems is warranted. If schools, or more accurately those who work within them, do have some agency to make a difference, then there is an ethical imperative to design more effective schools. The risk with focusing only on the structurally based inequalities and being relatively pessimistic about educational change is that we contribute to exacerbating existing inequalities through inaction.

The traditions behind optimism and pessimism are both right. They are both right because, on the one hand, there is evidence to show that teachers and schools can make a difference, which I will describe in the following chapters. However, on the other hand, schools are by default systemically structured to select some sorts of students over others; the evidence again which I will lay out in the chapters is that schooling outcomes stubbornly and comprehensively reflect ethnic identities and income levels. The discipline base of each position may have gotten in the way of a more informed view of the nature of schools, teachers, and learning but these are not mutually exclusive views. In the following chapters I take the view that psychological approaches to understanding development and learning in schools should be both cautiously optimistic and carefully critical about changing schools.

It turns out to be hard to be an optimist. The reasons for this are at once simple and complicated. The simple answer is that in any endeavor if you want to change something rather than just describe the present condition, you have chosen the harder path of going beyond description and explanation. But the more complex reason is that once you start trying to change something that has individual, social, cultural, and structural properties, and is located in settings that compromise experimental control, you find out how difficult the proposition really is. This book outlines what the science of learning development and teaching, a science of performance to design better schools, needs to do to be effective in the face of these challenges.

2

WEIGHING UP THE EVIDENCE

In this chapter the evidence is introduced for being relatively pessimistic or optimistic about what schools can achieve. We have two views of the same phenomena. Or are the phenomena the same? On the one hand a constellation of theoretical, empirical, political and ideological thinking convincingly suggests that class and culturally and socially based 'capital' determines success at school. The rich and powerful will always be rich and powerful because schools are instrumental in the stratification of society. Either intentionally or unwittingly, the dominant group wishes and acts to maintain its position. On the other hand an equally powerful constellation of thinking and researching argues that schooling can reduce inequalities in that very capital. Schools can create mobility, make social stratification more febrile, enable children to move out of 'poverty traps,' and in the extreme cases education and literacy can be emancipatory.

They can't both be right about the phenomena of concern to us in this book; the groups of children for whom high levels of literacy achievement in schools traditionally has been risky. An initial way out of the conundrum is to confront the usual suspects; perhaps the differences arise because the evidence is suspect on one side or the other. Perhaps there are weaknesses in the tools or the interpretation of the information generated by those tools. So, what is the nature of the evidence for and against optimism and pessimism? I will return throughout this book to this question of the forms of evidence and their interpretation, but this chapter outlines the general form of the evidence and the issues around interpretation. The chapter also begins to map out the rapprochement at the level of thinking about the evidence.

The evidence

The evidence for children's backgrounds determining their success in literacy achievement at school is easy to find. And it is stark. A common way of generating the evidence is to establish that literacy achievement at school is associated with a child's background. There are enduring and pervasive differences at whatever level one cares to look. The differences can be found at a national level across countries in the association of social, economic, and ethnic identity with achievement. The associations are found within countries at the level of regions and school districts. So pervasive and embedded are these differences that they can even be found within schools.

The association at the level of countries is well known. The programme of international research conducted by the International Association for Evaluation of Educational Achievement, reported in their Progress in International Reading Literacy Studies (PIRLS), was designed to examine 9 and 10 year olds' achievement in reading comprehension across countries. It uses multicomponent measures of comprehension processes in both narrative reading and reading information. It also probes characteristics of families and schools and their associations with achievement at school. The most recent PIRLS study (Mullis, Martin, Kennedy, & Foy, 2007) involved over 200,000 children in 40 countries. In every country the usual indices of status and position such as parental education level and employment status were strongly associated with achievement. Students with at least one parent with university education scored 120 points higher on the scale of reading achievement (which has an average of 500) than students from families whose parents did not complete lower secondary school. This is a difference of more than the average difference between all the achievement scores and the mean for the scores (the so-called standard deviation). The same appears with occupational status, to be expected because it is closely related to educational level. Children from homes where both parents work for pay scored 124 points higher than children from families where neither parent was working outside the home.

National databases such as the National Assessment of Educational Progress (NAEP) in the United States can be used to illustrate differences within countries (Vanneman, Hamilton, Baldwin Anderson, & Rahman, 2009). In 2002 the average Black or Hispanic 12th Grader was reading at the level of the average White 8th Grader. In 2005 White 4th Graders were on average about three grades higher in reading than Black or Latino students, the gap roughly standing at 0.7 of a standard deviation in reading.

There has been a view that if the children who are at risk in schools could be in schools that serve children who were not at risk then the differences would be ameliorated. That isn't the case either, although it depends on how one measures the difference. If overall differences between these students and the general population averages are of concern then being at schools serving high socio economic status (SES) communities can make a difference. Linda Darling-Hammond (2007) describes a study of two groups of African American high school students. The two groups were from families with similar low income levels, and at least initially had similar achievement levels. One group whose families were randomly placed in public housing in Chicago suburbs attended better-funded largely White suburban schools while the other group remained in city schools. The group attending largely White schools had better educational outcomes than their city-based peers; seen in opportunities to take more challenging courses, receiving additional help, graduating on time, attending college, and securing good jobs.

But if the differences are measured in terms of continuing gaps between students from different communities within that school then the differences are likely to remain. That is, better-resourced schools are associated with higher achievement for all students, higher than students in less well-resourced schools, but in relative terms the gaps remain.

In a recent development of a new reading comprehension assessment for New Zealand students the achievement levels for a nationally representative sample were analysed by school type. In New Zealand, schools are categorized into deciles. The decile category reflects socioeconomic and ethnic identity of the surrounding communities. 'Decile 1' schools are schools serving the communities with the lowest income and employment levels and have the highest numbers of Māori (from indigenous communities) and Pasifika children (from Pacific Island families). High decile schools have few students from these communities and serve relatively wealthy families in terms of income and employment levels. Students have largely been Anglo European New Zealanders (Pakeha) although this demography is changing for some decile 10 schools with new immigrant groups particularly from China, Hong Kong, South Korea and Taiwan, and other Asian countries. The decile category is used for targeted funding purposes, which means that low decile schools get access to funds from central government for the language and other needs of their students.

The development team found that while the overall scores on the reading comprehension assessment rose by decile level, a common finding, the gap between 'Pakeha' on the one hand and Māori and Pasifika children on the other remained across decile levels. This is shown in Figure 2.1. So the Māori and Pasifika children were scoring higher, the higher the decile level of the school, but so were the other children. In a decile 10 school, the wealthiest and the traditionally most Anglo European school, Māori and Pasifika children were scoring higher than Anglo European children in the decile 1 schools. But the gap remained between them and was still of the same order.

The development of inequality

The presence of enduring and pervasive gaps across and within countries and between and inside schools suggests these are fixed and immutable differences. But this initial approach to the question of whether schools make a difference is quite limited. First, it is a static picture of an association. There might be cause

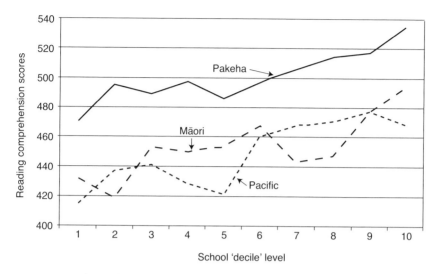

FIGURE 2.1 Relationships between reading comprehension achievement and the decile rating of schools for Māori, Pacific Island and Pakeha (Anglo European) students in Years 4–8.

Source: Hattie (2003).

for some optimism in trends over time, perhaps things have been getting better over time. Second, it doesn't tell us much about mechanisms. Looking at the picture over time might also begin to tell us about possible mechanisms of change if there were patterns in the trends.

The picture over time: 1

However, this static picture appears to be supported by evidence from countries that have been tracking these differences for some time. Take the situation in the United States (Darling-Hammond, 2007). National databases such as the NAEP, which has been available since the early 1970s, have enabled long term monitoring of achievement scores. On national assessments of reading and writing Black students' performance is consistently below that of White students, although there have been shifts. In reading there were large gains in Black students' scores during the 1970s and 1980s. But in the 1990s these gains were reversed and the gaps actually got larger. As noted earlier, in 2002 the average Black or Hispanic 12th Grader was reading at the level of the average White 8th Grader and since 2002 there has been no change in the gap either way. Scores in writing have declined since 1988.

This gap exists despite numerous initiatives. The picture from 2002 reflects a period of unprecedented federal spending and policy changes through the No Child Left Behind legislation. The Act was designed to raise achievement and in so doing close the achievement gaps because all children irrespective of racial/ethnic and poverty stratus should be 100 per cent proficient as defined by their states by 2014. The $13.3 billion spent in 2006 accounted for about 8 per cent of the total funding for K–12 education and mandates are in place for higher levels for teacher qualifications and accountability for schools, with requirements for schools to be changed if they do not meet adequate yearly progress indices. Despite all this the general consensus is that there is very little evidence three to four years into the programme that gaps have reduced (Porter, & Polikoff, 2007).

The picture over time: 2

The association between background and achievement seems impervious even to country-wide efforts deploying huge resources over time. But maybe the picture just painted is like the old problem with cross sectional studies of IQ, which suggested we lost intelligence as we got older. This turned out to be a reflection of the process of selecting cohorts, which in cross sectional studies are from different historical periods. In 2008 a 10 year old selected in a cross sectional study will have spent early childhood and early primary years in a society with tools and resources different even from the 25 year old of 2008 who was five years old in 1988 and was growing up in the early 1980s. The Flynn effect (Flynn, 2007) tells us that IQ levels have been rising over time so the cross section at one time may not be a good picture of what actually happened as children became young people and then adults. The cohorts in the NAEP data might mask how children from different groups achieve as they actually got older. But even so, if the Flynn effect applied equally to academic achievement by different groups then even with the effect in place we wouldn't necessarily see a difference in the gap, only parallel lines of increase.

Evidence that sheds light on this is provided by looking at patterns for the same children over time in longitudinal studies. A more complete approach to the association, in a longitudinal form, extends the association between background and achievement into a four step analysis. In a longitudinal analysis we can check whether children from different social and cultural groups arrive at school with different literacy knowledge. We can check whether any differences present at the beginning of school persist through school. We can also check whether differences that weren't present at the beginning appear in school, and finally whether life after school such as employment, income and access to further education is attributable to the earlier differences. With this approach the pervasiveness or otherwise of the developmental patterns of differences can be established and we can begin to understand the role of the school in changing or not changing those patterns.

The first two steps, examining the degree to which differences in literacy knowledge before school are associated with background and then the degree to which these very differences are predictive of literacy achievement at school, are often completed in longitudinal studies. And in general the associations are found.

Irrespective of the system it seems in general children from particular groups start school *scoring lower on standard measures of literacy knowledge* compared with children from *certain other more 'advantaged' groups.*

Although perhaps irritating to the reader, I have used italics in the above statement as a holding device, a signal that more work has to be done. The meaning behind these words and phrases needs to be unpacked, and this will happen in succeeding chapters. It is important to note that these are statements about averages (and not variability), that the differences only apply to some groups, and even then the definition of a community whose children find schools risky places or of a relatively 'advantaged' group needs to be considered carefully. It is also worth noting that the differences are differences only in relationship to particular sorts of definitions, tests, or practices of literacy.

With these provisos in mind, what do we know about the differences before school and the differences at school? To answer this accurately so that meaningful judgements can be made about the differences we might find, we need a model of literacy development from which to work. The most elegant and parsimonious model is one provided by the developmentalist Scott Paris (2005). He describes a set of 'constrained' knowledge and skills and a set of 'unconstrained' knowledge and skills developing over time. They come from different aspects of literacy experiences, they have different gradients of learning (children learn the constrained set fast and generally become competent before learning the unconstrained set) and learning the unconstrained set is dependent on but not caused by the constrained set.

Constrained skills include areas of knowledge of the sound system and its related written symbol system. In English this means ideas about and awareness of how words are composed of sounds (phonemes) and that they can be represented with discrete written symbols and that the relationships between them are both regular and irregular; they are not perfect. The constrained set also includes the concepts or basic rules that children need to operate by in order to read and write, such as starting from left to right or that the print (rather than the illustration) contains the message. All of these are constrained because the knowledge needed is discrete. It has boundaries because there are just so many concepts to acquire, just so many sounds and letters to know about. And the developmental patterns show these are acquired rapidly at school and the ceilings are hit very early on.

The unconstrained set of knowledge and skills are those that are not the items of knowledge. They are a more open ended language-based set. They include knowledge of words, the knowledge of syntax and language patterns in written form, and the strategies associated with comprehending. The set also includes the knowledge needed to understand the types and the content of texts used at school, such as narrative and expository texts, and their rules of operating, and overarching these areas the awareness of how to read and write effectively for different purposes. These are unconstrained skills because unlike the constrained set they are unbounded. Their development is more gradual and greater differences in progress can be expected. We do not all become professional writers or avid readers of historical novels.

Given these twin sets of skills, what exactly are the differences in literacy between children from different communities on entry to school and how are they related to progress and achievement at school? As far as the constrained set is concerned there is large variability in these components before school. In New Zealand the average difference (standard deviation) between children in letter knowledge is of the order of 15 letters (when the test is both upper and lower case forms). It is similar in the US. On average, these differences are reliably associated with social class and membership, in particular cultural groups. For example, Susan Neuman (2006) recently summarized some of these differences in studies from the US. The studies show 85 per cent of the highest SES children beginning kindergarten can recognize letters of the alphabet compared with 39 per cent of lowest SES children; 51 per cent of the former can identify beginning sounds of words while only 10 per cent of the latter can; 76 per cent of the high SES children can write their name compared with 54 per cent of the lowest SES children.

These constrained areas of knowledge and skills in English, such as phonemic awareness, knowledge of alphabetic symbols and rules and concepts about print, are strong predictors of continued development at school across many countries in which the language of instruction is English. Predicting progress in its simplest form is done by estimating the correlation with progress, say one or more years into school. A correlation is a measure of the degree to which two scores vary together; for example, the number of letters known at school entry on the one hand and the level of progress on some test after a year on the other hand. The closer to 1.0 the value, the greater the positive association. The number of letters one knows correlates substantially with progress after a year of the order of $r = 0.5$ or more, in the United States (Snow, Burns, & Griffith, 1998) and in New Zealand (Clay, 2001). In one classic study the probability of a low progress reader on these sorts of measures at the end of Grade 1 being a low progress reader in Grade 4 was 0.88. That is, in close to 9 out of 10 cases the prediction from after the first year of still being a low progress reader would be right (Juel, Griffiths, & Gough, 1986).

So levels of constrained skills on entry to school remain predictive of achievement in literacy some years into school. But it turns out that in later years this is largely because of associations with the unconstrained set of skills. And the latter set is the important one for further progress. Another way to put this is that one has to learn to decode (to get words off the page using sound and letter knowledge) and this is necessary to be able to comprehend, but it is not sufficient. Learning to read and write in the early stages means being in a better position to become a competent comprehender. The relationships between say alphabetic knowledge and success in the 4th Grade in reading comprehension tasks are mediated by becoming better at the unconstrained skills. Knowing more initially is related to being in a position to learn more of the unconstrained skills.

When all these relationships are sorted out, the unconstrained set, what Whitehurst and Lonigan (2001) call a second strand of development to do with language meanings and use becomes more highly predictive of further development and progress at school. For example, size of vocabulary in the first year at school measured as receptive vocabulary is highly predictive of reading comprehension in succeeding grades even after an impressive 10 years at school (in one study a correlation of 0.55, Biemiller, 2006). Similar relationships with high progress in reading comprehension can be found over long time frames with complexity of a child's language before school measured in terms of being able to use and understand language that is less reliant on familiar context, that contains more complex grammatical structures and that is more like written language (Dickinson, & Tabors, 2001). This is because what is needed for reading comprehension and for writing effectively for school tasks become even more heavily dependent on language-related knowledge and skills as children move through the grades.

Are the differences that are present at the beginning at school and that are associated with family background and identity changed at school, and what do the trajectories look like after school? The second two steps of a longitudinal analysis are examined further in detail in later chapters by asking the hard question of whether one can change schools extensively enough to overcome the insidious effects of poverty and discrimination. In sum, we often find the trajectories typically follow the initial differences. They are at best parallel trajectories when considered in average terms and in terms of months at school; at worst, the trajectories can often diverge further (Alexander, Etwistle, & Olson, 2007).

The differences in achievement upon exiting from schools in terms of graduation levels and access to further education also affect access to types of employment and economic, social, and political resources. The longitudinal studies also suggest long term effects of lower progress at school. Educational studies in the OECD countries estimate (OECD, 2006) that students who obtain higher qualifications at school tend to have more options for tertiary education and future employment. Those who leave school early have a greater risk of unemployment or low incomes. For countries in the OECD, half of GDP per capita growth from 1994 to 2004 is attributable to rising labour productivity and application of knowledge and skills are at the heart of economic growth. The estimated long term effect on economic output of one additional year of education is generally between 3 and 6 per cent. Analyses of human capital based on literacy scores show significant positive effects on growth. Private return to individuals (calculated by comparing future earnings prospects to the private cost of studying) show a return rate above 8 per cent (and as high as 22.6 per cent) for tertiary education in all OECD countries and generally higher return rates at the upper secondary level.

More specific analyses from the United States and the United Kingdom estimate that increases in achievement test scores in the early years in reading of one standard deviation (an increase of 34 per cent from the average score in a normal distribution) might be associated with higher lifetime earnings of between 8 to 20 per cent (Ludwig, & Phillips, 2007).

Looking for mechanisms

These time-based analyses tell us that over time, at least in some countries, in some regions and in some schools, the association between background and school achievement remains strong. Beginning differences in the two sets of literacy skills mean that students' developmental trajectories appear to be largely fixed. The predictability associated with the continuing differences suggests that schools haven't worked out how to make a difference, or that they can't (and shouldn't be expected to) and we shouldn't be optimistic. To add to the gloom there is the evidence that the gaps can get larger, especially in aspects of the unconstrained set of skills, over the course of schooling.

The associations with background are just that, associations. While powerfully challenging, they are problematic. If we left the analysis there we would be guilty of what the developmentalist Urie Bronfenbrenner (1979) criticized as a letterbox approach to understanding psychological phenomenon. We need to know much more than this, to get behind the social addresses of schools and families, to fully appreciate the power of the argument that schools can't make a difference. We need to know the school's role in this process and understand the mechanisms both within schools and outside of schools. We need to know just how much of a difference we could expect schools to make, under what sorts of conditions.

To do this we need good theoretical accounts and robust evidence. While the details of the explanations are contained in succeeding chapters, the question of what counts as robust evidence requires a statistical diversion at this point. Much of the evidence just presented showing the associations between background and achievement, is in the form of correlations. The wealth of evidence paints a compelling picture and the pervasiveness of the phenomena is striking. But correlations can be misleading, or at least in simple form may hide fuller explanations. The maxim that correlations don't prove cause bears repeating.

Imagine we surveyed foot size and progress in reading in a large sample of schools across ages, say across the primary school years. Progress could be measured in terms of the level of text at which a child can read. The scattergram of students when plotted in the two dimensions of foot size and progress in reading would look something like Figure 2.2. That is, in the bottom left hand, small foot size and low reading levels; and at the top right, large feet and higher reading levels. We might assume looking at this relationship that larger feet produce higher reading levels. So we find a means to enlarge foot size and we are able to solve literacy problems at school. We might conclude the reverse. If we want to produce more elite swimmers we make sure that budding swimmers progress to the highest levels in literacy.

Clearly, both of these conclusions are silly. The obvious point is that both foot size and text levels are related to another phenomenon – time spent at school. And the longer you spend at school the bigger you get, and the further up the text levels (generally speaking) you go. And time at school is in turn related to generally available patterns of teaching related to learning to read.

The correlations with background tell us some things but the use of 'letter boxes' means they are limited in what they can tell us about mechanisms and processes, and hence about the role of schools. What is it about having limited formal education as a parent that might limit school-related literacy levels, what is about poverty that reduces the likelihood of success at school, or what is about being Māori or Black?

Thankfully there are supports for further interpretations of the correlations. The supports come in the form of more sophisticated correlations using better-informed measures of the possible mechanisms. In bigger and better correlations it is possible to explore the contribution of different factors to the observed achievement patterns. In the foot example we could introduce time at school into the equation and look at how the two factors, foot size and time at school,

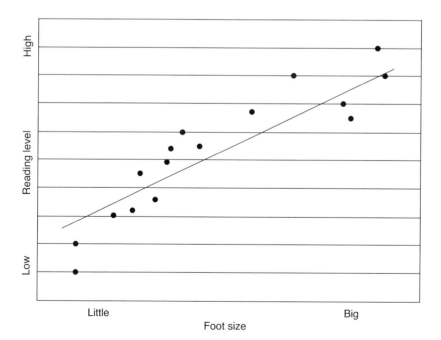

FIGURE 2.2 Relationship between size of foot and reading level at primary school.

interacted. We could get smarter and look at aspects of reading such as faster decoding and use of comprehension strategies, and look at the interactions. As we introduced these factors into our equation it would become apparent which ones provided the grunt of the association and which ones were peripheral or acted more like proxies for the others. So reading processes would 'predict,' that is, be associated with, more of the variation in differences in progress across time, and time at school would be related to these and foot size would likely have an insignificant relationship, independently of the association with these two things, because its influence on reading is entirely accounted for by time at school.

The explanations for why schools are ineffective have been greatly enriched by more sophisticated analyses of associations. But there is a second problem in the general picture painted by the evidence of schools being ineffectual. It arises because of the well-known problems with correlations, simple or otherwise. It is that correlations can't assure us about cause. They can suggest, even strongly so, but we need further evidence that is in some experimental form to add further surety. Allied to this is an old philosophical argument proposed by David Hume (1739–1740/1969) that you can't get "ought" from an "is." Just because the world is the way it is doesn't mean that it is the way it ought to be, or is immutably so (or causally so). Hume's problem can be applied to schools. So just because schools can't be effective, doesn't mean that they ought to be ineffective. Much of this book examines the experimental evidence for the effectiveness of schools. The correlational evidence helps us understand where to look for change and to understand why changes are not possible or are limited, but the experimental evidence in different forms provides a fundamental test of our explanations.

There is one final statistical point. Much of the tradition in quantitative analyses in social sciences and particularly in psychology is based on a model of behavior or performance or outcome that is essentially agrarian. The early statistical procedures designed by Ronald Fisher (1934) were drawn from studies of crop yields across fields. Within these techniques, which have titles such as t tests and ANOVAs, there is a reliance on measures that indicate what the central point of the sample or group looks like. The most obvious and well known of these measures of central tendency is the average or mean. The standard deviation adds to the picture of the central tendency.

In addition, the techniques attempt to control variability. That is, the tests are focused on finding what the average or core or essential features are like. But the focus is also on trying to reduce, minimize or account for all the variability in the information, so that the average, core or essential features are uncovered. So variability often comes to be seen as 'error' masking the essential and true phenomenon. What this in turn means is that we deal often in averages and see the variability in terms of qualifying those averages. Achievement tests and intelligence tests and the like are designed on the basic assumption that a student's results will be a combination of a true score and some error.

But the average doesn't really represent any one thing in any study sample. It doesn't represent a real child if children are the units being studied, and it doesn't represent a school if schools are the unit. An alternative is to see the variability as an essential property of human behavior, of learning and development, of schools and the ways in which social institutions function. It is in the variability that the details of the explanations lie. So perhaps we might find that schools on average are not effective. But if we also find examples of outliers, of very effective schools, what does this tell us in general about the explanations, and more importantly what does it tell us about what is possible?

Conclusion

Strong and enduring associations between achievement and one's background and identity exist at whatever level one cares to examine the associations; including when change over time is examined. The differences for those groups of children on which we are focused hover close to one standard deviation in literary achievement. However, evidence from experimental research including large-scale interventions needs to be added to this picture to move beyond treating the current state of affairs as a given. The next step is to more specifically review the range of explanations provided for the general picture of the associations between achievement and one's background and identity. This is needed in order to move beyond referring just to letter boxes. We need to check the evidence against the available explanations and so develop a more encompassing and informed view. There is considerably more to say about variability that will add complexity to this general picture of the pervasive association.

3

EXPLAINING OUR LIMITATIONS

Not surprisingly, given the dramatic and long-standing associations, there is a range of explanations for why schools and school systems seem to be relatively powerless to equalize the outcomes for children from different groups, either at the beginning or over the course of life at school. These range from explanations that argue schools are inherently unable to make much of a difference to those that argue we need more and better schooling. These positions are not as fixed as they are presented here and in certain combinations are not mutually exclusive. Also, I have deliberately put some explanations together that ordinarily belong in different disciplines and have different approaches. Paradoxically, creating more generic types of explanations is a means of being more precise about what the evidence suggests about the limitations of schools. The liberties I have taken help set up the core distinctions about where the sources of limitations might actually lie.

1. By default, schools select for social and cultural practices

One explanation locates the cause at an intersection. On one side are the schools that select for and promote certain types of knowledge and practices as institutions of a society. The other side comprises the socialization and funds of knowledge within those families who belong to less powerful, less well-resourced and culturally and linguistically different groups from more dominant groups. The explanation can be couched in different ways reflecting different sets of values underlying the explanation. But there is an impressively broad cross section of researchers in different disciplines who employ this core idea, although it may be expressed in different concepts if one is a developmental psychologist rather than an educational sociologist.

Sociologists using the framework of cultural capital theory argue that families have different access to social and cultural resources that are valued by schools. Developmental psychologists use concepts of how different family activities promote different forms of expertise, which then have different resonances with school activities. In both cases, the analysis is that there are family and community practices in the early years that have developmental sequelae. These are in the form of knowledge and skills that are more or less transferrable and functional at schools, providing different developmental bases on which schools can operate. The sociological account provides a means in its structural analyses of societies for understanding how the distribution of the capital has come about. The psychological account places the understanding in patterns of socialization across generations and how socialization itself is a developmental phenomenon.

Known literacy practices include those such as reading story books to children. When read in particular ways the practice develops children's awareness of story structure, their literate language, their awareness of how to activate background knowledge and make connections between the events in their lives and those written about in texts. These prepare children to enter into and make sense of classroom instruction. Teachers are then able to see and build on their expert knowledge.

Detailed descriptions of practices reveal how dynamic the psychological mechanisms are behind these figures. Telling examples of how the differences might track out (Neuman, 2006) include estimates of the amount of time children are read to prior to kindergarten – in the US, the figure is 1,000 hours for the highest SES children compared with 25 hours for the lowest. Or the accumulated experiences with words estimated to be 45 million for the former versus 13 million for the latter. Both reading to children and numbers of words experienced have known relationships with reading comprehension in the middle and upper primary years.

The differences are not just present before school. In later years the family and community practices include ongoing access to the highly literate language, and access to experiences and events that provide symbols and general knowledge valued by schools and essential to passing higher level exams. The amount of reading that a child does outside of school dramatically influences achievement at school, as we shall see in Chapter 4.

Sophisticated correlations tell us about the significance of these practices. The 2006 round of the PIRLS project went beyond the simple associations between SES and achievement in reading comprehension to examine, at a discrete distance, family practices. The PIRLS team (Mullis, Martin, Kennedy, & Foy, 2007) surveyed aspects of family practices, for example looking across countries at the relationship between books in the home and comprehension achievement. The score for children from homes with more than 100 books was about 100 points higher than the score for children from homes with 10 or fewer books. Countries with well-resourced homes in terms of numbers of books almost always had above the international average scores and the reverse was true. The differences between scores on these measures were even greater, a great deal more so, when examined within countries.

Most importantly, these relationships stand up even when the letter box variables are statistically controlled. For example, we know that irrespective of SES, actual book reading to preschoolers rather than simply number of books in the home is what makes the substantial difference. A US study of preschool children from low income families participating in the Head Start early childhood programme showed that compared with parents who didn't read to their children or read only around once or twice a week, parents who read three to six times a week had children with higher scores on literacy and language measures, and larger language gains over a year (Administration for Children and Families [ACF], 2003). This finding obtained even after statistically controlling within this already relatively low SES group for parent education level, parent literacy level and the presence of books in the home.

The fundamental effects of the practices have recently been shown even as young as 14 to 36 months. In a study of 1,500 children from families at or below the poverty line, children's language (words children produced or could understand) and cognition were associated strongly with reading several times a week after controlling for race/ethnicity, demographic risk, maternal education and verbal ability, gender, birth order, Head Start enrolment and even relationship factors (Raikes, Pan, Luis, Tamis-Le Honda, Brooks-Gunn, & Constantine, 2006).

What adds considerable robustness to these findings is that there is experimental evidence that shows that it is the reading with children that produces the outcomes (Whitehurst, & Lonigan, 2001). But what does this mean for the role of schools? A greater understanding of the role of family practices might inform us about the profiles of knowledge and skills children have on entry to school. This would enable us to better design and to target instruction. After all, one of the universals in educational thinking is to 'start where the child is at.' This was the argument I made in a book called *Meeting of minds* (McNaughton, 2002) and I will draw on that book and its core argument to support later claims about the (potential) effectiveness of schools.

But we have known about and have had good descriptions of different family practices and the profiles of knowledge and skills that develop from them for some time, with little evidence presented so far that this had made a difference. One reason might be that there is just too much ground to catch up. One of the most depressing (surprisingly pessimistic) accounts of this sort comes from two psychologists; Hart and Risley's (1995) study of vocabulary learning in different families. They compared the linguistic 'input' comprising the number of words children received in what they termed professional families (mostly families of college professors) with those in families receiving welfare. To make up the difference in the number of words experienced as input would require more than 40 hours of extra intervention with language per week in addition to the language input the children were already receiving; and this is before school. They interpret their evidence as indicating the sheer size of the educational task may be a major barrier to being effective.

Given that we have known abut the significance of family practices for some time one has to wonder about the responsiveness of teachers and of school systems. It does seem that the default mechanisms of schools are set to respond to only some sets of knowledge and skills, those of children from the majority and more powerful communities who have more of the knowledge and skills that schools value. And this default setting means that schools cannot and will not be able to make a difference.

The implication is that if schools are so impervious to the need to be more sensitive to practices of 'minority' communities, we should change the locus of our efforts and directly resource those communities to make conditions for socializing children in the relevant practices more possible. For example, if adults in a household have to work long hours and conditions of housing and employment mean constant shifting of location, there is very little opportunity to spend hours talking with children. Perhaps we should act on working conditions and employment so that they can access educational opportunities where they could develop the school-related language and literacy practices.

There is an important nuance in this generic view. Within it there are very different positions about the families and communities whose children are not well served by schools. Their language and literacy-related practices can be seen in two diametrically opposed ways. One is to view them as faulty and deficient. The other is to see them as culturally and socially resource-full, but mismatched on the other hand. These differing views in the general explanation lead to different approaches to resourcing families, which have different patterns of success (McNaughton, 1995).

2. Schools actively select for social and cultural practices

The first explanation that schools by default are selective can be extended. As it is, it suggests that schools are relatively passive in this process of selective filtering of children's funds of knowledge. The second generic explanation is one that views the schools as more active in the filtering. One could leave the first view at the point of seeing schools as relatively passive and the differences that exist at the beginning are accumulated and compounded through the years of teaching. In other words, schools might be effective but relatively equal in their effectiveness with all children. This view stresses the role of the original and ongoing practices outside of school as determinants for why schools don't matter. But in contrast to a passive incipient selection process operated by schools, the second view is that schools act in specific ways to create, maintain, or extend the differences in children's achievement.

The evidence shows that school instruction tends to identify, respond to, and act on the cultural capital that children bring with them to school. The responsive and active selection occurs from the beginning and continues as children's socialization outside of school develops and feeds into schools. Thus, recent longitudinal studies tend to show that while some differences in literacy are quickly reduced and most students become similarly skilled (for example in their knowledge of the alphabet or in their awareness of sound patterns in words' relationships with letters), the differences in the language and making meaning in reading comprehension can become more exaggerated (Paris, 2005).

The evidence that has been gathered over decades of research into classroom interactions also shows that instruction tends to be 'differential,' as Courtney Cazden (2001, p. 137) put it. Instruction responds to cultural and socially based differences in children in ways that can maintain or exaggerate the very differences. A simple example is the teacher correction of the errors children make when reading aloud. Some years ago a study of teacher responses to the children's errors showed that teachers were likely to respond to dialectical variations by children in the 'read alouds' as errors even though they were consistently used and did not interfere with meaning (Cunningham, 1976).

Again there are variations within this view. For example, detailed case studies of classrooms also show that the differential instruction can be exaggerated by what the students do. That is, students can act on teachers to collectively construct the differences. In one New Zealand case study the Pasifika girls in a high school class successfully manipulated their English teachers into teaching in a didactic recitation style of teaching, shifting from a more enquiry-based style. This was a more culturally preferred way of learning but it moved the instruction away from the style and content that would benefit them in exams (Jones, 1986).

Clearly the correlational evidence for the structural inequalities of societies being reproduced in classrooms is powerful. Is an experiment possible? Can we change the backgrounds of families and students and thereby see if we change the achievement patterns? A full experiment would require us to change some communities positively and some negatively or at least not change the status of some 'control' communities. To change power structures suggests the experiment would need to be revolutionary. If we were right and the disadvantaged communities or disempowered communities who became empowered now had the successful children at school this would provide a test. If a positive test occurred it would provide an educational spin on Solzhenitsyn's (1976) adage that in the revolution, only the hangman is changed.

Educators can't do this in classrooms and schools. Nevertheless, there is a sort of proof in the form of natural experiments. Experiments in social science occur when under the control of the researcher a planned manipulation of some condition (called an independent variable or the treatment) produces a change in conditions for the person or group under the microscope (subject or subjects) and where any change in the outcomes of interest can be compared with pre-existing conditions and with persons or groups who did not receive the treatment.

A natural experiment occurs where a naturally occurring change (that is not one under the control of the scientist) provides us with a means of looking at the effects of changed conditions on specified outcomes. Clearly social scientists cannot manipulate social class or 'minority' status to see if changing social class or 'minority' status produces an effect of achievement. But there are natural experimental versions of this. Cummins (2001) describes one such – the effect on achievement when families who are members of discriminated against communities in one country immigrate to another where their community is now part of the mainstream. The natural experiment reflects of course particular motivations and other attributes of the families. The resulting outcome of increased achievement reflects these, but it also reflects that it is the lived experience in a country that is a determining factor.

Other natural experiments are provided by looking at countries that are more or less equitable as societies over time and the effects on achievement. I will examine this in the next chapter. The evidence is that if communities' social, political, and economic position were to be changed, say through historical shifts within a society or through another route such as immigration, then educational outcomes can change. The position that this explanation and its evidence base leads one to is that it would be very difficult to change schools in the absence of changing power and other structural relations between communities outside of school.

3. Differential resourcing of schools causes differences

The third explanation has a different slant on the account of schools as selective mechanisms either passively or actively contributing to the achievement differences. It is that the school systems are rendered more or less effective by policy decisions and by the local and national systems for resourcing schools. This explanation locates the problem in the schools but the cause for the schools' ineffectiveness is the context within which a school operates. Linda Darling-Hammond (2007) has been detailing the systematic differences between schools that contribute to this in the United States. On just about every concrete measure ranging from the qualifications of the teachers to class sizes, text books, and access to computers and curriculum offerings, schools serving large numbers of low income and Black and Hispanic students have significantly fewer resources than schools serving mostly White students. In terms of qualifications it doesn't matter what aspect of qualification is chosen, certification, subject matter background, pedagogical training, selectivity of college attended, test scores or teaching experience, the differences are present.

How this state of affairs comes about is not hard to pin down according to Darling-Hammond (2007). One obvious set of drivers is unequal funding, and a situation especially for predominantly 'minority' schools where resources are declining but teacher demand is increasing. There are inequalities in property tax revenues, and funding formulas, which mean mainly White districts are higher spending districts and have smaller classes, more highly paid and experienced teachers, more up-to-date texts and other curriculum resources and a wider range of curriculum offerings.

Darling-Hammond (2007) has tested the resources explanation using correlational models. In different states in the United States she has looked at the simple association between identity and performance on high stakes state exams. Students' backgrounds (their poverty levels and 'minority' status) predict a large share of the variation of students not passing minimum standards across the school districts. But the school resources are associated with the background too. That is, school resources vary with who the students are and when estimates are made of the school resources alone they account for well over half of the variance; and this is the important bit, this accounting is independently of the students' background. Teacher qualifications were the strongest of the factors among the school resources in this prediction, more so than certification and salaries.

The more sophisticated correlational analyses provide strong support for the differential resources explanation. Yes, policies to do with funding and resourcing of schools, at least in the United States, conspire in creating the differences through a process of creating schools that have greater or lesser quality resources for their students. The next step in the logic is in Darling-Hammond's (2007) detailed proposals of how to make resources be more equitably funded and even targeted to make a difference. If that were done would that make a difference to the achievement gap? Behind this question is of course the prior question of why the funding is like that, why do the policy mechanisms severely under-resource schools? The answer to that question leads back to a bleak view of schooling systems as instruments of maintaining structural differences, either being passively complicit or actively collaborating in creating them.

4. Outside of school conditions and limited educational coverage reduce impact

The fourth explanation is a twist on the first. It is the argument that actually schools are relatively effective. By and large they do a good job of teaching and students from all backgrounds learn while they are at school. The problem is what happens outside of school; not just over the school year but also after a school year. The effectiveness of the school is severely tempered by the conditions in which communities live.

There are two arguments in this explanation. One is similar to the cultural capital argument, that it is family language and literacy practices rather than one's identity as such that are the important factors. The argument is that schools are relatively good at teaching while students are at school but the differences are exacerbated outside of school. There is a whole chapter devoted to this explanation where I discuss the 'summer effect' and the effects on progress from one school year to the next of not being at school, where some are learning, and some are not. Again, there is strong evidence that this explanation is at least partially right.

The fourth explanation says that schools are ineffectual because they do not operate 365 days a year. In the course of a full year students might spend 1,000 hours in school and almost five times that in their neighborhood and with families. Whereas the other three explanations say that schools are ineffectual because they default to creating the differences, or they actively conspire to make the differences, or they are forced to create the differences. The instructional coverage explanation predicts that in the absence of doing anything differently about resources and the nature of schools, if schools operated 365 days a year the differences would be smaller. The first three would predict exactly the opposite – the differences would be even larger if the schools were to remain open.

The second argument for this explanation is that schools are relatively effective while operating but what they can do is severely limited by those outside of school conditions about which schools can do little (Berliner, 2006). Again, I will have more to say about this argument in succeeding chapters. There is compelling evidence, not just from educational researchers, that conditions such as income disparities have marked influences on achievement patterns (Wilkinson, & Pickett, 2009). The more of these conditions such as poverty and poor housing that a community bears, the lower the achievement levels (Sampson, Sharkey, & Raudenbush, 2008).

5. We have yet to discover more effective processes in schools

The fifth explanation is really the counterpoint to the others. It is the position that we have yet to fully discover what makes schools more effective for those who find schools risky places; but we can. This explanation argues that the solution will lie in better understanding of school processes such as instruction and in research-based instructional design. Although not exclusively, this is the optimistic position often adopted by researchers and educators who use psychological frameworks to understand teaching and the role of schools.

We know that teaching can affect learning. Two sources of information are used to suggest we could do better. One is that when all the possible sources of influence on achievement are thrown into correlations, such as the family background, the type of school, the effect of the peer group, and leadership at schools it turns out that around 30 per cent of the variation between students in their learning, at least in some countries, is attributable to what teachers do (Hattie, 2009). Studies of studies, the so-called meta analyses, reveal more details. John

Hattie in his 2009 book *Visible Learning* uses the meta analysis technique to summarize the massive databases that are available on research into the factors influencing learning. Several emerge as especially significant, including the role of feedback. The evidence is clear that teachers can make a difference to aspects of learning and that there are well known properties of at least some dimensions of effective instruction.

The history of psychology applied to schools is a history of developing more and better understanding of dimensions of instruction. For example, we know a lot about the properties of feedback, such as the role of information and timing. There are studies in various curriculum areas, not just literacy, that show learning can be altered at the very specific level of everyday interactions as well as the general level of a programme of instruction. But knowing about how a specific act of teaching works, even how a combination of acts, say in an approach to reading like Reciprocal Teaching or Shared Reading, does not necessarily translate to being able to teach effectively with 30 students from a variety of social, cultural and linguistic backgrounds and to work effectively with the other teachers and students who contribute to the school's community in a school that has limited resources.

There are other problems with being overly optimistic about what analyses of discrete instructional events can contribute. Take for example a classic study from the front line of the phonics 'wars' in literacy education (Foorman, Francis, Fletcher, Schatschneider, & Mehta, 1998). In this very well designed study an enriched specific programme of phonics instruction based on detailed research evidence was delivered in schools serving children from low income families. Not surprisingly, large gains in the enriched phonics class occurred much larger in terms of gains over time than in comparison classes. But the programme, well designed and delivered as it was, made no difference to reading comprehension. The children were more knowledgeable in phonics and could decode more accurately and fluently but there was no generalized effect on what I earlier referred to as the second strand of development. Knowing about a piece of the instructional puzzle is important. But the issue of greater effectiveness with children with whom we have not been very effective may be to design comprehensively effective programmes of instruction and assessment operating across school days and school years.

Even when our sights are set on school-wide change rather than just one part of instruction, the picture is not very impressive. There are planned interventions, at the level of small-scale studies, that change teaching in some way, and larger-scale studies in which whole schools, clusters of schools, school districts, regions, and even countries have been involved. Some of this research is covered in later chapters, but suffice it to say here there are daunting problems facing the more optimistic view that schools can make a difference. For example Borman (2005) reviewed the evidence for large-scale projects of school reform in high-poverty schools in the United States. The review shows that they can produce widespread gains, but generally the gain is modest and it takes a very long period (five years or more) of concerted effort to begin to make substantial inroads.

A telling reflection on this fifth explanation comes from an influential educational psychologist. Having spent years testing and refining principles of effective instruction in classrooms and written seminal texts on these principles, David Berliner (2006) despairs of being able to make classrooms more effective. In an address to the American Association for Research in Education in 2005 he explained his 'gloomy conclusions' about national school reform movements in the United States. His analysis is compelling. Consistent with the previous explanation, he describes how poverty and other factors outside of classrooms severely constrain what schools can achieve.

Another focus of discovery has contributed to the school improvement or school reform movement and is implicated in the instructional design concept. It comes in a variety of forms that argue that we need to see schools as complex organizations. When researched as a system that develops we are discovering new features which contribute to being more effective; in leadership, in the coherence in the professional communities' practices and in the infrastructure needs of the school such as good evidence management systems (Timperley, Wilson, Barrar, & Fung, 2007).

This explanation argues that we could be more effective if schools were better organizations. One part of the organizational change explanation locates ineffectiveness in the leadership necessary to create and sustain effective systems within the school. If teachers are to teach effectively they need systems within their schools that enable them so to do. These include management systems and organizational structures that provide the necessary support and access to information and evidence.

The second version of this argument comes in the form of an explanation for why large school-reform movements have mostly failed to achieve widespread change. The cognitive psychologist David Olson (2003) asked this question in a book on the failures of educational reform. It was directed at the large-scale movements such as the shift to make education more child-centred and initiatives in school improvement. His argument is that schools are cultural entities. Teachers, teacher leaders, specialists, and managers; each of the members of the collective entity contribute to forming the culture. At a collective level the culture is defined by its shared practices, values, and beliefs. Becoming a member of the community involves becoming deeply immersed in the traditions of the institution.

This cultural practice explanation argues that the reforms have failed to treat schools as cultural entities. Change designers have not appreciated the dynamics of cultures and cultural change, including how new members who are initially apprentices and on the periphery of the cultural group become over time socialized into the community, and how this socialization into and the loss of core members out of the community can be poorly or well managed.

There is certainly research support for this view of how schools could be more effective. The schooling improvement literature identifies that programmes of change are more effective if they establish a 'professional learning community' in which there is school-wide coherent instructional and assessment systems and in which there is enhancement of the shared practices, goals, and values of, and belief in, the role and functions of the community to be more effective (Raphael, Au, & Goldman, 2009). But the provisos made above about the overall results of the schooling improvement work suggest this is not a simple solution either.

Yet another focus of discovery, which arguably is as important as the others, is the role of cultural responsiveness in our teaching. In a way the theoretical idea of cultural responsiveness takes over where the first explanation leaves off. The theory says that the day-to-day interactions and the instructional resources involve expectations, values, beliefs and culturally significant patterns. Like the first explanation it argues that traditional school pedagogy often takes forms that are antagonistic to or mismatched with students' culturally based knowledge, skills, values, and experiences. Theoretical advances and detailed, sensitive research are revealing how to make our pedagogy more responsive. The advances indicate how to incorporate children's backgrounds, their cognitive, social, and cultural repertoires into classroom activities. They also indicate how to better respond emotionally and cognitively to the children (Bishop, O'Sullivan, & Berryman, 2010; Lee, 2009; McNaughton, 2002).

Interestingly, there are few examples where the cultural responsiveness component of teaching has been systematically added to whole school reform processes to make changes. One programme of secondary school change in New Zealand entirely focused on this, called Te Kotahitanga (Bishop, O'Sullivan, & Berryman, 2010) involves changing the responsiveness of teachers to Māori students. The accumulating evidence from this programme with 12 schools is that gains can be substantial, especially in engagement and retention indices.

6. A comprehensive nested model of processes is needed, together with a science of perfomance

The final position is the one that is arrived at by the end of this book. It has elements of each of the above explanations and is sympathetic to the concerns raised by Berliner's (2006) analysis. It is a model of nested systems each of which needs to modified if schools are to make the optimal differences needed, to substantially change the achievement patterns. Each of the explanations means we have to change fundamental aspects of the policy context for schools serving those communities and children for whom schools are risky places. We need to change the ways these schools are resourced, the way their teachers are prepared and the instruction that happens, including the use of pedagogies that are culturally responsive. In order to do this systematically we will need to change some core aspects of research and development to create a more productive science to overcome the real pressing problems such as the summer learning effect and Matthew Effect, the phenomena that provide powerful brakes on what schools can achieve described in subsequent chapters.

The model at the end of the book draws on the socio cultural theorizing I referred to earlier. The primary unit of analysis is a child co-constructing, often in interaction with significant others, in the activities that go to make up the practices of families, communities, and schools. But this primary analysis is embedded in further analyses reflecting layers of social, cultural, physical, and other phenomena in which children's activities and the wider practices exist. A critical idea is that one can foreground for analysis an activity such as the child reading independently outside of school. However, the patterns and significance of this activity need to be seen against the background of the other layers, in addition to the previous history and development of this child and his or her activities. This model requires a science of perfomance if more effective schools are to be designed.

4

OPTIMISM IN THE DETAIL

In the previous chapters I introduced some of the evidence for being optimistic or pessimistic about whether schools can be effective for all groups of children, not just some. Based on this evidence a number of explanations have been proposed for how schools currently function or could function. In this chapter I review further evidence for the explanations, but now by focusing on the variability around the associations and the general experimental evidence for schools making a difference.

Variability

Variability is a problem for existing explanations of many educational phenomena. It is particularly problematic for the explanations about schools. The devil lies in the detail of the variability in the association between school success and background for just how pessimistic or optimistic we can be.

In psychology the issue of variability in phenomena has been treated in two different ways. One way is to see the variability as an irritant. That is, we want to know about the essential or core features of a phenomenon and because of our instruments and because of the fluctuations that are part of the human condition we design ways of measuring and comparing that control for that variability.

I noted earlier the most famous formula in psychometrics, Y (a person's score on a given measure) = T (true score) + E (measurement error). Much of intelligence testing is built around the idea that there is a core or true score and there is error, and that a measure, be it from an observation or a test, will contain peripheral fluctuations both around the measurement of the true score (no tool is perfect) and the fact that error can creep in. Research procedures used in education that draw on these ideas seek the ideal of an uncontaminated estimate of the true scores. This means in experimental methods seeking the essential differences between the experimental group and the control group. One way to increase the likelihood of focusing on the essential or true differences and not be overwhelmed by all the sources of error is by the size of the research. The more 'subjects' in an experiment the better, because the more subjects there are, the more all the possible sources of variability will be accounted for if there is random assignment to the experimental and control groups.

The second approach is to treat variability as the core. Rather than an irritant, in this view variability in psychological phenomena is an essential feature of the human condition that we need to understand. It is important to know why someone performs higher than expected or usual or higher than their past performance on an intelligence test. It is also important to know why a school performs better than expectations, given its community and resources. Greater numbers do no necessarily mean more confidence in an essential feature. Rather, painstaking attention to the detail of the variability, understanding its sources and then replicating and extending the analysis are preferred.

In a productive research enterprise we need elements of both these approaches. In particular, for research on schools and their effectiveness we need to know what the sources of variability might be as well as whether, despite that variability, one can reliably produce effective schools generally. This chapter considers the evidence that some schools can under some conditions beat the odds. If the evidence is robust this must mean the conclusion that schools can't make a difference needs qualification.

Earlier I reviewed the evidence for a substantial association between a child's identity when it reflects the inequalities in a society and their achievement at school. The association can be found at different levels; it is present across countries, within countries, across school districts and within school districts. But the correlations aren't perfect, there is plenty of variability and in this chapter we want to know what this tells us about schools.

Variability between countries

How do countries fare in this association between background and achievement? Are there countries where the association has weakened, where the differences between groups from different communities are small? And if there are, with what are these variations on the theme associated?

It may be that any variation between countries towards a narrowing of achievement differences is a reflection of more equitable societies and that the schools simply reflect the state of the society at large. This would still mean being more pessimistic about what schools could achieve without first making changes in the society at large. So if there are differences between countries, are there identifiable sources for these differences in schooling and schools rather than in less inequality in the society?

There is considerable evidence about the association from the international studies of achievement across countries. I have already referred to the PIRLS programme, which is an examination of reading comprehension. There are two others that can tell us about international comparisons and do relate to literacy at school. Boston College, which heads the PIRLS programme, also leads the Trends in International Mathematics and Science Study (TIMSS). TIMSS contains some information on literacy in so far as students have to read the items. More directly, the OECD's Programme for International Student Assessment (PISA) examines achievement in literacy in terms of reading, but also in mathematics and science, designing their tests to show how well students can extrapolate from what they have learned and apply their knowledge and skills in novel settings.

These are large-scale studies, and necessarily are limited in how far behind the letterbox or the classroom walls they can go. But they are capable of answering the general point about the degrees of variability and the possible sources.

The first thing to note from each of these planned comparisons is that there is variability across countries in patterns of achievement related to social background. The variation in achievement associated with school background is considerably different across different countries. The PIRLS (Mullis, Martin, Kennedy, & Foy, 2007) data reveal that the variation is very large in countries such as Turkey and Germany, moderate in countries such as Greece and the United States and very small in Scandinavian countries. What this means is that despite the existing differences in income levels and educational levels across these countries there are some countries where the variation in achievement attributable to background is large and there are countries where the variation attributable to background is small, compared with averages across all the countries.

In the PISA (OECD, 2007) comparisons Canada consistently has been a country in which the impact of socio-economic background is significantly below the OECD average. Canada also had an achievement profile that was significantly better than the OECD average. For Germany, whose achievement is around the average for OECD countries, the impact of background is significantly greater than OECD countries on average.

Andreas Schliecher (2007) has analysed the variability in the 2003 PISA data in great detail. He concludes that there are structural features of the school systems across countries that compound or reduce the effects of background. One of these features is how stratified the system is. That is, in countries where there is early streaming into different types of schools or programmes within schools the effects of background are stronger. On the other hand, the degree of autonomy schools have within a country when coupled with external centralized examinations is associated with reduced effects of background. There are high-performing countries in terms of overall achievement in which SES does not impact as greatly as other countries. These countries have relatively autonomous schools, where there is strong support for teachers and a focus on ongoing improvement in the school system, and they are not differentiated early on so they don't select students into different tracks or curriculum strands.

Further support for Schliecher's analyses comes from ongoing OECD educational data (OECD, 2006). In the 2006 summary of school systems in countries where students are placed into several different types of schools or programmes, student background accounts for 19 per cent of variation in achievement compared with 14 per cent in countries with only one or two programmes. One final feature that Schliecher identified is that the effect of background is influenced by how well systems introduce new immigrant families to success at school. The high-performing schools tend to be the schools in which first generation new immigrant students do well and second generation students do even better. Countries with more of these schools reduce the effects of background.

While what can be said from these studies about actual teaching is limited because they do not conduct detailed classroom observations, the patterns convince Schliecher about the nature of an effective teacher in the twenty-first century. He comes to a similar conclusion to that of researchers in the United States. He argues that teachers who will be effective in reducing disparities are those in knowledge-rich schooling contexts, who know a lot and who make informed professional judgements (including those related to benchmarks); he calls them "knowledge workers" (2007, p. 46). The US researchers Linda Darling-Hammond and John Bransford have a similar concept of teachers as "adaptive experts" (2005, p. 49). I will explore this view of teachers further in subsequent chapters.

Finland has become the darling of international studies because it has done so well in reducing disparities. Schleicher's (2007) general view of teachers has been filled out in close analyses of Finland's success. Researchers have attributed Finland's success at the level of classroom teaching to a dramatic overhaul of teacher education (Darling-Hammond, 2006). The key features that enable Finnish teachers to be 'adaptive experts' are their capabilities for problem solving derived from their preparation and an extensive base of knowledge of both content and the principles of learning. There is a focus in their knowledge on teaching for diversity. Teacher preparation in Finland includes a three-year Masters Degree programme, part of which involves completing research theses that develop a research orientation to school problems. Their preparation as problem solvers provides them with experience in cycles of planning actions and reflection or analysis. These features, it is argued, enable teachers to create powerful learning environments.

The commitment to effective teaching includes an ongoing process of school reform based on continuous evaluation of the preparation teachers receive. In addition, teacher education is highly competitive and well funded, as is educational research. The relatively autonomous schools noted by Schleicher (2007), however, are not isolated, they are often in partnerships with universities – yet another feature to which I will return when proposing effective research programmes.

Variability within countries

The international data also show substantial variation in achievement within countries at all levels of schooling that could be compared, such as between regions, local districts, and schools. Variability also can be found between cities in how well the children of that city achieve at school and this is associated with general indices of how literate the population in that city is. In the most recent rankings from America's 'Most literate cities' (Miller, 2009), Minneapolis comes out top in the analyses of 69 cities. The analyses involve six key indicators including newspaper circulation, number of bookstores, library resources, periodical publishing, Internet resources and educational attainment.

Given all that has been said so far about associations between background and school success, we would expect to find such variability within a country. It would be especially noticeable between schools if schools differed in their composition of students with different backgrounds. In the United States the variability between schools is large because of this. The data from TIMSS, like the data from the literacy studies, shows that in mathematics and science the difference between wealthy schools (in which less than 10 per cent of the student body are children in poverty, as defined by receiving free or reduced lunch entitlements) and poor schools (in which more than 75 per cent of the children are in poverty) amount to the ubiquitous standard deviation (Berliner, 2006).

The question about variability between schools can be asked in a more targeted way. Are there districts and schools that go against the grain, so-called outliers? The answer to this question is yes. There are shining examples. New York City's Community School District #2 was one (Hubbard, Mehan, & Stein, 2006). A very successful reform programme took place in District #2 under the leadership of Superintendent Anthony Alvarado. From 1987 to 1998 student achievement ranking rose from near the bottom of the thirty-two community school districts in New York, to second. In a later chapter I examine this success from the point of view of a comparison with another district with high proportions of low income students on the West Coast of the United States where an attempt to replicate the success of that district was not nearly so spectacular. But the district's success illustrates variability in two senses. It was an outlier in achievement despite the composition of students in the district, and it changed – it was itself variable.

Similarly, there are descriptions of individual schools where achievement is higher than expectations. The late Michael Pressley and his associates started a programme of research that study schools that produce high achievement in populations at risk from school failure (Pressley, Raphael, Gallagher, & Di Bella, 2004). One such school was a private K–12 urban school with an entirely African American student population. It had the characteristics described in the classic school effectiveness literature for a successful school, such as high expectations, strong leadership, and excellent management, an emphasis on academic success, a safe and structured environment, with frequent evaluation of progress. It also had what the instructional and psychological literature would describe as best practice. Teachers personalized their instruction, responding to the needs of individual students. They engendered trusting relationships and provided graduated and sensitive guidance using a variety of motivational techniques. The school had accountability systems for teachers built around student engagement and evidence of achievement; and strong community-schools connections. Finally, they had longer school days and school years.

There are other examples. Cummins (2007) describes another such school on a Navajo reservation. The school had implemented a bilingual bicultural programme that used a literature-based approach to reading and writing in both Navajo and English, with instruction focused on process. Subject matter instruction used culturally relevant themes. The evaluations of the school through the 1990s showed consistent improvements in oral English and English reading scores on a range of assessments, and overall levels in reading that were significantly better than comparison groups.

Within large-scale schooling improvement programmes involving many schools like Success For All (Slavin, & Madden, 2001), there are also wide differences between schools. These differences, of the order of more than half a standard deviation in the distributions, can be linked to how well the programme has been implemented. New Zealand school improvement studies also have shown variability between schools, but these differences tend not be as great as the variability within classrooms. In one study, the intervention had a substantial effect that meant overall achievement across seven schools accelerated by almost one year of academic progress in addition to that expected over three years (Lai, McNaughton, Amituanai-Toloa, Turner, & Hsiao, 2009). But some teachers were very much more effective than others. Students at the same schools made very different gains in reading achievement over the course of a year.

The spread across classrooms in that study in one year is shown in Figure 4.1. The gains over the school year are shown in 'stanines' (these are scores standardized for age level in a nine-part distribution, where five represents the average band of achievement and one is the lowest band). One would expect a zero gain over a year given that these are age adjusted, and zero would mean expected growth occurred. There were some teachers in whose classrooms students on average made zero or minimal growth, or even lost ground. In the great majority of the classrooms students made gains of a quarter or more of a year's growth in addition to the expected gain. All these teachers had been participating in the same school change intervention. But the difference in gain over the year in these classrooms was well over two stanines, about two years in growth. The between-school variation in Success For All (Slavin, & Madden, 2001) and the between-teacher variation in the New Zealand example illustrates that variability in programmes is common.

The shining examples of schools achieving with students significantly better than the averages would predict are few and far between and it turns out they

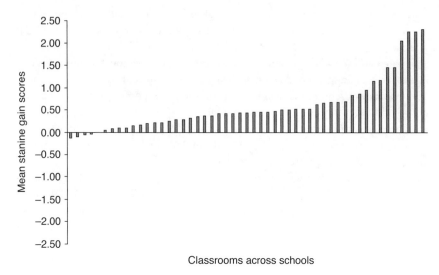

FIGURE 4.1 Achievement gains over one year in 52 classrooms involved in a
Schooling Improvement programme.

Source: McNaughton et al. (2006).

are very hard to repeat. This creates a conundrum because if many of the features
can be isolated why is success so hard to repeat? This is a subject of later chapters.
At this point we can note that the examples of variability between schools mean
that the picture of schooling is not uniformly dire. The schools do not inevitably
passively reflect inequalities in societies.

Variability within groups

But these accounts of variability can hide another detail, an important detail
that helps to illuminate the explanations and predictions for change. Variability
occurs also in the very groups for whose achievement the reforms are designed.
One can get this information also from the international studies. For example,
John Guthrie (2004) examined the PISA data from 2000, which included a
substantial amount of data from questionnaires of the 15 year olds in the 27
countries and added this to questionnaire data from the ongoing NAEP
monitoring in the United States to identify the significance of what he calls 'literacy
engagement.' The general concept includes the idea of extensive reading and
writing but additionally, the application of cognitive strategies for processing of
complex meanings from texts and being positive about reading and writing.

Two conclusions emerge from his analyses. For 9 year olds on the NAEP
in 1998 the correlation between one of the indicators of engagement, how much
reading occurred (not school-assigned or required reading, nor comics and

magazines), was highly correlated with reading comprehension achievement, and more importantly it was a better predictor, that is it is more highly correlated with achievement, than parental education and income. But a second conclusion was just how much the variation mattered for the usual associations. Those students who were highly engaged but from low income and low educational backgrounds substantially outscored students who were from families with higher incomes and higher education levels, but were less engaged. This same pattern emerged in his analyses of the PISA data. On the indicator, highly engaged 15-year-old readers from homes with lower material advantage had higher scores than less engaged readers with higher material advantage.

There is the usual problem of causal link here. Is it that engagement causes success or vice versa? Likely it is both and over time one feeds the other, creating reciprocal effects. But the essential point here is that as a group the low income/low educational level students have important lived experiences that make a difference to achievement. In keeping with the socialization explanations of the association, the lived experiences that create this mutually reinforcing development can be seen as happening without schools' influences.

But perhaps engagement can be built inside of school too. Guthrie (2004) claims that his research programme is identifying how teachers can increase literacy engagement. However, it is a daunting task. On this one indicator of engagement, amount of reading, he estimates that a Grade 4 student reading two years below their grade level at a Grade 2 level would need to read at least three hours a day for two years so that after two years, at 6th Grade, they were reading at their grade level. This 600 per cent increase in reading would need to be more than recreational reading, it would need to be also reading and writing about a range of topics, themes, and content that were purposeful in terms of school subject matter. The difference of two grades is less than a standard deviation and smaller than the differences that currently exist between the target groups (either based on ethnicity or on income) on NAEP.

Patterns that change over time?

Another way of approaching the phenomenon of variability is to examine patterns of change over time. So we can ask the question: are there examples where countries have acted through schools on achievement differences and have been able to change the patterns of achievement despite the presence of inequalities in the society at large? Are there schools and districts, and perhaps even countries, that have been able to change over time?

Changing countries

Many countries have implemented reforms aimed at increasing school effectiveness, often in the early years and often for literacy and numeracy. In the most recent of the PIRLS survey data (Mullis, Martin, Kennedy, & Foy, 2007), for example, Singapore made significant improvement from 2001 to be one of three top-performing countries in 2006.

In some cases the countries have deliberately focused on the achievement gaps between mainstream and target 'minority' groups. Ben Levin (2008), the Canadian researcher and policy maker who has reviewed the success of these policy developments, concludes that most education reform programmes turn out to have quite small effects on students' learning, like the evidence for the lack of substantial impact of the recent reforms nationally in the United States. But there are some positive areas.

In 1997 England committed to improve the literacy (and numeracy) skills of the 3 million elementary children in 18,500 primary schools through improving the effectiveness of their 200,000 teachers (Stannard, & Huxford, 2007). It had two large-scale objectives – to raise the overall achievement of children, and by so doing reduce the gaps, defined as raising the achievement levels of poorer performing schools. This was a large-scale enterprise, the total funding for which amounted to some six hundred million pounds over four years. Infrastructure change at a national and local level occurred. It included developing data systems for schools so that they had access to data on student achievement and increased capacity of schools to make sense of those data. External monitoring and compliance systems following cycles of inspections were put in place, as were hundreds of new positions and resources. For teachers in classrooms the resources included extensive professional development, and detailed specifications for how and what to teach including a specially designed 'literacy hour.'

Other policy initiatives designed to support literacy gains were put in place. These included an early childhood policy with parental leave provisions, tax credits for child care and expanded child care. The initiatives were directed especially at high-need or high-poverty communities and low achieving schools, and included extensive summer and after school supplementary programmes with these schools.

Did this large-scale and multifaceted effort produce the desired results? As I have briefly noted already, how outcomes are defined needs careful consideration. Among the concerns for any reform targeted on specific groups are questions about how much of the 'gap' actually reduced, and whether the target groups' achievement levels shifted to deliver more equitable outcomes. Unlike the next example of reform from New Zealand, the reform in England was not explicitly aimed at particular groups so much as the undifferentiated tail end of the distribution (and low achieving schools typically serving poorer communities), to raise overall achievement.

The reform produced important results. The first objective of the overall initiative for literacy of raising national levels was defined in terms of a real benchmark, the English curriculum level that 11 year olds were expected to attain. In terms of the English curriculum this was 'level 4.' The target for the reform was to have 80 per cent of 11 year olds at or above that level in 2002.

In the first three years overall achievement in literacy rose significantly and by lifting the 'tail' the gap between the top and bottom of the achievement range was narrowed. Results plateaued from 2000 to 2004, but then began to rise again. By 2006 a total gain of 14 per cent had occurred and only 21 per cent of the tested population was below the level. The reported results are particularly impressive for reading as distinct from writing, with 83 per cent at or above the expected level. Given the earlier gains the goalposts were shifted even higher in 2002, to be set at 85 per cent by 2006.

The benchmark has been harder to reach for writing. Writing rose by 14 per cent too but from a low base and in 2006, 67 per cent were at the expected level. Interestingly, internal benchmarks do not necessarily translate into international benchmarks. In terms of the international comparison in PIRLS (Mullis, Martin, Kennedy, & Foy, 2007), England had significantly lower overall scores in 2006 compared with 2001.

What is interesting is that the analyses of meeting the objectives focus on the raising of the tail but it is not immediately clear just how much students from poor families have benefited from this. Have schools taught those students more effectively? Questions about how different groups fare in reforms are important to raise because of the evidence of the Matthew Effects reviewed in the next chapter, which suggests interventions may affect some groups rather than others. At the very least we need to know if a reform raises the whole distribution but the gaps between some groups remain the same. In the England reform both boys and girls gained, but the gap between them in percentages of those at or above the benchmark was the same at the end in 2006 (11 per cent) as it was in the beginning; the differences were now at a higher level.

There have been costs, not just financial, for this programme of large-scale change. The programme of change was experienced in different ways by teachers and for some the prescriptive nature and compliance regimes were frustrating and undermined professionalism. New and evolving components and strategies added to confusion in some sites. Constant new initiatives often requiring time to prepare funding proposals and creating a sense of overload led in some quarters to what Levin (2008) calls 'initiative fatigue.' The initiatives in England also fuelled debates about the best ways to teach reading, reactivating the debate about phonics. Levin (2008) describes these as distracting in terms of the focus and effectiveness of the national strategy.

The New Zealand government also adopted a literacy and numeracy strategy, in 1998 (New Zealand Ministry of Education, 2002). Again the policy environment created important infrastructural changes that were introduced over several years. Examples included mandated annual reporting of achievement for target groups, and a change in the school guidelines to require a focus on literacy and numeracy in the first years at school. The policy was specifically directed at school Years 1 to 4 and specifically designed to address achievement gaps, in this country defined in terms of target groups (Māori children and children from Pacific Island families) and schools serving those children in the poorest communities.

Unlike in England, the changes at the level of instructional practices in New Zealand were not heavily scripted. In fact, resources that prescribed specific instructional practices in pre-specified sequences were not deployed. However, new foci and resources aimed at increasingly fine-tuning practices and introducing new emphases (such as forms of explicit teaching of comprehension strategies, and explicit teaching of phonics) were in place, including reformatting phonics instruction to be more explicit and tied to progress and a concern for rates of progress in reading texts. New texts including electronic resources became available.

Dedicated funding was made available especially for schools serving the poorest communities with the highest proportions of Māori and Pasifika students. The funding included contestable pools for innovative evidence-based projects in schools and clusters of schools. Specific school improvement programmes were designed for school clusters in the very poorest areas where there were high numbers of Māori and Pasifika students.

In New Zealand's case the achievement evidence had become well known and debated nationally since the early 1990s using the PIRLS (Mullis, Martin, Kennedy, & Foy, 2007) and other international comparative data. Starting in 1996 there was also four-yearly national monitoring of achievement using a raft of purpose-built literacy measures that were designed from the curriculum objectives (the National Education Monitoring Project – NEMP). Despite the high standing New Zealand had in international comparisons in literacy, New Zealand had recognized that there were large gaps even by international standards between mainstream Anglo European students and both Māori and immigrant Pacifica students.

As in England, New Zealand has seen marked changes in some areas. The NEMP programme has been collecting data on features of reading at Year 4 (9 year olds) and Year 9 (14 year olds) since 1996 (Flockton & Crooks, 1996; 2000; 2004; 2008). There has been substantial change in the reading accuracy of Year 4 students. In 1996, 19 per cent of the representative sample of students assessed were reading below expected levels (judged in terms of accuracy of reading texts at defined levels). The percentages dramatically reduced to 12 per cent and 7 per cent in 2000 and 2004 respectively and have remained at lower levels.

Importantly, the measures of reading comprehension do not show the same consistent improvement and the evidence suggests the gaps may be widening for comprehension. Similarly, in the cycles of assessments for writing from 1998 to 2002 there was no evidence from a portfolio of 35 different tasks that changes had occurred either in overall raised levels or in closing the gaps for poor schools or for Māori and Pasifika children. But by 2006 overall achievement in writing had been raised in some areas (for example overall 8 per cent more 4 year olds succeeding in the writing tasks) and there was evidence of reduced differences between ethnic groups.

Explaining these patterns is difficult in the absence of a planned research design for the whole strategy. The early thrust of the strategy was on reading in the first four years of school and to close gaps. New national developments in writing, such as new types of assessments for writing, became available later in the strategy (a major online resource was introduced first in 2003). The reason for the disappointing pattern for reading comprehension was discussed earlier. Changing the accuracy and fluency of reading is a necessary but not sufficient condition for changing reading comprehension.

In New Zealand, as in England, the achievement gaps between the bottom of the distribution and the top in terms of reading accuracy have been reduced. Did the reform affect the gaps in terms the target groups? It did. For example, there was a substantial reduction in the differerence in reading accuracy at Year 4 between Māori children and others, and Pasifika children and others, in overall levels of accuracy. But although the differences were now much smaller (dropping on average below half a standard deviation), they still existed.

Changing districts and schools

I have already noted that there are districts and schools that have changed from being typical in terms of the associations between background and achievement, to being high performing against expectations. Districts such as New York City's Community School District #2 provide examples and their variability, in the sense of change over time, indicates what is possible. What is the evidence from experiments to change schools and clusters of schools?

The idea of an experiment here means more than a policy and resourcing shift. It means a deliberately designed and implemented programme of change that has certain design features. In the science of educational research this means that the programme is constrained in known ways, and has in-built, pre-planned tests for different explanations for why changes did or did not occur.

New Zealand's major intervention, like England's, was an experiment in the colloquial sense, but not in the formal scientific sense. It had multiple components that were introduced in ways that were determined by policy and financial and political factors. The changes were added to and modified over time. There were no design features built in from day one that would rule out alternative explanations. This means that the evidence that reading accuracy changed from 1996 through 2000 to 2004 has several possible explanations. Did the training of principals change over this period of time, which enabled teachers to be more focused? Was there a burst of funding for IT unrelated to the literacy strategy taking place, which changed classroom practices in using written texts? Were new and powerful educational television programmes for children introduced coincidentally, which provided opportunities to learn words and be more accurate?

The veracity of some of the explanations can of course be examined after the fact. For example, was it the case that the circumstances of families in New Zealand changed, perhaps through changes to New Zealand's economic well-being through patterns of international trading, to which New Zealand is vulnerable? Did their income levels and degrees of poverty change and did this cause the improvement? This can be checked. The social indicator of relative poverty, the ratio of the 80th percentile of household income to the 20th percentile actually rose over this time, indicating increasing income inequality (New Zealand Ministry of Social Development, 2007). So we can exclude that explanation. But there are others and it is hard to exclude them.

An additional problem is the presence of so many components that were drip fed into the programme. We can't know what combination of factors in what arrangements actually caused the change. How much was it the result of the professional discussions and reflection of practices in the mid 1990s created by seeing and understanding the significance of the evidence about gaps in achievement? How much was determined by resources and professional development? What was the contribution of the parent information programme designed by advertisers and carrying powerful messages through television advertisements about how parents could help their children read?

Experiments are designed to answer some of these sorts of questions about alternative explanations and the role of components. The classic approach to experimentation in educational research is to set the gold standard as some form of randomized control group design in which there are controls for all the reasonable and possible causes, including history and maturation. This may be a kind of 'fool's gold' in that the model is not generally applicable to everyday educational phenomena. Indeed, there are examples of where this approach is dangerous in that designing the experimental constraints leads to a simplifying of the complexity of educational systems. The simplification means that conclusions about the effectiveness of a procedure, implemented under highly constrained conditions, are inappropriately generalized to the real world.

But to provide a scientific basis for changing educational phenomena it is critical that we test ideas out. And this needs to be done in ways that are deliberate and that through their design enable us to increase our confidence in explanations. Educational researchers can deliberately change circumstances to test theories. We can use experiments to try to understand the conditions that produce stars in our classrooms – out of grey matter perhaps, and by avoiding black holes of despair.

Several general conclusions come from the planned experiments. The first is that small changes are typical. Borman (2005) has done the analyses for the United States. He summarized research-based data from 40 years of Title 1 programmes (started in 1965 as part of President Johnson's 'War on Poverty,' it provided funding to reduce the achievement gap for poor children) and more recently 29 models of comprehensive school reform. He concluded that aggregated and considered nationally they have had 'modest' effects in changing the achievement patterns of high poverty schools.

Borman (2005) uses the index of the size of the effect to evaluate the significance of the change. This index, the effect size, is a measure of the difference the intervention has made. The measure might be based on a comparison of the same groups of students and schools before and after a programme of reform or an intervention has occurred, or it might be between the gains made by experimental groups of students and schools in an intervention and a control group of students or schools not in the intervention. The difference in their average achievement levels or gains in achievement are compared with the common standard deviation across the groups being compared.

The effect size measure indicates how far apart the students are on average after an intervention, compared with the average variation across the entire group (for example, in a direct comparison between groups, all the students in the experimental and the control groups). So if there is a large spread of scores anyway even a relatively large difference between the averages in an experimental group compared with a control group might not be all that meaningful because the students' scores were so variable. Similarly, even if the average difference before and after an intervention was large the gain might not be all that meaningful if there were wide differences between the students. If the average difference in the comparison was equal to one full standard deviation of the groups' scores, the effect size would be 1.0. If an intervention had managed a shift equivalent to half a standard deviation, the effect size would be 0.5 and so on.

In Borman's (2005) analysis the effect sizes range from 0.11 to 0.15, meaning in essence a little over 10 per cent of a standard deviation increase in achievement is the norm. That is only 10 per cent of what would be needed to make a difference of the sort required for the gaps to be closed, assuming that the achievement of the non-poverty schools remains static. They require something like a standard deviation change.

It is important to qualify this general conclusion using the theme of this chapter, variability. The second conclusion is that there is variation in the degree of effectiveness. This is partly because despite reform policy in recent years being federal, there is substantial state and local variation in what programmes are designed and used to meet the policy. Some reform programmes are much more effective than others on some measures of achievement, and only at some grade levels, For example, *Success For All* (Slavin, & Madden, 2001) reports effect sizes on measures of early reading components for fully implemented programmes in the early grades that are very large, of the order of 0.5. Schools even vary in their effectiveness within this highly structured and prescriptive programme, usually linked to the degree to which the programme has been implemented and the consistency of staff using the programme.

A third general point from the experimental evidence about school reform is that time really is of the essence. The effects of comprehensive school reform increase, but not immediately. The effects are relatively flat at around 0.15 for four years but gradually rise after five years. Borman (2005) finds that schools that have implemented reforms for five years have effect sizes of 0.25 and in a very few schools that had systematically engaged in reform for more than eight years the effects sizes were 0.5, or half a standard deviation and half what might be needed. The average span of a reform is three years, so not many schools show this promise. Moreover, it is not apparent whether this reflects schools who have been successful continuing to engage in a programme with that level of success when other schools have long dropped out, or whether it is a cumulative effect.

Changing poverty

There is another impressive set of data about the variability that can be examined as change over time which provides a somewhat sobering assessment of possibilities for schools. The data come from the effects of changes in poverty.

In a previous chapter the evidence was reviewed for changes in the achievement of students in the United States and how in recent years there is little evidence for significant changes in the gaps between White, and Black and Hispanic students, and between children from families that are poor, and children from those that are not poor. In the set of PISA studies it actually doesn't matter whether you examine achievement in maths, science or reading literacy, the differences between 15 year olds in terms of ethnicity (but undifferentiated by social background) is about 100 standard scores, the ubiquitous standard deviation. These figures and others led David Berliner to his "gloomy conclusion" (2006, p. 949) about what school reform can actually achieve.

Berliner (2006) also drew his conclusion by reviewing evidence about the significance of poverty, including what happens when the condition of poverty changes. There are studies that have followed families over time as their family income changes. When poverty is defined in terms of the ratio of the income available compared with their needs such as housing, food, and transportation costs faced by a family one can track what happens to children when the circumstance of families change this ratio.

When circumstances change for poor families whose available income is substantially less than their needs, their children's school-related development, such as their early literacy and language, also changes. This change can be either up or down. If families move from being poor to being a lot less poor the change is positive and their children come to be the same as, if not better than, non-poor families. But if their circumstances get worse, so too do their children's school readiness.

One analysis of Chicago children's development over seven years calculated the impact of what the authors termed the "effects of concentrated disadvantage"

(Sampson, Sharkey, & Raudenbush, 2008, p. 849). They looked at movement into and out of neighborhoods with concentrated disadvantage, giving them a means of calculating the effects in a natural experiment. The measure of concentrated disadvantage was comprised of the highest levels of welfare receipt, poverty, unemployment, single parent-headed households, racial composition, and density of children. Moving into and living in an area of concentrated disadvantage compared with moving out was associated for African American 6 to 12 year olds with disparities in school-related reading and vocabulary after seven years equivalent to missing about a year of school.

Other studies have shown positive effects on children of families who have moved out of poverty because of newly available income. Children's psychological health became more positive in one such study reviewed by Berliner (2006) associated with the change from being poor compared to those families who remained poor and those families who were never poor. There was a thought-provoking study that compared the effects of educational efforts with changes in poverty. This study estimated the effects of the large-scale programme Head Start on children's development (social and academic) with the effects of raising income levels. Similar gains for children's development would accrue from a $13,000 increase in income levels (in 2004 dollars). This cost was a bit less expensive than the annual cost per child of attending Head Start. Berliner (2006) draws the obvious dramatic point. What would we be able to achieve with both approaches to school improvement; with both high quality programmes, and better incomes for the poor.

What can we conclude?

This foray into the evidence for the effectiveness of schools in closing achievement gaps suggests the following conclusions.

Changing schools at a national level, or a district level or even in one school is difficult, time-consuming and very demanding on resources. The extent of change possible, given unchanged social and cultural conditions, especially in features of relative poverty and the stratification of economic and political power, may be limited. On current evidence under best circumstances the changes are around half of the gains needed. The extent of change is determined by the policy context operating at the national or local level. Nevertheless, there are pockets of promise that suggest two further conclusions. The achievement gaps are not immutable and schools can have a significant role in producing more equitable outcomes. Is this cause to be positive, and how positive can we actually be?

5

PROBLEMS FOR AN OPTIMIST – MATTHEW EFFECTS

Even if on the evidence from the detailed variability we can be more optimistic about the degree to which schools can make a difference, there are problems to confront and solve. The next chapters deal with these problems. These are problems on the ground; that is, problems facing schools and teachers' practices. They are about what schools and teachers need to solve in order to be as effective as possible, given circumstances under which schools exist. As I have noted already, these include the policy environment for funding and hiring teachers, and the layers and conditions of social and economic inequality. The question sitting behind each chapter is how solvable are these challenges without changing existing conditions outside of schools first?

In this chapter I examine the problems posed by the phenomena in education that collectively are called Matthew Effects. These effects have been recognized for some time. In educational studies they have a biblical derivation, although the idea can be found in other belief systems. The effects refer to the rich getting richer and the poor getting poorer. The original moral tale is about how two people were given resources by the power who dispenses worldly resources. But the two differed on the uses to which these were put. The person who put their resources to good use was given more resources as a reward. The other person buried his, wanting to protect them, and his were taken away because he didn't put them to good use. In a dramatic twist his were given to the rich protagonist.

There are problems with applying the morality lesson uncritically to education. Is the child who does not work well, does not make the progress we would like to see, really guilty of misuse of resources? But in general, the effect of resources generating further resources and the lack thereof making one susceptible to further limitations, is pervasive. In education the phenomena mean roughly that those who already have greater knowledge or skills get access to more knowledge and skills, and the corollary: those who have fewer skills or knowledge in a particularly competitive environment run the risk of receiving even less of what they need.

To illustrate, first consider a major flaw in children's sports coaching. It happens in the ways that children are selected for more or elite coaching. In collective and competitive sports such as football or hockey the children are organized into year groups. In the pre and early pubertal years the likelihood of being selected for further or elite coaching is determined largely by one's birthday, unless the selector is very careful. If a child's birthday was 1 January and the designation of a year grade is from 1 January to 31 December in that calendar year then the child with the early birthday is older by about a year than the youngest child. And age matters, because size goes with age. Selection for further or elite coaching, if it is blind to the age differences, means the older child who is already better endowed gets more resources and all that this entails in terms of further access to coaching and teams, while the younger one is denied access and cumulatively gets less of what they would need to be able to compete (Baxter-Jones, 1995).

Education can be like this coaching problem. The Matthew Effects are pervasive in education and can be found at the level of classrooms, schools, and school districts, cities and countries. They are of course pervasive in other domains. Indeed the original idea came from medical science. Keith Stanovich (1986) first introduced the term in education. His aim was to explain individual differences in reading acquisition. He argued for a core process occurring when differences between learners in their knowledge and skills mean differences in accessing opportunities, creating opportunities and getting the most out of opportunities to learn more. He called these Matthew Effects. He applied this analysis to vocabulary learning and summarized research showing that children with more vocabulary are likely to be better readers. They therefore are likely to create or at least engage with environments where they read more texts and are more engaged in reading. Through their reading they are better prepared to learn more words, which means their advantage creates an accelerating feedback loop of more opportunities to learn and better capabilities for learning through those opportunities.

The Matthew Effect in classrooms

Here is an example from the very beginnings of schooling. It comes from the classic longitudinal study that was Marie Clay's (1966) doctoral thesis. She followed 100 children from the beginning of school, which in New Zealand is on a child's fifth birthday, irrespective of when in the year that falls. In New Zealand at that time children started to read simple books quite early on. The reading series started with repetitive caption books such as a book with an animals theme which says "Here is a cat", "Here is a dog" and so on; and progressed through texts with an emergent narrative structure with one sentence per page with a repetitive structure matching the illustration such as "Mother is washing the car", "Father is washing the dishes"; through to more and more complex texts with more than one sentence per page, with increasing complexity of words and sentence forms without a one-to-one relationship with the illustration.

Children arrived at school with different degrees of knowledge that enabled them to engage in the reading of these texts. Clay (1966) showed they differed in terms of their word knowledge, their alphabet knowledge and their concepts of how books work (which is the front, where does the 'message' come from, where do you start reading, etc.). Those children who could engage and get underway quickly made rapid progress through the book levels. Their success meant that they got increasing exposure to more and more complex books and more and more textual resources, and to more and more complex discussion and instruction from the teacher.

In terms of their access to written words, by the end of a year at school Clay (1966) calculated that the fastest progress children, the top 25 per cent of the children, had encountered around 20,000 words, many of them different and complex. In contrast, the lowest 25 per cent of children were stuck in the simplest books by the end of the year. They had encountered 5,000 words, mostly the same ones because of the controlled vocabulary in the starter texts. They had systematically less of what they needed to begin to make the sort of progress the top children did.

In some similar studies these bottom children were found to get even more simplified tasks than the faster progress or more advanced children, such as work sheets. These by definition are largely stripped of meaning and textual complexity, and entail actions of matching upper case and lower case letters. They often get systematic and extended phonics instruction, which means they are denied even

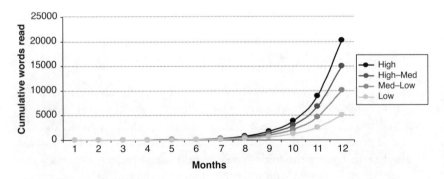

FIGURE 5.1 Cumulative words read by quartile groups over first 12 months.

Source: Estimated from Clay (1966).

further rich language resources and teacher interactions. There is also evidence that the very children targeted in programmes to reduce achievement gaps may receive even more structured and prescriptive instruction in these items and basic building blocks which, when overprescribed and used extensively over time, reduce even further their access to the rich instruction which is what they need (Cummins, 2007). The rich get richer and the poor get poorer.

As Stanovich (1986) noted, the phenomena are observable beyond the first stages of reading. There are studies of how teachers' elaborations of new words when they are reading books to a group of children enable children to learn new vocabulary, at a faster rate than if they just read the book to the children. The base rate of working out meanings of new words from just hearing a book being read is surprisingly high given the right sorts of books and engagement; around 15 per cent of the unknown words in one study. But in experimental studies teachers add considerable value to this, more than doubling the base rate when they defined and explained target words on the run as they read to children (Elley, 1989). However, here is the rub – the more advanced readers or language users in the class often get more out of the book and the teacher elaborations than the less advanced readers or language users, learning more words (Penno, Wilkinson, & Moore, 2002).

Another pattern of Matthew Effects occurs in reading instruction; where children are reading books and receiving guidance for their accuracy and effectiveness teachers may act differently with high and low progress readers (Cazden, 2001). In one study teachers with high progress readers tended to prompt and correct readers' mistakes (miscues) in ways that increase their self-regulation, for example by delaying the correction, and focusing instruction on how to make sense using a variety of cues to decode words. With lower progress readers in the same classroom, the teachers interacted more immediately, dominating the correction process and focusing more singularly on letters and sounds reducing the making of sense and the ability to use a variety of cues. The predicted outcome was the high progress readers make even more progress and the lower progress readers struggle further.

Matthew Effects across a city

Neuman & Celano (2006) have an impressive demonstration of Matthew Effects at the level of a whole city. Twenty million dollars was deployed in a five-year project to transform 32 neighborhood libraries in Philadelphia into a technology rich modern urban library system. The collaborative community-based project had a goal to enhance access to print and technology for all children and families in Philadelphia, but focusing specifically on closing the achievement gap in school literacy between children from poorer and 'minority' communities and other communities. This was a deliberate strategy to equalize resources on the assumption this would equalize opportunity for literacy development.

Architects designed spaces to reflect each branch's local culture, heritage, and talents; special collections were purchased to match the language and cultural interests of those in the neighborhood; and children's librarians and technology specialists provided special programming for children after school. New computers, even for preschoolers, were made available with educational games, there were 1,000 new books and software, professional development for librarians in family literacy practices and children's development, technology assistants to help parents, open shelving to increase access. This was a major investment in new resources.

The researchers made a very important discovery before the massive intervention. They found that the assumption, based on circulation figures, that low income communities used their local library less often than middle income communities was wrong. There was widespread use by both middle income and low income communities with similar numbers of school aged children, similar amounts of time, and similar numbers of books selected to browse. But they also discovered before the massive development that the quality of time differed greatly between these groups; and was even greater after.

Differences in the quality of time spent in the library occurred in several ways. For school aged children there were differences in what books were selected, with the children from the middle income communities selecting books appropriate to their reading level or even more challenging texts. Half the time children from low income communities read below age level picture books. For preschool children stark differences were found. Children from middle income communities always went with an adult who was a mentor for library use, who assisted their children making choices, and visits ended with a check out of a book. Children from low income communities more often came alone, or with a peer or sibling who provided little specific help or coaching to select or choose books. The new computers took time away from reading for the children from low income communities whereas adults continued to coach and help the middle income children who often did homework and online research. With the new technology these children were reading approximately three times the amount that the low income children were, and using materials of far greater challenge.

Like the children's television programme 'Sesame Street' 30 years previously, the intervention did not produce equal outcomes (Ceci, & Pepierno, 2005). Rather than closing the gap the project had exacerbated the gap. Classic Matthew Effects were operating.

Explaining Matthew Effects

What is the explanation for these effects? There are several. The general explanation is the more you know or can do which is relevant to an activity or domain, the more sense you can make out of new experiences in that activity or the more accessible new experiences within that domain become. Considering this in terms of basic cognitive processes, the reason is the relationship between one's current knowledge base with one's interconnected concepts and understanding and what one can learn using strategies, and ways of attending to and perceiving new information relevant to that knowledge base.

Robert Siegler (1986) explained the cognitive basis 30 years ago in the well-known balance beam problem. Children are asked to judge whether a scale which has weights at different distances from the fulcrum will balance or on which side the scale will go down. Different combinations of weights and distances require different rules of solving. Children can be assigned to groups that use particular rules, for example some children will only consider weight and irrespective of distance from the fulcrum will judge the side with more weight will go down. However, children of different ages using this same simple rule benefit differently from learning experiences, given that the learning experiences involve repeated examples of the balance scale problems so children can see the result, that is what the scale did. Older children learn more than younger children. They adopt more advanced rules.

The reason for this age difference, which Siegler (1986) proved in a series of experiments, was that the older children attended to the display differently. They noticed (encoded) both dimensions of weight and distance whereas the younger children hadn't. Seigler (1986) could prove this because if you teach younger children to also encode the second dimension they can learn as much as the older children. Improved encoding heightens their ability to learn. With more experience in attending to multiple dimensions, perhaps with more experience on see saws and every day experiences of balancing, older children came to the tasks with more knowledge and also with greater strategies for attending to critical dimension which enabled them to pick up more information.

Language acquisition researchers use similar models of the psychological processes. The models also focus on the knowledge base in networks of understanding based on detailed memories of specific and generic proprieties of words and rules (Pinker, 1999). This is why a child with a larger base of words, a bigger kit of lexical items, is able to pick up more new words and the properties of those words when reading the same text as another reader with a smaller lexical kit bag.

This explains the child's side of the phenomenon. The explanation for how a teacher's instruction can contribute to the Mathew Effect arises from what Cazden (2001) calls preactive and interactive influences. The preactive influences are those from teachers' training and their beliefs and expectations that lead them to treat children in systematically different ways; as Cazden (2001) put it, to differentiate their instruction. Sometimes this is very appropriate and fundamental to good teaching, the need to match instruction to individual needs. But when this applies to children from culturally and linguistically diverse communities who are not economically, socially, and politically advantaged, and when it means that a systematic reduction or restriction of provision of effective 'resources' occurs then it contributes to Matthew Effects. In the Clay (1979) longitudinal study the teachers did not set out to keep low progress children reading little repetitive books, but believed that the structure afforded by their simplicity is what the children needed and hence continued to select those books, a judgement call reinforced by the children's continued lack of progress.

The second process, interactive influences, takes place in the moment by moment interactions with a reader. The need to adjust feedback and the forms that guidance take to better match individual need is, as I noted earlier, core to good teaching. But when this is systematically done so that it reduces access or further learning it contributes to the ubiquitous Matthew Effects. A teacher can be reinforced for decisions to provide help, which means that they are more controlling than they need to be, or that they try to simplify too much by compartmentalizing instruction into smaller bits than is necessary. This means the overall intention to read for meaning is harder to activate and integration of the variety of sources of information into fluent and accurate decoding become even harder to achieve. These effects are exacerbated in an environment where there is competition for resources. There is a limit to the time and energy a teacher with 30 children can devote to any one individual or group of children.

In the case of the libraries in Philadelphia the explanation is about what the current family practices enable them to do with the new resources that have become available. Having a parent who has the time and can act as a mediator for selecting books and using computers for school related literacy tasks, already knowing how to participate in the selection and use of books at an appropriate reading age, means that a family more practiced in those areas is able to access and use the new resources made available in the library more effectively for school related literacy experiences.

Pervasive Matthew Effects

Ceci and Papierno (2005) extend the analyses of these Matthew Effects even further, showing how gaps widen in education as a consequence of many different types of intervention. They occur in the field of student loans and work study provision in universities in the United States. Wealthier universities garner even more federal resources than less wealthy universities to provide low interest loans to students, thus enabling those universities to select even better students and support those students, which increases the productivity of the university further. They occur in advanced placement programmes in high school where families with higher SES over-utilize offerings. They occur in the availability and use of computers in schools, with increased and more effective use in schools serving high SES students.

Of course the effects are not limited to education. In medicine and health care disparities between groups who access and use health interventions are exacerbated by new technologies because unequal access through insurance and other mechanisms leads to even greater differentials in health.

The issue for improving schooling outcomes for students and families who are not typically well served by schools is that there is a high risk that Matthew Effects will operate; curriculum changes, resourcing changes, and changes in pedagogy may have the unwanted side effect of exacerbating the disparities. The evidence for this can be seen in large-scale innovations in school systems such as the library intervention in Philadelphia. There are those that argue the nationally implemented programmes such as 'No Child Left Behind' in the United States (Cummins, 2007) have not had effects on closing the gaps because instruction has defaulted to treating children from low income communities with more compartmentalized and explicit teaching in phonics, given the policy environment that mandates the use of phonics instruction. Flexibly used, this instruction may be useful in the short term but counter-productive longer term when used in ways which at the same time reduce access to a broad range of literary experiences and progress in meaningful reading and writing (Paris, 2005). This is why the question was asked earlier about what gaps the major reforms in England and New Zealand have actually reduced. Or to put it more positively in terms of the themes in this book, have the schools taught children more effectively so that the groups of children who need more effective instruction most, have come to be like their peers in their achievement?

Avoiding Matthew Effects through targeting

The analysis provided by Ceci and Papierno (2005) adds an important distinction to help our understanding of how Matthew Effects operate and how they might be overcome. They point out that these effects occur with universally applied interventions, as distinct from deliberately targeted interventions. The former may exacerbate. The latter may reduce disparities.

This is the lesson learned by the researchers associated with the Philadelphia library intervention. They suggest a different strategy be used in large-scale programmes. While the initial step should be that we need to keep on going, and consider first leveling of resources to equalize access, there should be a second step. This should then tip the balance *in the other direction* by providing more resources and additional supports to low income children. This would be a targeted intervention.

A ground breaking experimental study in which Matthew Effects did not occur helps in understanding the patterns. The study was of vocabulary teaching in classrooms conducted by Warwick Elley (1989). He was able to show that teacher elaborations of target new words during the interactive reading of books with 8- and 9-year-old students increased their pick up of new vocabulary. Importantly, the rate of learning new words was the same for both low and high ability groups; no Mathew Effect.

There is one crucial drawback to the study. His finding has been difficult to repeat. In study after study high ability or high progress readers are found to learn more new words from being read books, with and without elaborations, than do low ability or low progress students. Despite this there is every reason to conclude these effects are not inevitable, and with careful planning can be overcome. The key to what could happen is in one of the replication studies (Penno, Wilkinson, & Moore, 2002). In this study the comparison between low ability and high ability groups used the same texts but examined the learning of word meanings under two contrastive conditions; without teacher explanations of target words and with teacher explanations. Although under the same conditions the high progress children outstripped the low progress children, a comparison across conditions reveals a more complex picture. Lower ability groups could pick up as many words with teacher explanations as higher ability groups could without explanations. The comparison suggests what might be possible if instruction is targeted in ways that provide appropriate support.

The probable reason for the failure to replicate Elley's (1989) original study is because the methods used reflect the conditions that give rise to Matthew Effects; the failure is a methodological artifact. Because of the need to control variables in a tight experimental design the books used in the interventions have been carefully selected, among other things for the specific vocabulary that can be tracked in children's learning over the experiment. The need to control for differences both known and unknown across texts has meant that the same books have been used across different groups. Both the high and low progress or ability groups get the same treatment; that is, the same books.

This is admirable experimental control, but the result of the same treatment is that there is a lack of match with needs. In this case it is a lack of match between the language levels of the texts and the ability levels of the different groups in a classroom. And what that means is that the higher progress groups get more out of the same book because they can use their more extensive knowledge base and their strategic attention to identify and locate words within their networks of morphological and semantic knowledge. Perhaps in the original Elley (1989) study the books used were sufficiently varied to be well suited to both groups of students.

The vocabulary studies may provide a further element in thinking about how schools can be effective and not fall into the Matthew Effects trap. Much of the more positive evidence about what schools can achieve comes from targeted interventions. The more effective of the comprehensive school reforms in the United States target particular schools, teaching particular children in particular areas of achievement. The specificity of the programme of intervention and how it is targeted has emerged as a crucial dimension of school interventions (Rowan, Correnti, Miller, & Camburn, 2009). But there is a fine line between targeted interventions that provide the resources to make further progress and inappropriately differentiated instruction that restricts further opportunities.

The risk in a targeted intervention is that what is targeted does not provide what is really needed. The risk is in gains that are limited because of over simplification and compartmentalization, the risk noted earlier. Another risk is that the gains don't meet the acceleration criterion against which effectiveness should be judged, a standard introduced in the next chapter. If different books are used in the vocabulary studies and there is always a differential use of books with those for the lower progress children containing less complex and more familiar words, the lower group may never catch up. The rate at which children in the low progress groups learn new words under both conditions, with and without teacher explanations, needs to be increased in ways that don't just match what high ability readers can do, but actually go beyond their rate. This is the longer term challenge associated with the need to accelerate rates of learning.

Targeted but discriminatory?

There is one last issue to confront. It comes from Ceci and Papierno's (2005) analysis. They also point out that if interventions are to be targeted there are larger political, economical and philosophical issues to confront. What if there is a national need to have students achieve better, to have more capably high achievers? They argue that elevating the top students pays off in terms of the science and business leaders of tomorrow. Is this more important than bringing up the bottom, reducing the long-term consequences of inequality both for individuals and for societies?

In one sense this should be a spurious conundrum. The obvious answer is to do both. But Ceci and Papierno (2005) paint the worst case scenario where a society believes it has limited resources for doing anything. Gloria Ladson-Billings (2006) has presented a compelling rejoinder to not targeting the students and communities for whom schools have been risky places. She recasts the answer in terms of needing to repay an educational debt and in her analysis the needs for a society to pay debts and to reduce the potential for disharmony are great.

There is another rejoinder. It is to say that the idea of bringing up the tail of the achievement distribution, or reducing the gaps between the lower achieving groups and the average, is not what the target should be anyway. In the next chapter I argue for a different target that is a radical departure from the idea of reducing the gaps. It meets Ceci and Papierno's (2005) challenge. The issue is to raise the whole distribution of achievement as well as raising low achievers. Is there evidence we can do that?

Overcoming Matthew Effects

So, is it possible for the poor to get richer despite the pervasiveness of and potential for instruction and schooling to default to Matthew Effects? I have already presented initial evidence for the affirmative located in the variability around the usual associations. But that evidence also suggested overcoming these effects is both limited and difficult. It requires considerable knowledge and skill on the one hand and resources and time on the other.

What this investigation of Matthew Effects enables us to do is to refine the argument for how to be effective. There are five refinements coming from this literature. To be as effective as possible school interventions need to have the following features.

1. Targeted. There are two related senses of 'targeted' suggested by Matthew Effects research literature. One is targeted in the sense of being directed at the particular needs of the students for whom we need to be more effective. The need is to design instructional programmes and deploy resources for what is essential to sustained progress. In the example of vocabulary instruction this means designing programmes that optimize the acquisition of vocabulary. But not just any vocabulary. We know that some words and some combinations of words, say for middle grade readers, are going to be more useful to progress in the tasks confronted in schools than others. These are mainly words that are Graeco-Latinate in origin, those most often found in literary texts used in schools, as well as figurative and idiomatic words and phrases, and words with subject specific meanings (Corson, 1997). And not just any teaching, but teaching that builds the capability to acquire increasingly more words without reliance on the teacher so that through specific strategies such as morphological analysis, metalinguistic awareness (sometimes called 'word consciousness') and through motivational effects engagement is increased across texts (Nagy, 2007). Related to this sense of targeted is not designing an omnibus programme because that is likely to maintain or at worst exacerbate gaps. An omnibus programme needs to be differentiated, but differentiated in ways that avoid the risks of the very differentiation creating further differences.

2. Developmentally progressive. The meaning of 'progressive' used here is very specific. It means creating conditions that optimize the likelihood that further development in the literacy pathways that are critical to school success will occur. The notion of effects that bootstrap other effects is part of this sense of appropriate. Stanovich's (1986) original application of the concept of Matthew Effects was to vocabulary development *and* reading comprehension. The longer term goal is reading comprehension. Vocabulary learning, when it has the features noted above, could bootstrap further longer term learning associated with reading comprehension, creating feedback loops that enable more vocabulary to be learned and hence greater access to more complex books. An omnibus programme is problematic if it does not provide exposure to the texts well suited to particular groups of learners, or it does not contain a workable ratio of new (or unfamiliarly used) words that are of the sort that will be barriers to further learning if they are not learned or it teaches in a

way that reduces the ongoing engagement of the learner with capabilities of controlling learning with exponential growth.

3. Other things being equal – being early. An implication of the presence of Matthew Effects is that altering the processes early is likely to be more effective than doing so later. Previously, I described Guthrie's (2004) estimate of what it would take to boost progress to grade level for a 4th Grader who was reading two grades below average. It would take three hours a day for two years to catch up. Stanovich (1986) calculated how many words different sorts of students in the middle grades are likely to read over an academic year. For the least motivated readers the estimate is 100,000 words. For an average reader it is around 1,000,000. For a voracious reader in the middle grades it might be as high as 10,000,000. The order of the problem at this point is obvious. But early is not necessarily always better, and for many children later is when the gaps may become more obvious or more able to be targeted. For example, rapid decoding is a precondition for being able to engage extensively in texts to acquire words through personal reading. Although building habits of personal reading in the early years of school should be the goal of an effective beginning reading programme, promoting personal reading across texts may need to be targeted later. In addition, a paradox that we will encounter in following chapters is that early interventions may not solve later ones. So, other things being equal, earlier is better, but we need to be able to design interventions that solve the problem for later too.

The literature also holds some caveats. There are substantial risks in targeted programmes whenever they occur. These are encapsulated in a telling case study of school change that follows up on the high performing Navajo school described by Cummins (2007) in an earlier chapter. His case study is of what can happen following an intervention programme, in this case the Reading First programme mandated under the No Child Left Behind legislation for use with low income students in underperforming schools. On the basis of the performance on English standardized tests the school was identified as underperforming. The categorization was applied to the school using English test scores despite the bilingual nature of the schools' programme and its consistent improvements. The bilingual programme ended and a prescriptive phonics programme replaced the process oriented, literature-based approach. Achievement test scores actually declined, comprehension scores were lower in 2003 than they were in 1999.

The risks can be easily identified and the list of principles for being effective also needs to include the following.

4. Avoid defaulting to easy to teach components. The easiest and most teachable items are not necessarily what is developmentally appropriate and may be counter-productive to longer term gains.

5. Avoid defaulting (without close monitoring of effectiveness) to explicit intensive and extensive highly scripted teaching. Following teaching routines for specific items to be learned is very effective pedagogy. But widespread use of overly scripted and intensive lessons leads to two fundamental problems. One is it undermines the expertise of the teacher and in the context of culturally and linguistically diverse students, and students whose social and cultural identity means that schools are risky places, the need to be innovative, adaptable and imaginative in teaching is even more critical. The second is that overuse reduces teaching that enables transfer and independence to develop, diverting the focus away from problem solving, critical thinking, and meaning related activities that need to be more open ended.

6

WHAT IS BEING EFFECTIVE?

Accelerating and distributing achievement

It would be a substantial achievement if in designing a way to make schools more effective we were able to overcome Matthew Effects and could make a significant difference to the disparities in achievement. But what would the evidence for this be? What would the evidence be that we have enabled schools to make a difference to those children not well served by schooling? What differences are educationally significant? The answers to these questions introduce several important concepts, which are partly statistical, and partly to do with defining educational significance. The concepts are *acceleration*, *matched distributions of achievement*, and *shifting distributions*.

At the most important level, what is educationally significant is a deeply cultural and political question, as much as it is a developmental one. In the context of New Zealand, the cultural aspirations of Māori communities for educational success have been recently couched in the strategic goal for education to be "Māori enjoying education success as Māori." The national policy that established this goal is called 'Ka Hikitia' (New Zealand Ministry of Education, 2009) meaning to lift up or step up performance. It proposes principles of a "Māori Potential approach" (New Zealand Ministry of Education Group Maori 2009, p. 19) to educational change and innovation in which success includes enhancing one's identity as Māori. The Māori potential approach emphasizes partnership, working together and sharing power, and seeing Māori children as culturally advantaged by virtue of who they are and having the potential to achieve at the highest levels.

In this chapter, and for the remainder of the book, I want to take the subset of criteria from this set of values that may be common across developed countries. Within the cultural and political aspirations that communities for whom schools have been risky places hold, and within public or mainstream schools there is a common core of concern. It is that schools should be effective for their children in terms of learning and achievement.

The question of how to measure the effects of educational interventions has taxed the educational community for years. We measure children's learning in a number of ways, often simply by counting units of knowledge or performance and how they change. Take, for example, an intervention that had a focus on children's writing at school. Measures could be designed that tell us how many more new words children had in their writing vocabulary at the beginning of the intervention and at the end. Being able to write words is one component of writing. There are others and more complex judgements could be added to the simple measures. For example, does a second sample of writing after an intervention contain more examples of agreement between pronouns and subjects across sentences and in so doing is there evidence from the second sample that children are writing with increased linguistic coherence? Even more complex indices of the quality of writing could be used which tell us whether the use of linguistic devices that reflect an awareness of what the 'audience' of the writing needs to know, had changed.

The same basic logic can be applied to complex attributes of performance such as reading strategies and the effective use of those strategies. In reading comprehension there are a number of strategies that are needed to be deployed to comprehend effectively. We can indirectly test for them by measuring outcomes of their use such as being able to answer inferential questions or recall questions after reading passages. More directly we can probe for their presence using procedures that make their use overt, such as through read aloud protocols.

Using such measures we can test whether a change has occurred from before the intervention until after. Has more been learned, has the rating of quality increased, can the learner be more strategic? In the simplest design of an intervention we could simply ask whether such a change had occurred, and we could use statistical procedures to show the amount of change. But each of these measures, ranging from simple to complex in reading or writing, would not be sufficient.

It may be that the change is trivial. It doesn't take a great deal of educational knowledge to work out that for an 8 year old using three more new words in their writing after 10 weeks of an intervention isn't very significant. It takes quite a lot of extra knowledge to figure out whether a change of one level of writing quality over a 10 week intervention is trivial or not.

This is essentially a question about time and expectations. Pegging any change to amount of time of the intervention, say 10 weeks, helps but doesn't go far enough.

Time matters, but it isn't a cause, alluded to in the title of Neil Young's (1979) record *Rust never sleeps*. Processes take place in real time, and time is a proxy measure for those processes. Elapsed time, even if you are sleeping, means ongoing opportunity for a process to occur.

Rusting is the result of oxidation, which requires time. We may know that in general, under typical conditions a non-galvanized nail will become rusty at a particular rate. If we were interested in how well a galvanizing protection worked we would be interested to know how much oxidation is typical under what circumstances (say away from direct weather or outside and exposed to direct weather) and over what period of time. And then we would be interested in how much we could alter the process relative to the typical process.

So, too, with educational concerns. The issue for an intervention is to know first what would be expected given certain conditions, over what period of time, and the relationships between what happened in the intervention and those known features. Usually what this means is that we need to know what children typically learn over that period of time under specified conditions – what the usual timing for learning is. The traditional approach taken by educational research to meet this objective is to have some sort of comparison group. This basic idea is essential. We need to know what might happen if we had not intervened and whether the gains would have occurred anyway.

But this raises yet a further issue. Whom do we compare? The first choice might be to compare with similar children in similar classrooms and similar schools. Then we find that typically over 10 weeks 8 year olds in these circumstances do learn three new words, or go up half a level on average in their writing. That tells us something and statistical analyses might tell us the gains the children in our intervention made are statistically significant differences, compared with like children in like circumstances.

But this is clearly not sufficient either. The discussion of Matthew Effects alerts us to this. Is the gain in three new words or being able to answer 10 more comprehension questions correctly educationally significant? In the context of being able to show that schools can make a difference to those groups of children from communities who have not been well served, the issue is one of knowing whether a difference has been made to their standing relative to other groups of children including those who are well served in a society. And this requires us to examine three aspects of the change in their knowledge and skills over time. One is the acceleration in their learning, a second is the match between their distribution of achievement and the distribution normally expected, and the third is the equity in the match.

Acceleration

The acceleration problem was recognized 30 years ago by Clay (1979), in the early intervention programme Reading Recovery. In the 1970s she set about designing an intervention for children making low progress in literacy after the first year of instruction. At that time in New Zealand early intervention for low progress readers in the first year of school did not exist and children were not eligible for any extra support until they had been at school for two years and were assessed as needing special education. Whereupon they would be taken out of mainstream classrooms and placed in special education classrooms along with other children, who had received similar diagnoses.

There were several problems with this system, including the delay in special help. Her Reading Recovery programme filtered out children making slow progress relative to their cohort in a school after only a year of instruction and gave them intensive daily one-to-one instruction over the course of about 20 weeks. The argument was that the bulk of children making slow progress were capable of normal progress and needed a burst of very intensive teaching that drew on well trained and highly knowledgeable specialist teachers. In addition the programme would act as a screening device for severe problems requiring more clinical and specialist roles. In essence these would be children who did not respond to the best set of teaching conditions, our best 'second wave' teaching over this period. This screening process through an intervention is now known as Response to Intervention assessment.

This is where the acceleration problem comes in. Her developmental argument was that in order for an early intervention programme to be educationally effective for an individual it needed to change the rate of acquisition to a rate of progress faster than the cohort to whom the individual belonged. This was needed so that over the brief but intensive period of the individualized intervention a learner would come to function within the average bands required for their classroom.

This is illustrated in Figure 6.1. Low progress on entry to school is apparent by reference to expected growth from the school cohort. The problem is to do more than simply get progress back to the expected rate of growth; that is, the same rate of progress as the cohort. That would at best produce parallel growth over time. Under this scenario, the learner never catches up. Rather, the challenge is to increase the rate of progress relative to the expected growth to get the learner back to an expected level.

In large-scale studies of the effectiveness of Reading Recovery the same logic about demonstrating acceleration also applies. That is, national evaluations of Reading Recovery, such as those in the US, analyse rates of gain for aggregated Reading Recovery children compared with classroom matched random samples of students over fall, mid-year and spring (Gomez-Bellenge, & Rodgers, 2007).

This acceleration in achievement gains needs to be a non negotiable criterion for judging effectiveness. The full judgement of effectiveness depends upon knowing what the usual or expected rates of gain are for the focus of the intervention. The challenge is to define appropriately against whom to compare the effects of the intervention. In the original Reading Recovery application of this criterion in a school the comparison was the middle band of achievement for the child's cohort at the time of the intervention. The issue was getting the single child back into that band of achievement whereupon the Reading Recovery intervention would be 'discontinued.' The identification of a child as 'discontinued' was a judgement that sufficient acceleration had occurred to get that child back to functioning in reading within the average band of the school cohort to whom that child belonged.

Matched distributions of achievement

The general issue of acceleration for groups of students from particular cultural groups and from poor communities who have not been well served by schools is similar to the one faced by Reading Recovery. It is also is to make accelerated gains, to come to function like other students at equivalent levels. Their rates of progress also need to be higher than comparison cohorts. The longer the gap widens, as shown in Figure 6.1, the more ground there is to make up, and this is the same for the groups of children with whom this book is concerned. If, as the national databases suggest, groups of children such as poor Black or Hispanic children in the United States, or Māori and Pasifika children in poorest communities in New Zealand tend on average to be two or more years behind other students in achievement levels of reading comprehension, then making adequate yearly progress defined in terms of an expected rate of gain over a year, would not be enough. The children simply never catch up. This is the acceleration challenge. If levels are low, then the rate of gain in achievement terms needs to be faster than the average rate of gain.

But against whom should groups of students from particular cultural groups and from poor communities who have not been well served by schools be compared? The acceleration issue for those students not well served by schools is not exactly the same as in Reading Recovery and not exactly the same as shown in Figure 6.1. The target is not for that group of students to come to function *as a group* within average bands. Yes, the rate of acceleration needs to be higher than the average rate of gain. But the acceleration should have a more profound outcome. Our expectation should not be that the group in its entirety would function as average. It should be that the rate of gain changes the distribution of their achievement levels in a way that matches what should be expected nationally in the distribution of achievement.

A distribution of achievement is a spread of achievement scores. In classic psychometric design an achievement test is constructed so that scores in a large enough sample fall along a bell shaped curve. The items of the test are graduated in difficulty and during the design process are written and rewritten and rejected or accepted depending on whether they discriminate in a way that means that if all the target group of children, say 8 to 13 year olds, did the test most would pass the majority of the items. Some would pass almost all and some would fail almost all. Spread out along a graph that plotted numbers of students passing against numbers of items passed would give us the bell curve; few students in the extreme tails and most students in the middle.

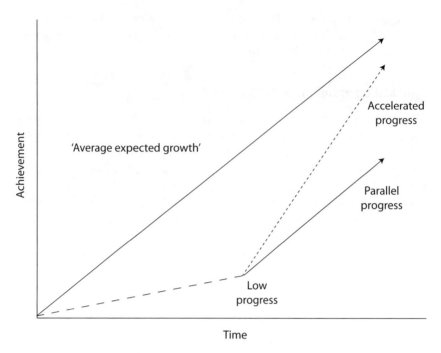

FIGURE 6.1 The acceleration problem.

To return to the criterion – a matched distribution means that the probability of being in the lower (or indeed the upper) 'tail' of the distribution should be no less and no more than would be expected in the population at large. Similarly, the probability of being in the middle portion of the distribution would be the same. The standard then is that the distribution of the group of targeted students, say Māori children in schools serving low SES communities, should match the distribution of achievement one would expect nationally in New Zealand.

There are some technical difficulties with this concept. Not the least is that if we could change the achievement of the groups currently at risk in schools and they make up a big enough group within the overall population, then the national distribution of achievement on the current items of difficulty would likely change.

A second is that typical test construction has involved a normalizing process in which the difficulties of items have been deliberately designed to create the bell curve spread. The test is designed to create tails of achievement and, crudely put, against the average 50 per cent of students will pass and 50 per cent will fail in an age group. But increasingly educational systems also use more criteria referenced assessments or tests against standards of performance. These entail setting specific tasks to be accomplished that are judged to be what is required to have achieved some set performance standard at some level within a curriculum. These are not normalized in so far as it is technically possible for everyone in the target age range to meet the standard or pass the criterion level of performance. What does a distribution of achievement mean under these conditions?

Both these technical difficulties can be solved. The normative change problem can be solved by renorming exercises and the like. The second problem, performance based assessments, can be solved by comparisons that are based on typical pass rates against the criterion. In many circumstances there are still levels of pass to be considered and the outcomes of matched pass rates still applies.

There is one major flaw in this rosy picture. It arises if the active selection explanation in Chapter 3 applies, which argues that the creation of differential outcomes is created by middle class and 'mainstream' capture of schools and schools are complicit in this outcome. If the explanation that schools actively teach and credential in ways that reflect the knowledge and skills of 'privileged' students is correct, and it must be at least partially correct on the evidence, then this would lead to a concern. It would be the prediction that the renorming or redesign exercise would result in more deliberate privileging (that is, selection) of one groups' knowledge and skills over another and hence change the goalposts. This would result in reconsigning more of the students who were not 'mainstream' to the lower parts of the distribution (or to more often not meeting the standards). This possibility would need to be closely monitored.

A matched distribution would be a more equitable criterion than simply closing the achievement gaps on the basis of averages. As a group, the children for whom the intervention is designed should be indistinguishable from what the expected distribution should be; illustrated in Figure 6.2. The left hand part of the figure shows two very unmatched distributions. One distribution is markedly skewed to the left of the normal distribution. There is some overlap. Some children in the left skewed distribution are as good as and even better than the average children in the so-called normal distribution. But the bulk of the children in the lower distribution, those 63 per cent who are one standard deviation either side of the skewed mean, are way lower than the bulk of the children in the higher distribution. The standard deviations are contiguous.

Beside this first set of distributions is a second set. It is an idealized representation of a successful intervention. The skewed left-hand distribution has moved to more closely overlap the normal distribution. There is no difference in the probability of a child being in any part of the other's distribution.

The figure is a schematic to represent the concept. But although stylized, it is very close to what a cluster of primary schools have achieved in New Zealand (Lai, McNaughton, Amituanai-Toloa, Turner, & Hsiao, 2009). Their distributions compared with national distributions are shown in Figure 6.3. The distributions summarize the changes over three years in reading comprehension achievement for 238 children in school Year 4 (9 year olds) to Year 8 (13 year olds). The children were in seven 'decile 1' schools. These are the schools serving

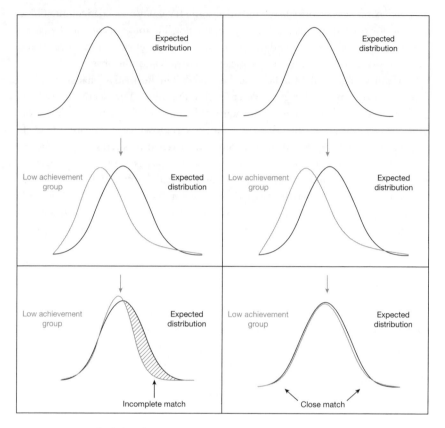

FIGURE 6.2 Matched distributions.

communities with the lowest incomes and highest unemployment. The school communities were overwhelmingly made up of Pasifika families and Māori families. Of the 87 per cent from Pasifika communities, about half had a first language other than English (mostly Samoan, Tongan, Cook Island Māori, and Niuean).

The intervention was designed to raise reading comprehension. The measure of achievement in reading comprehension is from a normalized assessment. The scores are represented in stanines where 5 represents the average for any age group (but reflecting different raw scores) and stanines 4 to 6 represent an average band within which there should be 54 per cent of the children. At the beginning of the intervention there were only 39 per cent in the middle bands of stanine 4 to 6 and less than 1 per cent in the highest bands of stanines 7 to 9, where there should in national terms have been 23 per cent of the children.

After three years of intensive research and development using a three phase model of intervention, the distribution went from looking like the first (top) set of distributions in Figure 6.3 to closer to the second set. The shift in Figure 6.3

is from left to right; from Time 1 (the beginning of the first year) to Time 6 (the end of the third year). After three years the percentage of students in the lowest achievement bands (stanines 1 to 3) had dropped from 59 per cent to 32 per cent (and 23 per cent would be expected in these bands) and now there were 59 per cent in the middle bands (and 54 per cent would be expected). Close to but not at the desired outcome. Although statistically speaking the two distributions were the same, there were still only 10 per cent of the children in the upper bands of stanine 7 to 9 (23 per cent would be expected from the national distribution to be in the above average and outstanding bands).

Matched distributions are possible but it takes considerable time, effort and resources. A case study of one of the decile 1 schools involved in an ongoing research and development partnership is described in the last chapter. After multiple cycles of problem solving, each of three years' duration, this school even surpassed the expected distribution. The distribution of achievement in reading comprehension at the end of the year in 2009 was skewed to the right of national distribution. The picture was the same in writing achievement.

This equity criterion is very different from standard practice in educational research. Usually the comparison is another group of like students, other poor and 'minority' children in the same sorts of schools. It is not hard to get significant but educationally and developmentally trivial results from these sorts of comparisons. Educational research into the effects of instruction and school effectiveness is littered with thousands of studies making such comparisons and showing significant results.

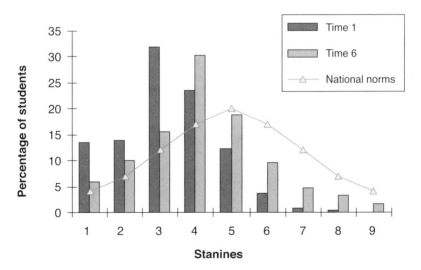

FIGURE 6.3 The distribution of achievement of 238 students at the beginning and end of a three-year intervention with seven schools, compared with the expected national distribution.

Source: Lai et al. (2009).

Hattie (2009) reviewed many of those studies looking for what the average effects of different sorts of instructional changes were in educational research. His list of interventions includes the effects of giving feedback in studies where one group receives high quality feedback (descriptive and informative and personalized to the student) compared with no feedback or low quality feedback. It includes studies of homework, again often in the form of homework versus no homework. It includes size of class and grouping. There are effect sizes, the index described in Chapter 3, calculated for each study of each area and these can be added together, adjusted for sample size and other features of different study, and averaged so that Hattie (2009) can give an estimate of the effect of that area of instruction on learning. When all of the effect sizes across all areas are considered, the average effect of planned interventions so to speak, we have an overall estimate of the effect size and it is 0.4.

Hattie's (2009) estimate is that on average classroom change in carefully designed studies that compare one form of change with what is typical produces a gain of less than half a standard deviation. The most effective areas, such as the area of well designed feedback, produce a gain over 1.0 standard deviation. But these results are in carefully controlled circumstances involving well scripted and monitored changes over a brief period. And they are not studies specifically about the effects for the children about whom we are concerned and do not ask the distribution question. We need to know how much difference a change makes over the long haul to their relative standing compared to a distribution, not of their peers but of the general population.

To summarize the argument so far; it is important to be able to demonstrate that a programme can lift achievement for students from a particular community relative to similar students and schools. But that doesn't tell you whether this is an important or equitable difference. The statistics that are applied in these circumstances can be misleading. A significant difference may not mean educationally valuable change. The criteria of acceleration and building matched distributions provide both developmental and equity criteria. They are tough but transparent, and require a demonstration that the distribution of achievement has been altered for the group of students such that there is the same probability for them as any other child for being in any part of the distribution (high, medium, or low).

The same logic as applied to students from particular communities applies to schools. Schools that serve the poorest and most diverse communities who do not have the same economic and political power as mainstream communities should be spread out along the distribution of schools and their achievement, with as much likelihood as being anywhere in that distribution as any other school. From what we have learned from the international evidence that is clearly a daunting challenge.

Acceleration with matched distributions are criteria which set an aspirational goal. Just getting acceleration to average levels in a classroom poses Reading

Recovery with a very difficult benchmark. The programme is recognized as the most successful one-to-one early intervention designed and partly this is because a very tough challenge was set for success. The formulation of acceleration provides a concrete means for judging whether or not educationally and developmentally significant gains have occurred. The former part of the criterion means a rate of gain occurred that actually takes the child to a level that is equivalent to the level expected, while the latter part means that the success is defined by being able to cope at the levels required in a real lived context.

This tough criterion has turned out to be achievable for a large majority of individual children going through Reading Recovery (eg Gomez-Bellenge, & Rogers, 2007). But it takes an intensive pull-out programme providing one-to-one tutoring with a highly trained expert who is well resourced with texts and professional support. It is an early intervention occurring after only a year at school.

Shifting whole distributions

There is more to consider about the idea of affecting a distribution. Acceleration so that a more equitable distribution eventuates is a punishingly difficult benchmark to set. But there is yet another, even more punishing. It was raised in the previous chapter on Matthew Effects. The challenge was posed by Ceci and Papierno (2005). Their challenge was partly political and partly economic, as much as it was about equity. The issue of targeted interventions, essentially those like Reading Recovery or some forms of schooling improvement, can be effective. But isn't there a need to universalize the power of an intervention or at least the resourcing of new developments so that others have access and can be accelerated? Haven't those students in the upper bands of the distribution also got a right to be extended? Isn't a country also interested in even better and brighter graduates from schools?

Ceci and Papierno's (2005) challenge was about targeted interventions that might enable specific schools to be more effective in teaching children whose achievement is typically low and which may be able to equalize distributions. Interventions that lift the tail end and the distribution might satisfy equity issues but may not satisfy other systemic goals to raise the entire distribution. Districts, regions and nations are keen to improve their performance as a whole for diverse political and economic reasons. On that basis they query whether this is funding well spent.

This is not the place to tease out the political and ethical bases for such a proposal. However, it is the place to answer such challenges from the point of view of ideal educational change. The ideal position to take is that these positions – equitable outcomes and shifting a large system – are not mutually exclusive. Both the make up of the distribution and the level of the distribution can change.

That is, the probability that children from particular communities should inevitably be over represented in the lower part of the distribution needs to change. But regions and countries should properly be concerned with where the entire distribution is and raising that entire distribution.

Countries such as Singapore have recognized the latter need and the evidence through international comparisons suggests they have been very successful as a country. The critical question for Singapore and indeed similar countries is whether the shift in the entire distribution contains within it an equitable distribution of achievement for children from different communities.

The case study single school in the last chapter shows that the idea of shifting the distribution of achievement for children is not just about bringing up the tail. It can be about a system change too.

What distribution?

Distributions are derived from assessment tools and choosing the right assessment tool is not straightforward. In the case of school literacy the choice involves selecting both when and what parts of the developmental pathways to examine. The model of literacy development from earlier chapters identifies pathways for both 'constrained' and 'unconstrained' skills. These have different developmental properties. For example, the constrained skills are learned early and quickly. The unconstrained skills are slower developing. The former are necessary conditions for the development of the latter ones, but are not sufficient to guarantee adequate development.

Earlier too I introduced the idea of developmentally progressive interventions in order to counteract Matthew Effects. Checking on what is being assessed and hence what provides the distribution or the evidence for acceleration needs to be well understood in the light of this concept. Showing that acceleration for a group of children has occurred in gaining knowledge of the alphabet, or in understanding and using letter sound combinations accurately is important. But it may be a limited demonstration of having made a substantial impact on reducing disparities because this may have no bearing on later developmental gaps in reading comprehension and writing.

The case of New Zealand's literacy strategy was described earlier where a policy context and resourcing and research and development projects were associated with a drop in Year 4 students who could not read accurately for their age level. The drop was substantial, from 19 per cent of Year 4 children in 1996 to 12 per cent in 2000 and just 7 per cent in 2004. But the same monitoring that shows this change over time also shows that reading comprehension levels and purposeful writing did not improve over the same interval for Māori and Pasifika children compared with other children either at Year 4 (9 year olds) or at Year 9 (14 year olds). Other research studies have confirmed this picture. The New Zealand case shows that, by taking a broad view of assessment, the question of where the changes in acceleration and in distribution have occurred across constrained and unconstrained skills, in the earlier aspects of development and the later aspects reflecting capabilities in the harder areas of the curriculum in the upper primary school can be checked. The policy context and research and resourcing has shifted to focus on these later stages of reading and writing in school.

What is possible?

How possible is it for a country to accelerate achievement and change distributions for children who have typically not been well served by schools? The need for acceleration is shown in the patterns from the National Assessment of Educational progress, which has data on 4th Grade children's reading achievement in the United States over a 30 year period (Fuller, Wright, Gesicki, & Kang, 2007). As I noted in earlier chapters, the gaps between these groups at any one time appear to be large and immutable.

The known long-term trend data on 9 year olds in the US provide representative comparisons in achievement patterns between three ethnic groups, White, Black and Latino. Within such data it is possible to look for evidence for acceleration. Looking at trends over the long time frame of 30 years we can detect an overall gain by the Black students of about three grade levels compared with Whites gaining one grade. The Black–White achievement gap closed dramatically over this time frame. But it has not happened in a smooth incremental fashion. The dramatic gain happened notably in the 1970s and 1980s. In recent years, from 1992, White students had made gains of about half a grade level. Black and Latino groups have had more up and down progress but overall have gained over one grade level. These gains were discernible up until 2002, after which no further reduction has occurred.

Acceleration on such a grand scale is possible but clearly needs to be sustained. Closing these gaps is a big ask. Another perspective is provided by Borman's (2005) review of title 1 programmes, those designed for schools serving poor and 'minority' children. His review of just these schools and the changes in achievement shows little change from the 1980s in measured effectiveness from gains in effectiveness from 1965. The effect sizes have plateaued at about 0.15 (that is, schools with these programmes make gains of a little over 10 per cent of a standard deviation), although the variability has reduced, suggesting that efforts have become more consistent albeit with modest effectiveness. Since 2002 there has been a huge federal push to boost student achievement and close these gaps promoted in the No Child Left Behind programme. Researchers are examining the trend lines very closely to see whether and how the federal policy, operationalized by individual states and districts in their own school programmes, will have an effect over the longer term.

The challenge facing a country

New Zealand, a much smaller country than the United States, and one with a centralized policy and resourcing agency (the Ministry of Education) and national assessments but with relatively autonomous self-managing schools, also faces an acceleration and distribution challenge. It can be seen in the actual distribution of achievement on one of the international comparisons. This comparison shows the average as well as the percentages of children around that average. In international terms the average is high but there is a 'long tail.' Hidden in that tail is a disproportionate number of Māori and Pasifika students.

New Zealand needs to be internationally competitive in niche industries and products. It needs to be able to generate wealth from primary industries such as farming, milk production and timber, and it also needs to be able to develop leading edge skills, knowledge and technologies. But given its size and position these need to be in very specific areas in which the country might have advantages and might be competitive. Literacy levels are part of this continuous imperative.

The distribution has to be changed in three ways. First, its tail needs to be reduced so that more children are literate and able to engage in the activities that are to do with both collective and individual well-being. Second, the mix in the distribution needs to be changed so that the distribution of achievement by children from different communities is made equitable so that they are not unequally represented in the tail and are equally represented in the high achieving leading edge. Together these two things are critical for the social cohesion of the country. And third, the whole distribution needs to be shifted to the right (to the upper end of the distribution in international terms), or shifted upwards.

In this and the previous chapter, two conditions have been identified that need to be met if schools are to make a difference. Under ideal conditions change requires targeted interventions sitting within omnibus programmes and they need to accelerate and change representations in the distributions. The targeted programmes are necessary to reduce the risk of, or provide an antidote to, Matthew Effects. But in the ideal case the developments accruing from that research should be able to inform the system as a whole. The omnibus programmes should be designed to lead to further improvement of the system as a whole.

This case will be put in later chapters when the significance of developing a science of performance and the need for research and development partnerships are discussed. But the evidence is not strong that these ideal conditions can be met.

7

SUMMER LEARNING

The summer break in the United States or New Zealand is a major event in the calendar for both children and their teachers, to say nothing of what it means for families. The six weeks or more of the interregnum mark different phases and different activities for all three groups. What do children do over the summer break? The answer is all manner of things, except in large measure what they do in regular school. But, ironically, what happens over that period of time may be more important to the challenge of creating effective schools than what happens during the school year. And far from being an explanation for why schools can't be effective or for why they are limited in how effective they might be, this needs to be seen as a challenge that schools should help to solve, thereby increasing their effectiveness.

The third of the challenges for an optimistic view of schools' effectiveness has been called 'summer learning.' It is the case that some children are learning what counts at school over summer and some are not. If one summarizes studies that have tracked achievement over more than a school year including the summer break the estimated summer learning compared with what is learned over the school months is equivalent to a loss of at least one month of instruction. In recent estimates in the United States children's test scores on average are at least one month lower returning to school in autumn than they were when they left in spring. Summer loss affects not only reading, the focus of my analysis in this book; it affects other curriculum areas such as maths too (Cooper, Charlton, Valentine, & Muhlenbruck, 2000).

The classic description of this phenomenon comes from Heyns' (1978) study of 6th and 7th Graders in Atlanta schools. Her study contributed strong evidence that schools did make a difference to poor and 'minority' children by clarifying competing interpretations of a previous influential study on schooling, the Coleman Report published in 1966 (Coleman, Campbell, Hobson, McPartland,

Mood, Weinfield, et al., 1966). That report often had been seen as showing that differences among families account for more of the difference in achievement than differences between high schools.

The data in the report do essentially show this. But the next step often taken by readers was to interpret this to mean that high schools had no effect on achievement. A startlingly different conclusion can be drawn from Heyns' (1978) work. Many high schools were able to promote achievement with children from different communities and from both rich and poor families, and the differences in how much achievement they could promote were not great. Heyns (1978) showed that the high schools in her study were indeed effective. Students from different backgrounds made discernible gains, and for these students the gains in achievement were similar when they were at school.

What Heyns (1978) contributed to the analysis of schools' effectiveness was the finding of summer learning. Students from poorer communities and Black students make less growth than other students over the months when schools are closed. Over time, the cumulative effect is to make a substantial contribution to a widening gap in achievement (Cooper, Charlton, Valentine, & Muhlenbruck, 2000; Entwisle, Alexander, & Olson, 1997).

Heyns (1978) showed that between half and two thirds of the annual learning gap between White children from high income homes and the poorest Black children accrued during the summer months. The gradations between the groups in their profiles of achievement in word knowledge over a calendar year were stark. All income and ethnicity groups gained over the school months, somewhat surprisingly for those who took the negative interpretation of the Coleman report. The major differences appeared between school years. For some, gains continued albeit at a lower rate over the summer. For others the rate was reversed and achievement steeply dropped over the summer. Low income Black students lost almost a quarter of a school grade in word knowledge and the lowest income White students made almost no gains over the summer.

The explanation for the summer learning effect is related to family social and cultural practices and families' access to resources. Together these provide differential exposure for children to school-related literacy activities over the summer. Heyns (1978) used a standardized instrument, the Metropolitan Achievement Tests, with well-known features of reliability and validity. The pattern of results was the same across the nine sub tests. Picking the most reliable of the subtests, word knowledge, she found that the single most influential activity which was related to achievement over the summer was reading. It didn't matter whether this was measured in terms of books read, or time spent reading or use of the library, and these were measured in well-designed surveys and diary records. The relationship between reading and vocabulary learning as tapped by the standardized test was very robust. Most importantly, it didn't matter whether you were rich or poor or Black or White, the relationship held.

The average child in Atlanta read more than five books over the summer, but there were substantial differences between families around this average. Heyns (1978) calculated some very precise relationships. Each additional hour spent reading on a typical day, or every four books completed over the summer, were worth an additional vocabulary word, irrespective of income and ethnicity; equivalent to an extra month of achievement on the standardized tests. One word may not sound much but the word knowledge test does not of course measure all the actual words added to children's lexicons. It is like a generalized measure, a proxy for all those words, in the form of a graded scale of the sorts of words associated with school success. Learning one more word on this scale represents a significant impact for these months when what is usual is not a gain but a loss. How much was read was associated with such things as income level and access to (measured in distance from) a library.

What Heyns' (1978) study means is that even if schools who serve the poorest and traditionally less well served communities do as good a job as schools serving wealthier communities, the communities with more of the practices and resources that are linked to school achievement, the gap between achievement in the schools will still get wider because of the summer effect.

The significance of family practices over the summer receives support from an unlikely quarter, the farming and small town communities of rural West Coast New Zealand. The summer learning effect is found here not with the poorest linguistically and culturally diverse children but with children from a variety of homes living in rural and small towns in a remote part of the South island of New Zealand.

Using statistical modelling techniques it is possible to estimate the level of the summer learning effects on achievement at the 33 rural schools together with two sets of urban schools, each with seven schools serving almost entirely Māori and Pasifika students from communities with the lowest income and employment levels. The estimates for the three sets of schools are shown in Figure 7.1. The graph plots the longitudinal growth in the cohorts of students in each set of schools over three years in reading comprehension achievement measured in age adjusted stanines. The size of the cohorts range from 98 students to 573 students. The trends over time for the urban schools show a gradual movement towards the average. Gains are made during the year and these plateau or drop over the summer (which is between December and February in New Zealand). The reading achievement across the schools from the remote West Coast area starts higher and trends upward too. The majority of the students in these schools were Anglo European, with about 16 per cent of the students Māori. The students' families were from a range of income and employment groups.

These students also gained over the course of the school year but the mathematically calculated effect of summer has even more of a negative effect on growth than for the urban students. The teachers attribute this effect to attractions of the rural and small town lifestyles and students enjoying activities

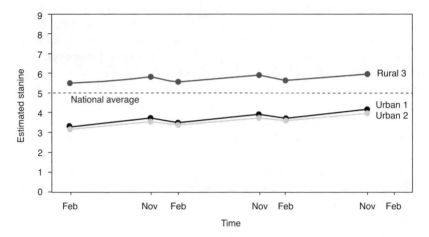

FIGURE 7.1 Estimated growth models in reading comprehension in three sets of schools over three school years and two summer breaks (November–February).

to do over summer that do not include 'recreational' reading. The analyses reveal that in all three sets of schools lower achieving students in particular were more likely to drop in achievement scores over summer, and the effects were similar irrespective of ethnicity. Interestingly, the patterns suggest more access to and use of school related literacy activities in the urban settings over summer, especially activities associated with neighbourhood libraries and churches. The presence of these variations across regions and the likely explanations are consistent with the fourth explanation in Chapter three for not being more effective; we would be more effective with more educational coverage.

A tougher acceleration problem and even more profound Matthew Effects

There are two possible implications for schools arising from this finding of the significance of summer learning. One is that the schools serving the communities who traditionally find schools risky places need to be even better at teaching than other schools. Their children need to make better than average rates of gain. Heyns' (1978) study contributed to a rethinking of the value that schools add to learning. All groups made some gains during the school months and at somewhat similar rates, more similar than some interpretations of Coleman, Campbell, Hobson, et al. (1966) had predicted. But the gains over the school months in the Atlanta schools were not equal. The White children from the wealthiest homes gained more than three quarters of a grade score while the poorest Black child on average gained a little over a half of a grade score. On average

Black children gained 0.61 of a grade and White children 0.70, the expected gain given the test design.

The differential gain over the whole year comprised of small differences while at school and larger ones while not at school poses the acceleration problem I identified earlier in a new form. The presence of the summer learning effect (SLE) means gaining a fully matched distribution of achievement a very difficult proposition over the long term. In the last chapter I presented some evidence that under the best conditions we can design currently, schools that serve the poorest and children from communities with the lowest political and social power in an intervention phase, can accelerate achievement gains and change the distribution patterns so that the children's achievement matches a more normal distribution. The substantial issue is whether that can be sustained over the longer term, to cumulatively maintain equitable outcomes. And that means dealing with the SLE in some form.

To add to the challenge, researchers have identified the severity of the challenge posed by SLE when accumulated over years. This is a repeat of the second problem I identified; it is a problem of Matthew Effects but in a new form. The SLE creates a barrier that gets larger over time. In their remarkable longitudinal study of these effects the researchers at Johns Hopkins University have plotted the cumulative effects from the start of school (Alexander, Entwisle, & Olson, 2007). Their study followed a representative sample of Baltimore children from 1st Grade through to age 22 years. Starting in 1982, they have been describing the SLE in papers and books, drawing the attention of educators and policy makers to its significance.

Recently they examined the cumulative effects. The extent of the differences over the first nine years surprised even them. The SLE differences contributed to more than half of the overall differences in achievement between low and high SES youth. Over the first five years the effect accounted for a larger component of achievement difference than that built up over the preschool years. Moreover, as these researchers put it, the difference continued to 'reverberate' into high school. The achievement gaps contributed to differences in high school placements, drop out rates, and college attendance. They described the cumulative effect as a 'lasting legacy.'

Being more effective implies being able to either overcome or minimize the SLE. One possibility is by super teaching over the course of the school year. There are two routes to doing this. One is accelerating so much that we nullify the drops because the net gain is so large over the years. But is it reasonable to expect schools to produce gains that over a calendar year and beyond are so large that despite drops over summer cumulatively a normal distribution can be achieved and maintained? The acceleration challenge and the Matthew Effect phenomena associated with summer would seem to pose insurmountable difficulties. And there is little evidence for that degree of acceleration.

But there is a second route to doing this and this is the second implication of the research on summer learning. A second route is to do something more directly about summer. But this begs a prior question. The question is whether dealing with what happens when school is not in session is a school's concern. The answer to this is an emphatic yes. Not to solve that 'problem' alone or even completely, but it is the school's job to contribute to solutions.

Not by schools alone

The slump in achievement over the summer occurs because the literacy and language activities in which some children engage with their families do not provide, to the same extent as in other families, school related literacy experiences. In the language of cultural capital theory from the first explanation for the ineffectiveness of schools, families have different access to social and cultural resources that are valued by schools. For those who have practices valued by schools further learning and development occur in school-related knowledge and skills.

Furthermore, isn't the influence that schools can have over access to and use of these practices over summer at best likely to be indirect, unless of course schools continued to remain open (an option to which I will return)? A psychological approach to this problem can be posed in this way: being able to influence activities that are distant in time and place is a classic problem of transfer or generalization. This is dependent on building processes or actions that are carried out perhaps through such robust and well practised activities that they continue off site, perhaps with generative strategies that enable children to modify their own learning and develop control over that learning without the continuing immediate guidance; perhaps through guidance or supports that have been put in place to bridge the gaps to prompt and to pace; or perhaps by providing children with the capability to modify their own immediate surroundings to create a more conducive context for the school, like literacy activities. Can teachers and schools actually do this, that is, influence the likelihood that these practices will more often occur?

The case of vocabulary

One possible way for schools to be influential is to be so effective at enabling children to be readers that more children more often generalize the reading practices of school at home. Is this possible? There is very little evidence to answer that question and given what we know about how family practices are dependent on resources such as access to appropriately challenging books, it is seemingly a daunting challenge.

Following on from Heyns' (1978) groundbreaking findings, a concrete example to examine for possibilities is vocabulary learning. There are additional reasons for exploring the case of vocabulary including how central it is to the development of reading comprehension and hence widespread success at school from the middle grades (Biemiller, 2006). Vocabulary size is related to reading comprehension.

The size of vocabulary on entry to school is a very significant predictor of reading comprehension, not greatly in the 1st Grades but from 3rd Grade onwards and in some remarkable studies 11 years into school. The reasons for this are not hard to fathom. Vocabulary provides building blocks for making meaning. The vocabulary one has acts as an amplifier of thoughts and capabilities to communicate and receive communication. The more words one knows the more words one can discern, acquire, and develop the shadings of meanings of. The more words one knows the more sense one can make out of books. And even more importantly the more one can work out the meanings of new words and their linguistic properties, adding these to one's lexicon. Matthew Effects are present in vocabulary learning; the more vocabulary one has the more one can gain.

From where do the opportunities to acquire new words come? They come in the early years from the language input from one's family and community. Increasingly in the preschool and then early school years the books being read to children and the other literate exchanges are also sources. In the middle school years, being able to read becomes an engine for getting new words, both from the books one reads but also the other literacy environments one enters such as the Internet. Writing becomes a vehicle for developing one's sense of words too.

What we know is that the words that matter at school are initially the basic words in early texts that reflect high frequency words in widespread use across communities who use the language of instruction. But after that they are complex academic words or words used in literary ways, in analogies, in metaphor, in figurative ways that are the language landscape of writers. After the early years children meet in books phrases like 'the rock face,' words like 'induct,' 'unfurl' and 'alias.' Part of the source of these words is the exposure to and use of texts for reading and for studying at school. At least three influences that teachers have direct control over affect learning new words from these texts. One is the breadth and intensity of immersion in that literary landscape. A second is the teacher's deliberate teaching of vocabulary both with these texts and through other means. A third is the incidental acquisition associated with how teachers introduce and use words in the context of classroom activities.

There are several pieces to the puzzle of how children at school can be fast, efficient and increasingly productive learners of new words. The role of the teacher is one piece. Under the best practice designs for deliberate instruction researchers have shown the rates of adding new words via deliberate instruction in the early grades can reach about 12 new words per week and in extended studies for six weeks or more in older children up to 50 words might be added (Biemiller, 2006). But this rate is a small proportion of what average children acquire in a year; it is many hundreds of word meanings, in one estimate six new words per school day (Biemiller, 1999). There is a second piece to the jigsaw. Perhaps half of these new words come from children acquiring them through their own strategies applied during their personal reading. Under ordinary reading conditions with appropriate level texts children will work out and learn the meaning of about fifteen in every one hundred unknown words they encounter (Swanborn, & de Glopper, 1999).

If we are to capture effective teaching and learning for all children then these pieces, deliberate teaching as well as incidental exposure and acquisition through reading immersion, need to be aligned. We know some details about the role of the teacher in orchestrating this. There is the teacher's selection and introduction of texts that provide the right exposure, where the books are well matched with children having the types of words that they need, at the right frequencies in the appropriate linguistic contexts. There are the embedded explanations during reading to children and in other contexts; the on the fly extensions of an idea or connotation for using a partially known word, or elaboration of new and unfamiliar words. There is the explicit teaching of words, of how to parse words studying their morphology, creating the networks of knowledge that will be generative. There is the motivational influence of the teachers, as models and energizers for wanting to learn new words and new meanings, developing the sheer fascination with words and the need to know more. There is the community of readers teachers can create and foster in their classroom.

Interdependent with all of the above is the developing expertise of the child. The knowledge base they have about words, the strategies they have for identifying and solving, using for example their understanding of morphology and their capabilities to use analogies. And there is the awareness, their reflection and evaluation of their own learning that enables them to be metacognitive about learning.

A critical piece is the awareness students have. Being aware contributes to children being the source of their own development. In word learning this means promoting 'word consciousness' and rekindling the capabilities for learning in children who have become relatively uninterested. To bring them back to being what they had as young children, something like being 'word detectives.'

Each of these pieces for the puzzle of how children can be expert learners of vocabulary needs to be in place to maximize learning, but is this enough to produce the generalization that is needed to influence summer learning? Even if we get all of that right over the school year is it enough to generalize to when the school texts, the teachers and the class community are absent?

These come together for some children and not for others, as Heyns (1978) found in her study of what happened over summer. Time spent reading outside of school, at home and in libraries contributed considerably to achievement during summer. The relationship is also true of when children are at school. The more books children read recreationally at home the better they are at comprehension at school. Richard Anderson and his colleagues (Anderson, Wilson, & Feilding, 1988) established that twenty years ago. In their remarkable study of reading at home, 5th Graders in a small town from mostly middle class families filled in detailed diaries over several weeks. From these diaries the researchers determined number of words read at home. Staggering differences between the least and the most exposure to words emerged. Children at the extreme end would read by their calculations nearly 5 million words over the course of a year. At the other extreme the figure would be less than 10,000 and comprized mostly of words not in books. The former child would spend nearly two hundred times as many minutes per day reading books as the children who read least.

The range is a powerful finding and the patterns support the conclusion that home practices are a major source of differences between children in literacy experiences. But the study also considered the significance of the relationship when compared with (controlling for) other possible influences. The researchers also looked at a number of at home activities such as doing chores, homework, eating dinner, listening to music, all the usual things that might occupy a 5th Grader's time out of school, and relationships with reading comprehension in school. Reading time was by the far the more influential.

The researchers also factored in one other potential influence. A major influence on how well you read in one grade is how well you have read in earlier grades. Once that relationship was accounted for, the best predictor of a child's overall reading comprehension level in 5th Grade and growth in reading comprehension from the 2nd to the 5th Grade was time spent reading books. Vocabulary levels and growth from the 2nd to the 5th Grade in these levels were also significantly affected by time spent reading.

Teachers' roles influencing out of school practices

Once again these complex ways of teasing out a relationship confirm the significance of the practices. But what is very important for our understanding of the limits of schools is what Anderson, Wilson, & Fielding (1988) discovered about the effects of schools on this reading at home. The surprising finding was of a close relationship between time spent reading at home and the particular classroom a child came from. The relationship with an individual teacher was substantial. Children from the class that read the most at home averaged 16.5 minutes per day whereas children from the class that read the least averaged only 4.1 minutes a day.

The argument I made for searching for variability leads us to the obvious questions. What were those teachers doing, or not doing? What were the sources of the variability in student outcomes associated with individual teachers? We can make some tentative predictions from case studies and snippets of evidence such as the detail coming out of the Johns Hopkins research team (Alexander, Entwisle, & Olson, 2007) looking at the SLE and their design of teaching programmes through which teachers might influence the SLE in a number of ways. These ways include deliberately promoting appropriate books and increasing access to engaging texts at suitable levels of difficulty; selecting appropriate books to frequently read to children; providing time for extended reading in class; developing the awareness of children to take the initiative and further develop practices of literate uses; and generally creating a vibrant and sustained community of readers. In this sense their role as part librarian, part bookseller, part sales person and motivator and part model for what a reader can be, is substantial and apparently able to impact on reading practices at home, despite not being present at home.

Unfortunately, in the Anderson, Wilson, & Fielding (1988) study observations of teachers that would unravel these possibilities were not undertaken, and being a correlational study the usual caveats apply. Perhaps in the allocation of children to staff at the schools there was an unintended effect whereby the children more likely to be readers at home were placed with certain teachers, and those less likely to read at home were placed with others. We need added evidence both in the form of natural experiments and deliberate experiments to fully test this suggestion out that teachers can have effects beyond the walls of the classroom, through their actions in the classroom that can change children's actions outside the classroom.

This is yet another point at which the search for variability yields important findings. The summer learning effect is variable, even within ethnic and social groups and between like schools and even between like classrooms. As Anderson, Wilson, & Fielding (1988) showed, some classrooms do not drop in their achievement over summer. In the set of urban and rural schools referred to earlier, over three years losses over summer were the norm. But in the second year of the study of the rural schools, in eight schools this did not happen. The students in these schools gained over the summer months and these were not just the higher SES schools. Anecdotal information from those schools suggested that they did a range of things, such as keep their school libraries open over summer for families to access (in remote rural communities this would be the only library available).

A more direct test of the potential influence of teachers was carried out by researcher James Kim (2006) with 4th Grade children and their teachers. The 550 children, about half of them Black and Latino children, were from 10 high poverty schools. This study employed several pieces of the jigsaw. There was a teacher preparation and guidance piece, there was a child self-development piece and there was a piece about family practices.

The students were guided by their teachers while still in school to practice oral reading at home with a family member and to use comprehension strategies during independent silent reading at home. The guidance included an oral fluency component in which children learned to read out loud to a family member who in repeated reading checked expressiveness, intonation, and word knowledge. Five comprehension strategies were taught to the students to enable them to activate and monitor reading for meaning (questioning, rereading, predicting, activating background knowledge, and summarizing) who then practised them to be used during silent reading. The guidance occurred in the last month of school with all children.

The design of the research was such that all children got the preparation and guidance. What differed for half of the children was they got extra components aimed to boost their personal control, their awareness, and to activate family practices. Eight personally matched books were sent home biweekly over the two months of the summer together with postcards that had prompts to students to check the use of strategies and to have parents sign off that 'read alouds' had happened. In this respect, the study was carefully designed to provide a matched programme in that all children got the training at school but only half got the full package. Through surveys of reading habits and book preferences and text based measures of difficulty levels the eight books were well-matched with each child. Spring and autumn (pre and post) testing occurred and surveys of summer reading activities were conducted on return in Grade 5.

The surveys suggested that both groups of students read silently about the same amount over the summer, but the package did increase engagement in the oral reading activities with family members. The overall rate of engaging in literacy activities either personal or reading aloud was around once a week for the treatment group and slightly less frequently for the other group. The study compares one group against the other in terms of achievement levels when back at school in autumn. There was a difference favouring the group that got the postcard prompts and the books actually delivered at home. While the overall gains were relatively small for the groups that had the summer reading intervention, effect sizes for Black and Latino students in the treatment groups were 0.22 and 0.14 respectively.

The study was designed to compare the end result for the two groups. However, what is interesting is that while the overall group on average tended to drop in scores over summer, reflecting the ubiquity of the SLE (the autumn score was 13 per cent lower than the spring score), the gains by students who got the full package with all the pieces appeared sufficient to overcome the drop. The important finding was that the teachers' actions had a detectable effect on fluency and comprehension when the students were not at school and family practices were brought into play. In the results is another important finding. Family income level was not associated with greater or lesser effects. It was what practices occurred in families that was important.

This voluntary reading programme illustrates what needs to be solved to create an effective programme that could make a difference over the summer using the potential of teachers' roles. In this study the teacher prepared and organized to increase the likelihood of reading occurring over time and over sites. The study also shows that schools by themselves may not be able to overcome this summer learning effect. Families were involved, both directly in hearing reading but also indirectly as they made family time and space available for the reading to occur. But this study certainly shows that schools (or more generally educational endeavours to which schools contribute) have ways of influencing what happens over summer. It shows how the SLE is a problem to which schools can contribute solutions.

Teachers' roles in overcoming SLE

The first role therefore that teachers and school personnel can have is developing children's capabilities for being word learners outside of the classroom, putting in place the pieces that increase the likelihood that school related reading will occur. In the Kim (2006) study these include well-prepared children (motivated and skilled with strategies and aware of the goals), and appropriate resources (the selected texts) that were systematically and repeatedly made available for the children at home.

The component of providing appropriate books as an indirect way of influencing home practices has received some research attention. One New Zealand programme called Books in Homes gives books to Māori and Pasifika children. These are children from homes which have few books who are in schools serving the poorest communities. The children can choose which books from a range and over years can own up to seven, which they take home. An evaluation of the programme that followed children over a year including the summer found the 10 and 11 year old children's scores on a composite reading test which included comprehension and vocabulary increased over and above what the average gain in reading would be expected, in fact a 35 per cent gain by the 83 children. How much reading took place over summer is not known specifically but the reflections from children suggest several times a week during school, which continued over the summer (Elley, 1997).

There is a second role that teachers and school personnel can have. It is to be more directly involved with the development of family practices that support faster, more efficient, and more productive vocabulary learning. In other words, to not only prime children but also to prime their environments. This is in keeping with considering the need for summer learning as a problem to be solved, rather than being an explanation for why schools can't be as effective as we might want them to be.

In the early years of reading there are ways teachers can support parents to hear their children read books taken home from school. The research evidence shows that if specific guidance and techniques are given to parents and there is a flow of information between parents and teachers then children's early decoding accuracy and fluency can be improved and their progress in their reading texts can be boosted. One programme with a substantial experimental base enables parents to use techniques that are disarmingly summarized as "pause, prompt, and praise" (Glynn, 1995).

There are a number of studies, including larger scale programmes, that show how it is possible to change family literacy practices (Hannon, 2003). But these are not often directed from the school showing the effectiveness of teachers or school personnel to influence practices over summer, in reading comprehension generally or vocabulary learning in particular. The general literature shows that large gains are possible. One very influential set of studies from the UK did go over more than one year and hence the summer break (Hewison, & Tizard, 1980).

Parents who regularly interacted with their children through hearing them read aloud books sent home had children who had the highest scores in a large group of children from 'working class' families. If this went on for three years the scores were at the highest level, higher than if parents regularly interacted but only for two years. But even these parents had children whose scores were higher than parents who only regularly interacted for a year or those that never interacted. Without regular reading children were typically 20 per cent below national average levels, but with regular activity at home children were at average levels. Once again, it was the actual practice that predicted the outcomes much more than any other characteristic of the family.

This approach, to identify summer learning as at least in part an *educational problem*, is not the same thing as saying that a community's families and their practices are a problem to be solved. Families and their communities are not necessarily deficient in the cultural, social and linguistic resources they have. Their practices of language and literacy are not necessarily deficient in any absolute sense. Having a resource rich view of families is critical if we are to solve these educational problems. The alternative, seeing the families as deficient and their practices as poor or inadequate forms of parenting, has two predictable effects. These effects are in addition to the ethical and cultural offensiveness of the position. One is that there are limits to how much families will change in the context of outsiders, or representatives of mainstream communities giving messages that they are a problem and mainstream practices are inherently better and the right way to do things. The second is that the cultural imperialism undermines existing practices and parents' socialization roles are weakened. The educational problem to be solved is helping families and communities to build the sorts of extra resources they need if they are to also support, along with all their other socialization tasks, children's development in school related literacy (McNaughton, 2005).

We know that it is possible to add to families' literacy practices. And that these can contribute to school achievement. Most of that evidence comes from systematic changes in early literacy and language practices. There are well known principles about how to add value to family practices in ways that make a developmental difference. These include the need to be clear about guidance, demonstrating by using aspects of practices already in family repertoires, appropriate resources, and explicitness in sharing ideas and goals related to language development (McNaughton, 2005).

What about later at school when the issue of summer learning becomes critical? There are studies of how families add to their practices, either directly from guidance from teachers or indirectly by observing and incorporating aspects of school activities. These are not studies that are able to show effects on summer learning. What they do show however is the potential for families to add to what they can contribute through their practices to learning at school.

Like the Kim (2006) study there are studies of teachers providing guidance for how family members can hear their children read books for instruction that are sent home. A style of guidance can be built that has key elements which are significant for school learning. In the "pause, prompt, and praise" programme (Glynn, 1995), for beginning stages of reading these elements were pausing around errors (to enable self-corrections to occur), prompting to use cues to solve difficult words, and praising (providing feedback for accurate reading). Added to these elements of guidance are books that were at suitable difficulty and interest levels for children to be reading in a band of accuracy in which there are opportunities for learning but which do not pose too great a difficulty. This "pause, prompt, and praise" programme (Glynn, 1995) has a solid research base which includes its effectiveness as redeveloped for the indigenous community in New Zealand, for Māori for use in Te Reo Māori (the Māori language) (Hohepa, & McNaughton, 2002). Low progress Māori children and low progress children in general whose parents use the key elements in related sessions make significantly better progress in fluent and accurate decoding than children whose parents are not engaged in repeated sessions.

The role of parents' ideas and beliefs are clearly evident in these studies. A descriptive study of Samoan parents in a New Zealand school serving communities with the lowest employment and income levels examined how parents heard their children read books sent home by the teachers (McNaughton, Amituanai-Toloa, & Wolfgramm-Foliaki, 2009). The children were in bilingual classes, but were learning to read in English. The parents varied in how they approached this task. Those that had some experience with schools in New Zealand adopted a more "pause, prompt, and praise" (Glynn, 1995) approach. But all the parents added something that they had not seen but believed was important. The parents also checked their children's comprehension of the story that was read by requesting they reread the story in Samoan. They believed that they could check whether the children understood their reading if they could retell it and in so doing would practice their first language too.

It is possible to promote more learning over summer. Teachers can influence family practices that support school related learning, and they can influence their children's reading over summer. These are ways of solving the problem as a generalization problem, to use the traditional psychological framing. But there is another possible solution, which does not involve the regular classroom teacher in the dual roles. It takes the idea of school and adds that to the summer.

Summer schools

Summer schools are widespread in the United States and are designed for a variety of purposes. But among the summer schools are those designed to provide remedial programmes or provide catch up programmes for children who are low achievers or from communities where lower achievement at school is often the case.

A recent review of these programmes revealed that they can be very effective in reversing the achievement loss over summer for particular groups (Cooper,

Charlton, Valentine, & Muhlenbruck, 2000). On average, the achievement gains can be equivalent to the gains made during the entire regular school year. The average gains are about 25 per cent of a standard deviation, effect sizes around 0.25. This summary of the effects comes from studies that look at gains from the beginning to the end of a programme and at gains in one group going to summer school versus other groups.

The review comes to several strong conclusions about what works best. Programmes are more effective if they are targeted on academic content and instruction in subject matter. This conclusion comes from a curious finding that more gains occurred for children at either end of the school system. More gains were associated with programmes catering for the early grades and those catering for the later high school grades, rather than those programmes catering for the middle grades. The reason for this is that the programmes at beginning and end levels were usually more targeted on specific school-like content. At the lower grades successful programmes were focused on specific things to do with learning to read and write, and at the later grades focused on specific curriculum content.

Programmes that were more successful were targeted in a second way; they were more like school not only in content but also in terms of regular attendance. The hours of the summer schools varied but the most effective were between 60 to 120 hours over the summer. Finally, and not surprisingly given what I have said about the significance of family practices, the reviewers also found that the summer schools were more effective if there was some sort of parent involvement. This could include conferences with the teachers, observing in class, and even hearing reading at home.

Two provisos emerge however. One is the old bogey of Matthew Effects. In those programmes where there was a mix of students from different socio economic backgrounds it was found that middle class students made greater gains. The second proviso was something like a recency effect – there was evidence from programmes that went over more than one summer that gains might diminish over time.

Even with the best design features noted above, the effects of summer school can be moderated by context effects over which the designers and educators have very little control. This was dramatically demonstrated in an evaluation of a summer school programme operating across three years (Borman, & Dowling, 2006) that has many of the features of best practice found in Cooper et. al.'s meta analysis (Cooper, Charlton, Valentine, & Muhlenbruck, 2000). It was targeted on kindergarten and Grade 1 children from 10 high poverty urban schools. It was carefully designed with comparisons between those who went to the summer school with children who didn't. It involved a full day school like programme specifically for literacy learning with reading and writing skills in the morning and comprehension in the afternoon.

But after three years there were no differences detected on the reading vocabulary or reading comprehension measurers for the group of children going to the summer school. Both groups made gains during the school months and dropped or plateaued in achievement over the summer. In school terms, and only in school terms, over three summers there was essentially no extra learning for these children in elementary schools from high poverty urban neighbourhoods.

However, the researchers explored the large differences in attendance which varied substantially across the three summer sessions; only one in three children attended all three. Attendance patterns mirrored attendance at regular school and mobility. When analyses were conducted of what happens with full attendance versus not going to summer school the results were much stronger and the effect size for vocabulary rose essentially from zero to 0.32 and to 0.28 for comprehension. The treatment effect for 'compliers,' those attending at least two of three summers, was a gain of 50 per cent of one grade level in vocabulary and 40 per cent of a grade level for comprehension.

Conclusion

Two possible multi component solutions to the SLE may be possible. One is through schools working more deliberately with their children and communities to find ways of building access to and use of practices over summer. A second is through extending schools themselves. In a sense taking the summer break out of the SLE.

The research evidence raises questions about both approaches. Despite indicative support for the components, getting all the pieces coordinated in a powerful demonstration has yet to happen. On the other hand, increasing the schools' coverage raises a number of questions. There are societal as well as local questions. In some countries and for some groups more time at school even in summer school may not be acceptable or an option. Is compliance in attendance at these yet another problem schools might have to solve? This is unlikely, although through highly motivating and closely connected programmes some increased attendance might be created. But attendance also is at least partly to do with policies around employment and housing. And this leads us back to the central argument in this chapter. Yes, the summer learning is a school issue. And it is something that schools should attend to and probably can. But it is only partially solvable by schools. The solution is not by schools alone.

The conclusion about the SLE is that this should be seen as a problem for educators and schools to contribute solutions, rather than an explanation for why schools cannot be effective. So schools wishing to be effective are faced with not just an acceleration and distribution problem in the short term. They are faced with a threat to cumulatively being able to make and sustain a difference. They need to be able to contribute to solving the summer learning effect.

The fourth explanation for why schools are not as effective as we would like them to be came from the findings about summer learning. One conclusion that can be couched in terms of that explanation is that school learning is not extensive enough. That is, more schooling is needed. The summer schools prove a point about the effectiveness of schools and they also show how overcoming Matthew Effects needs targeted programmes. But they are limited in their effectiveness. Under the best possible conditions of full attendance in well designed programmes the gains are unlikely to meet the acceleration criterion.

Postscript

The evidence reviewed in this chapter raises a very important methodological issue about evaluations of school effectiveness. The presence of the SLE means that studies that simply examine gains over the course of a school year, as well as those studies that only measure gains over a calendar year, misrepresent the nature of both learning and development of children. In the former case just measuring gains over the school year does not give any indication of the impact and extent of summer learning. This may substantially over-represent gains for children. In the latter case, only measuring across a calendar year may substantially under-represent what schools can do in terms of learning while at school.

8

SUSTAINING CHANGE

Not just accelerating learning, but at the same time overcoming Matthew Effects and the SLE pose significant challenges to the enterprise of designing more effective schools. Being able to change a school to make the sorts of differences that matter is hard, but it also turns out that changing a school then sets up two further challenges. These are: how to sustain what has been changed and how to reproduce, or scale up that change, elsewhere. Both are harder to achieve than getting the right conditions in place for the change in the first instance. There almost seems to be a self-limiting principle operating. It is easy, relatively speaking, to get the model demonstration in place; but thereafter not so easy at all to make it last and take it to other sites.

Sustaining changes

Sustainability, the challenge to maintain gains that have been made, has become a buzz word in educational discussions. The buzz has come about because numbers of studies with schools have found that the effects of an initial intervention may not last (Coburn, 2003). Schools that have successfully implemented reforms have found it difficult to keep the changes going. Those programmes of change that have involved external agents are especially vulnerable and the literature contains many examples of when the influx of resources, professional development and the supports available through the programme finish, the practices implemented also finish in that they dissipate over time (Borman, 2005; Coburn, 2003).

Kamehameha

One of the most compelling descriptions of a programme of change that was sustained and rolled out on a large scale was the influential programme in the schools of the Kamehameha district in Hawai'i (Tharp, Estrada, Dalton, &

Yamauchi, 2000). The Kamehameha Elementary Education Program (KEEP) was a programme for Native Hawaiian students at kindergarten through to 3rd Grade, and aimed at building higher achievement levels in reading than the typical low levels for indigenous Hawaiian students. It started in 1970 and pronounced gains in reading achievement occurred. It continued with effective instruction faithful to the design in the original programme in the original schools and was extended to 15 multicultural public schools over an 18 year period. Achievement results continued to be above those of comparable non KEEP schools for 18 years. Then in 1997 it was formally terminated.

The original designers of the programme had constructed a multidimensional programme that used innovative theory. One aspect of its cutting edge design was evidence-based incorporation of the cultural resources of the students including their preferred ways of speaking and turn taking and their preferred ways of learning. This was done without compromising other aspects of innovation in the instructional design. Teachers developed extensive knowledge about instructional practices from research-based principles, and specific forms of instruction were honed through professional development. Schools implemented a five phase process that the designers had tested experimentally. The most recent analysis of these design features carried out at the end of the intervention identified many aspects of what are, in more contemporary eyes, now seen as best practice. Why dissipation?

The reasons are complex. The designers, reflecting on this question, see it as caused by two threats (Vogt, & Au, 1994). One was "too rapid expansion and reduction of resources," and, ironically, second was a problem arising from their own design. The former could be called the Napoleon syndrome; with enthusiasm to extend coverage, coupled with a course of action that requires continuous resourcing, a stretching thin of the research and development resources can occur. By 1992 classroom practices in the schools to which the programme had been extended had changed away from the original design and the programme no longer retained its core properties; the programme has lost 'fidelity' to the good features of the original design.

The second problem arose from their design focus, which was not on a whole school programme and did not involve change across the curricula. Rather it had a primary focus on literacy and was designed to impact on the lower elementary grades. Both the fidelity issue and the scope of the programme issue have become key determinants in sustaining what schools have achieved. What would have been needed to retain the programme in its robust form, continuing to have important educational effects for Hawaiian children, is a core issue for sustainability.

What is sustainability?

The general challenge of demonstrating sustainability is the requirement to show that when an intervention finishes, the process and programmes that have been put in place are able to continue, and that they continue to have the effects for which they were designed. In the case of trying to accelerate achievement and achieve equitable distributions of achievement, the issue in the first instance is whether the equitable distribution can be sustained for the schools' students. Despite this seeming to be straightforward as a goal, it is by no means clear what this requirement actually means.

The primary meaning of the idea is that the school continues to engage in the practices that produced the impact that was obtained in the first place, including such practices as the assessment, instruction and teaching resources as well as the features of the professional community of the school that have developed and its organizational properties. If the science is right, sustaining those components known to be necessary and sufficient to produce the effects should continue to have the effects initially established. The effects on which this book is focused are primarily student learning outcomes. In the ideal case the outcomes are accelerated rates of learning and an equitable distributions of achievement. (These goals, as I argued in the first chapter, sit within more encompassing goals that include achievement outcomes but include cultural goals and goals of well-being.)

But embedded within this simple definition are several issues. To begin with there is the question of when an intervention ends. The answer to that is very apparent if the change process is one that is designed by and driven by external agents. The end is when the external agent departs. There are some change programmes that are like that and if a restricted view of research design and experimental format is adopted this is almost a necessity. The idea is that there is a planned period when the experimental 'treatment,' often sumamrized as an omnibus 'independent variable,' isn't in place. Then it is, and the external agents implement the treatment. Then, in classic design terms, there is a planned point when the treatment has happened and the outcomes are assessed against the hypotheses. Did change consistent with the hypothesis happen and was the change detectably different from some control or comparison groups? Under these circumstances the question for sustainability is what happens next, whether generalization of the changes after the end of the planned period of the treatment occurred.

The problem with this formulation is that the end may not be very obvious. There are those school programmes that involve an ongoing relationship with external agents who continue to work with the site for change. Charter schools or research collaborations with clusters of schools are examples. The question of when a change process ends in one sense becomes nonsensical if it involves an ongoing relationship with external agents and this creates challenges for the research formats and the design of research into the effects of the 'intervention.' No simple 'before,' 'during' and 'after' design is possible.

These are not insurmountable challenges and I will return to this question. But they throw into relief a knotty problem that needs to be untangled in any programme of change. What would we expect to continue? One sense of sustainability is the expectation of the treatment continuing in the sense of continued school practices and their effects with new cohorts of students. Demographic change is a constant in many settings and especially urban settings, either in the short term at frenetic pace with new town planning and local employment developments or over the longer time frame in which local populations gradually change their composition through changes in house pricing and immigration. Such changes beg the question about whether the practices have the right mix or have the most effective components for new cohorts of students. Does this notion of sustainability across new cohorts of students apply in the face of this change?

Another meaning of sustaining is whether the practices are able to be maintained with new cohorts of teachers. In some urban school districts there is massive turnover of teachers. Studies of Memphis schools in the change programme Success For All (Slavin, & Madden, 2001) show that in the large school district of 104 elementary schools serving poor communities with high numbers of African American students, the typical rates of mobility were 17 to 22 per cent per annum. Interestingly, mobility went up in the first year of intervention, apparently reflecting the demands of teaching with Success For All (Slavin, & Madden, 2001), to above 30 per cent and up to 40 per cent (Ross, & Smith, 2001).

In the face of a third or more of staff changing in a year should sustainability refer to being able to maintain the processes and practices when the community of teachers and leaders has changed markedly? Put another way, perhaps sustainability is best conceived as being able to reproduce what the original groups of teachers achieved and whether they and new teachers can continue to do that over time. If this is the goal then presumably each new group of teachers would need to go through the same process. This is a question of the sustainability of the school community and their practices. This is a tall order for any small to medium sized business, to maintain productivity with an annual turnover of up to a quarter of its staff.

Yet another question is whether sustaining covers the continued progress of children once they have left the school or that part of the school that was the focus of the original intervention. This question is whether the learning is robust over time for the original group of students, a kind of developmental sustainability. Like the other forms of sustainability there are certain consequential questions such as how long one should look for continued effects for a group of students.

Each of these is a legitimate concern for judging sustainability. On pragmatic grounds there is an obvious response to these questions. If a programme of change for a school is dependent on only that group of teachers or leaders who implemented it, or is only applicable to that group of students who received it, or is only applicable to the current make up of the student body, or is only expected to occur while the change process is present and then rates of learning return to pre existing levels, then this is surely a very limited programme of change. But pragmatic concerns may not equal scientific concerns here. Each question requires consideration of what could be expected given the current science, our research and knowledge base in these areas.

Developmentally sustained

Let me take the last question first, the issue of developmental sustainability. The question is whether gains that have been made with a group of students under the most effective change process we could design could be expected to continue. Is change more than a brief phenomenon, detectable not only when the intervention might officially end but as the students progress across further year levels.

What this means in detail for literacy can be described in the following way. A programme of school change could be directed at early grade levels, the beginning part of what really is a long sequence of learning; the acquisition of school literacy. Given this, would learning continue at other levels of acquisition and use. If we got the first step functioning well would later steps be affected the same way? For the early levels of schooling the first step for literacy learning might mean affecting changes so that students more rapidly and comprehensively came to decode accurately and fluently with meaning, and more rapidly and comprehensively developed initial skills in writing to represent accurately words in simple texts. For sustainability to be demonstrated these changes would continue and affect students' later reading and writing, say in-depth reading comprehension and effective writing using a variety of writing genres. A similar requirement applies if reading and writing achievement in the middle or upper primary school years were the target of the change. Would the intervention impact on later learning and achievement in high school, perhaps seen in better performance in high school exams?

The answer to this question introduces two sobering caveats. Unfortunately there are few phenomena in education to which the idea of an inoculation is applicable. Also unfortunately what you design is mostly what you get. Both caveats are in evidence in recent reviews of schooling improvement projects in the United States.

The effectiveness of different programmes at different levels

In the United States by early 2000 over 100 different comprehensive school reform models (CSR) aimed at improving instruction and student achievement had been developed and implemented in between 10–20 per cent of the elementary schools (Rowan, Correnti, Miller, & Camburn, 2009). Less than a third of these (Borman, 2005) were widely replicated sufficiently to enable systematic and reliable analyses of effects. Just like the earlier large-scale attempts in Head Start to change the educational lives of poor and 'minority' children in the 1960s, which involved many models, this massive investment in educational change has produced mixed models with mixed results.

I have described in earlier chapters how Borman (2005) has been plotting the outcomes using the presence of variability in types and implementation as a basis for making judgements about effectiveness. The models differ in substantial ways. They differ in the design of the change process, in the specificity and focus of the instructional design, and in terms of the roles of the external agents and the teachers and leaders at the schools.

Researchers from the University of Michigan also have used this variability between models of change to advantage, as a means for understanding the effects of the different properties that models have. They have compared three of the most widely disseminated CSR models with each other and with schools without models in place, in over 100 schools (Rowan, Correnti, Miller, & Camburn, 2009). They have been looking at how the schools have implemented the models, how their instruction has changed and how these instructional changes map on to the achievement results. These models serve more disadvantaged students than average across the US (reflecting the schools adopting reform); half the sample of over 7,000 students, were African American.

They describe one, the Accelerated Schools Project (ASP), as using a pattern of 'cultural controls.' Facilitators working with schools act to develop a collective vision around 'powerful learning' with a view of children's learning as arising from an inherent need to understand and construct ideas about the world, which means a focus on authentic learner-centered and interactive forms of instruction. What distinguishes ASP from the two others is that it is not prescriptive and does not target particular subjects. That is, it has generic goals, changes are not formally specified and teachers are given autonomy to discover effective forms of teaching. Schools with this programme reported lowest levels of instructional leadership and the improvement plans were weakly specified.

In contrast, the America's Choice (AC) programme used 'professional controls,' and the programme was built around specific curricula content, typically beginning with writing. AC provided detailed guidance to teachers who were trained in a set of routines through workshops and had the professional support of locally appointed coaches and facilitators for the routines, assignments, and rubrics for assessment. Well-specified standards for the curriculum were grounded in professional consensus. In each school there were two leadership positions – a design coach and a literacy coordinator; the former working with principals and the latter with teachers. Teachers viewed their school improvement plans as well specified and were characterized by strong leadership. But the flip side was that the teachers reported lower levels of autonomy than other schools.

The third model, Success For All (SFA) (Slavin, & Madden, 2001), used 'procedural controls.' This model had the clearest and most highly specified plan of all three with tightly specified instructional routines for teaching reading in the early grades including weekly sequences designed around scripts for 90 minute lessons and with specially written books in the early grades. Schools were more centrally managed with a full time literacy coordinator responsible for school wide coordination of the programme. Instructional leaders in the schools and SFA personnel supervised the use of the instructional routines. Levels of leadership were perceived to be as high as in the AC schools and much higher than in the ASP schools.

These three models had different patterns of implementation and distinctive patterns of literacy instruction and student achievement. They varied in how tightly organized the teachers and leaders were, how specified the programme was, and on what the programme was focused including the actual forms of teaching in the classrooms. Two models, SFA and AC, had more highly specified and standardized programmes than the third model and than comparison (non CSR) schools. Leadership was different also, with AC schools higher than other models and non model schools in involvement of leaders in staff development, advising teaches, and setting goals. AC schools relied on having school leaders work closely with teachers to develop the design while SFA teachers relied on scripted lessons for implementation. ASP teachers had the highest autonomy of any model and other comparison schools. The strength of the professional community was assessed in a variety of ways, for example the prevalence of collaboration and critical discussion amongst staff and ASP schools was high on this measure.

These features were associated with distinctive instructional practices. ASP schools were no different on the various measures of literacy instruction from schools without models; that is, they had not changed their practices markedly and had the same variation in approaches as you would expect in a range of schools. AC schools were very different from other schools, with a substantially increased focus on writing and the production of written texts by students. Their teachers taught a broader range of writing components and had a distinctively greater emphasis on comprehension than comparison schools, and integrated work on comprehension with work on writing. There was more explicit teaching of writing, with instruction on literacy techniques and different genres, and students more often shared their writing and did substantive revisions. Students in these schools were more likely to write multiple connected paragraphs than students in other models and comparison schools.

SFA schools were different from their comparison non model schools. They were focused on teaching decoding skills, and word and sub word components of reading. Teachers in these schools were more likely to teach comprehension on a daily basis, teaching comprehension in 65 per cent of all lessons compared with 50 per cent of all lessons in comparison schools. They used direct instruction more often with a focus on comprehension strategies, checking answers and having students discuss with each other. They were no more or less likely than other non model schools to focus on more advanced strategies or write extended text about what they read. The instruction, unlike AC schools, was not 'literature based' and students in AC schools received far more exposure to direct instruction for writing and to work on extended assignments. SFA has been characterized as a skills-based reading instruction with a tendency for students to provide brief written and oral answers to check for basic comprehension.

The researchers examined outcomes at the early grades of K–2 and also at later grades, 3rd to 5th. This decision to cast the net more widely than is typically the case is very important to this question of developmental sustainability. If they had not done this they would have missed a major finding. Not surprisingly, achievement outcomes were different. What was surprising was that they were different at different levels.

As noted already, patterns of achievement in ASP schools were indistinguishable from the variability in achievement in the comparison non model schools in reading and in writing. But in contrast, SFA schools were very different from the comparison schools with a pronounced increase in early reading proficiency. The changes are impressive in terms of the criteria I established earlier. Over the two years K to Grade 2, SFA students moved from the 30th percentile (the average student is ranked at 30 per cent on the national distribution) to the 50th percentile, the average student now ranked at average levels on the early reading tests. The average child in comparison schools moved to about the 40th percentile. But these impressive results were not matched by results in later grades and the explanation is that the skills based approach had its most pronounced effect in promoting early reading proficiency, especially skills associated with decoding.

AC schools also differed markedly from their comparison schools. But unlike SFA, in this model the important differences emerged more clearly at the upper grades. The average students in comparison schools began 3rd Grade on the 40th percentile and ended the 5th Grade at the same level. The equivalent student in the AC school ended on the 50th percentile. The literature based approach focused on writing was better suited to stimulating later reading growth and writing than stimulating early growth.

These results are very close to what are predictable from the research literature on the development of literacy and teaching and learning. The developmental pattern explained in earlier chapters means that early effects are not sufficient to produce later effects. Being able to decode accurately and fluently, and with meaning, is necessary for the development of sophisticated comprehension, but not sufficient. Early decoding does not guarantee later writing skills. The reasons for this have been clearly explained by Scott Paris (2005) in his model of constrained and unconstrained skills (see Chapter 2).

Similarly, the research literature on the effects of teaching suggests that in many settings the effects of teachers will be such that variability of the effectiveness of the teacher from one level to the next will be influential. Certainly, the levels one has achieved in an earlier grade, what one has learned at one point in time, is highly predictive of what the level of achievement will be in a subsequent grade. But even so, there is considerable variability. Hence the conclusion that educational interventions by and large do not act like inoculations. This is a major reason why it was found that the early childhood gains in Head Start needed to be maintained by a schools based programme Follow Through, and why Reading Recovery's effectiveness is at least partially determined by the transition between the withdrawal setting and the classroom teacher's capabilities to teach effectively.

A disturbing by-product is possible with focusing on the necessary but not sufficient stages. There can be a 'child of Matthew Effects' in these developmental patterns. One can alter circumstances so that resources are planned and targeted and desired outcomes happen. The risk here is that by concentrating on one area, we inadvertently set up a more subtle form of Matthew Effects. This may happen for example where students are given a lot of instruction in decoding to provide basic knowledge and awareness of sounds and letters. But if this is done so that the instructional focus on language and comprehension is reduced, either concurrently or cumulatively as other children get more and more access to comprehension resources, and the target children are getting even less of what they need in the longer term.

And there is a potential conundrum in these results too. General programmes developing teachers' knowledge about the nature of development and learning may not be specific enough to change practices effectively. On the other hand, the more specific and detailed the programme, the greater the possibility that impressive effects will be developmentally limited. The solution to this conundrum is the same answer that is needed to solve each of the other forms of sustainability.

Sustained across cohorts

New students come into schools all the time. Should a change be able to be sustained with students who were not part of the original group of students with whom teachers learned to be more effective? The pragmatic answer to this is yes. The logic of traditional psychological science would argue that generalization to similar students should be expected if it was planned for. There is a parallel in applications of psychology to clinical practice. In their training in therapeutic procedures there needs to be a sufficient range of clients to enable generalization of the treatments to new but still similar clients, and with professional ideas in place to ensure that the differences between clients were attended to. This is what happens in training Reading Recovery teachers (Clay, 1994).

The parallel with clinical training is close, but the general school situation is somewhat different. The similarity of new students to original students is not simple. Some things may appear to be similar, say in the mixtures of gender and ethnicity in the student body. But even within these seemingly fixed categories there can be profoundly important differences. The mix of languages and control over those languages in new groups of students from the same ethnic backgrounds can change over years. The degree of access to political and economic resources may change. These have important bearings on the effectiveness of instruction.

Sustainability might mean expecting a programme of change to be sufficiently adaptable to adjust to these changed circumstances. If it did, studies need to track changes over time with new groups of students with known backgrounds in those characteristics that are important to the effectiveness of instruction. These would include language and cultural backgrounds as well as (given our focus) literacy and language practices in the local communities.

There are few studies that provide a systematic analysis of trends over new cohorts of students. In general Borman (2005) found larger effects in a first year of implementation followed by a dip (reflecting the general challenges of sustaining), but also that interventions that are kept in place with fidelity may get to be more effective after five years. The notable exception is SFA. The data on SFA schools suggests that effects with successive cohorts (in Grades 1–3) get larger after the first year as schools get better at the programme and teachers who are not comfortable with the programme leave and others who are well trained in the programme consolidate their practices (Slavin, & Madden, 2001).

Sustaining a community

The question of sustaining in terms of teachers' and leaders' practices introduces a different concern. Given that a programme of change is highly dependent on the personnel who lead and who implement that change, the question of change in the personnel is critical. What happens to a programme when new teachers arrive and when new leaders are appointed? And possibly more problematic is the question, what happens when teachers and leaders who are the old guards, the stalwarts in a programme of change with the institutional knowledge and practices, leave?

Taking the pragmatic approach again would suggest that a programme that was worth duplicating and expanding would need to be able to withstand these pressures. The challenge here is complicated by two things about schools and change, which are both a source of problems and a source of solutions. The first is that teachers have ideas and their practices reflect these. Another is that school communities are cultural entities and some cultures are better at succession planning than others.

People have ideas about learning and teaching, something systematically studied for almost a century. Wundt's concept of 'folk psychology' from 1916 originally applied to our general (mostly tacit) assumptions about the nature of minds. Olson and Bruner (1996) extended this to teachers' theories. They argue that teachers also hold a body of beliefs and assumptions about teaching including what children's minds are like and how one might help them learn. Moreover, they argue that changing teaching requires directly examining these:

> Any innovations will have to compete with, replace, or otherwise modify the folk theories that *already* guide both teachers and pupils.
>
> (Olson, & Bruner, 1996, p. 11, their emphasis)

Subsequently, Olson (2003) has developed the significance of these ideas further in his book on why school reforms largely fail. His answer – because they do not take into account the beliefs that are part of the cultural practices of schools.

The significance of having ideas is that those that teachers hold interact with the implementation of new ways of teaching. Lefstein (2007) describes how the partial implementation of the National Literacy Strategy in England was determined by the pedagogical beliefs of the teachers, because teachers cobble new ideas onto existing practices that reformers are trying to supplant. He uses a social practice perspective to understand this process, focusing on routines and interactional rules (largely unspoken) in the classroom and how these interact with a teacher's rationales. Several processes determine adoption or change in existing practices, including the degree to which knowledge and skills are well articulated in the new programme and the resilience of the interactional routines that already exist.

This sort of mixed implementation is generally seen as problematic. Davis and Sumara (2002) voice typical frustration over interventions with teachers. They studied teachers who used the vocabulary of 'constructivism' to plan, justify, and reflect on their teaching. But what they did often bore little relationship to the core original constructivist frameworks. Partly this is because of how in interventions ideas may not be adequately articulated (Cohen, & Ball, 2006), but it is also because of the ways teachers reconstruct and reframe their practices in idiosyncratic ways.

There is a general challenge here for reforming or improving teachers' practices. Teachers are like other learners and experts and they construct and reconstruct their ideas. This is a challenge in the first stages of implementing a change. It continues to be a problem when new ways of teaching and organizing a school to be more effective have been in place. The ideas that new members have will interact with those critical to the effectiveness of teaching. What this means is that planned induction into the ideas that are critical to the programme and that underpin the practices in the community is essential. The ideas of the incoming personnel are the challenge, but those held in the community are the source of the solution.

There is an even more positive slant to the role of teachers' ideas that needs to be picked up in an additional fourth idea about sustainability, sustaining innovation. Rather than seeing the role of ideas as inherently problematic in making schools more effective, it may be better to see teachers' active reconstruction of ideas as a dynamic, albeit risky, resource.

Ideas such as succession planning and inculcating the deeply held ideas underpinning the practices are understandable needs when the professional community of teachers and leaders is seen as a cultural entity, as Olson (2003) suggested. By considering this part of the total community (the whole school community is of course wider and includes students and families) as a cultural force we can begin to map out what might be required to create longevity in the face of the threat of staff turnover to continued effectiveness. With that view the issue becomes a question of socialization. The existing community socializes the new leaders or new teachers into the practices of the community.

This socialization enables the novice participants to move from being peripheral to the community to more central and knowledgeable members (Lave, 1991). Teachers may initially need considerable support but as they come to be knowledgeable and through the guidance of and collective engagement with other members they can develop as more adaptive experts. In that sense the community is a collective to which new members, including new leaders (and even new researchers), are apprenticed.

Two implications

There are two implications that follow from this analysis of the types of sustainability. One is that the emphasis in programmes of change needs to be on the processes that produce the content as well as the content itself. Change is a constant. The presence of new students with different backgrounds and cultural and linguistic resources from previous students requires flexibility in content and ways of teaching and assessing. Changes external to the schools, such as new assessments and new technologies, to say nothing of new curricula and new policies around the features of schools, also may require adaptiveness and innovation. Reliance on the content that was the outcome of the initial intervention is self-limiting.

But herein lies the conundrum. Being very specific about the content of the programme to be implemented is very significant in schooling improvement. The consensus from the evidence is that clearly specified practices are needed because changing existing practices requires deep knowledge and well-targeted practices, and hence clarity and elaborateness on the part of the design team (Cohen, & Ball, 2007). Being specific is also required for a basic need of science – the need to be able to specify what was done and from that be able to guarantee effects. These basic elements of being prescriptive and very specific about content enable programmes of change to have that sought after characteristic of high treatment integrity (Borman, 2005; Coburn, 2003) and this was what was undermined in the Kamehameha programme.

But the evidence also suggests being overly specific and prescriptive may undermine other features that go to make up effective interventions. One is the developmental sustainability noted earlier. But another is sustainability of communities and their preparedness to adjust to change. A degree of local autonomy is needed for the community to develop and to continue to develop as a community, and hence importing a set of procedures, particularly if they are highly specified, risks undermining local autonomy and efficacy (Coburn, 2003; Newmann, Smith, Allensworth, & Bryk, 2001). Indeed, approaches in which professional development focuses on joint problem-solving around agreed evidence such as student achievement outcomes are more likely than highly prescribed programmes to result in sustainable improvements in student achievement, particularly reading comprehension (Coburn, 2003; Hawley, & Valli, 1999; Timperley, Phillips, & Wiseman, 2003). But, as the reviews of ASP showed, a more collaborative development of common procedures risks not developing a well-specified and articulated programme, losing instructional coherence, and losing the specificity needed to be able to meet the basic requirements of treatment fidelity.

These tensions can be solved by distinguishing between the specificity of a process of change and the point at which the content itself should become specified. We know a lot about the processes by which a community needs to engage in order for it to be effective. This includes the collaborative and informed use of evidence to make decisions about instructional needs, and the testing out of the ongoing effectiveness of the instructional practices that have been developed from those processes. On the basis of evidence from across the schooling improvement literature we can specify the core processes now. These core processes, such as the evidence-informed interrogation of practices, can and should lead to a highly specific programme of instructional practices.

Here is the fundamental point for sustainability. Highly specified processes can be the basis for practices that can change in the future. The advent of new students, of new teachers, and of new external drivers such as new knowledge about instruction and newly designed curricula can be incorporated into the processes. A specific process can still lead to specific programmatic content, specific instructional designs to teach reading and writing, but the content of that programme is derived from a relatively more open ended starting point than starting with a prescriptive instructional programme that is externally designed and implemented.

This point is very important to the question of scalability also, which is the topic of the next chapter. Having a highly specified process of changing means that programmes can be developed that are adapted to local circumstances. Making the distinction I have made here means we can talk of fidelity to a process that can still deliver a high degree of programme specificity, which has been localized. The object then would be to develop fidelity to a programme that has been strongly contextualized by developing a highly focused collaborative context. The issue for researchers would then also include examining the suitability and effectiveness of the process where different types of local adaptation occur and where there may very well be differences in both short term and long term outcomes for students and teachers with different ways of developing the content.

The second implication that follows from this analysis of sustainability is that the basic models of school change need to be modified. Change should be able to be conceived as a process, however short or long; rather than as a discrete event that is enacted with external agents, who then move on. This is the core limitation of the classic experimental design applied to schooling contexts. The process needs to be reconceived as one in which partnerships are developed where needed expertise particularly in the content of change is accessed and negotiated. And where ongoing partnerships with external agents are still needed, not necessarily in the original form, but in some form which means reciprocal flow of ideas and practices. I will discuss more of this idea when we look at a science of performance.

Postscript: sustaining innovation

The challenge of solving the need for more effective instruction in schools serving diverse populations of students is clearly not easily or quickly solved. But the last part of this chapter introduced yet another twist. The rub is that getting the instruction and outcomes right for this group of students at this time and in this place is not all that is necessary. It is not the only thing on which we should be focusing. And it is not just being able to guarantee outcomes further up the school and with new students and staff. It is sustaining the process of being able to change to be more affective: to be innovative.

9

SCALING UP

We might be able to design a very effective intervention in a school that can be sustained over time with new staff and new students, and even over time with the same students as they develop through the school. But can this intervention be made to work with more and more schools? It is not much use if it is only workable with one school or a small set of schools because in most countries the children for whom we want schools to be more effective are not just in one or a small set of schools. Can the intervention be scaled up?

Scaling up is the planned extension of the first instance of change. It is the extension of the programme developed with the first school or schools involved in the programme of change to another set of schools. The point of the exercise being that if the improvements are worth anything then a whole district, a region, a state, or a nation would benefit from it. Scaling up is the basic process of making more of the same because it maximizes the benefits.

In the previous chapter I made a distinction between sustaining a process and sustaining a product, the programme for teaching and learning that resulted from that process. The significance of this distinction, between having a specific process that can lead to a detailed programme and having a detailed programme, is important to scalability. Planning the extension has typically been in terms of duplicating the programme, taking the programme of instruction to more and more schools. But the evidence about school change suggests that the idea of discovering something and then only repeating the content of that discovery is not what schools need.

The how and what of scaling up

There are three general approaches to scaling up that reflect different scientific strategies for the initial implementation. One is to design the best programme in terms of a possible product and implement that programme in school after school; a 'prescription' approach to changing schools. A second is to harness all available resources and to try to create the best example of an effective school one can; and then repeat that example in school after school. This is an 'exemplary model' approach. The third is to work with the resources of selected schools trying to make selected schools better and then grow those solutions; a 'retuning' approach. Each approach has benefits and each has limitations in terms of scaling up.

The three approaches have different strategies for scaling up. The first two tend to replicate the solution as it has been designed either in terms of a programme or in terms of the best resourced and most exemplary school possible. The benefits and limitations of the first two approaches can be illustrated in the patterns of success and failure in a well-researched example of repeating a solution. The attempted replication raises concerns about the limits in the first two approaches and their consequences.

Scaling up change with mixed success

Hubbard, Mehan, and Stein (2006) describe how in 1998 the San Diego City Schools (SDCS) attempted to reform their schools using a reform programme developed and implemented in the urban schools of New York City's Community School District #2. The evidence was that the District #2 reform had been highly successful. Under the leadership of Superintendent Anthony Alvarado student achievement ranking rose from near the bottom of the 32 community school districts in 1987 to second in 1998.

The goal of the San Diego reform was the same, and the architect of the initial reform in New York, Superintendent Anthony Alvarado, was brought in to oversee it. There were some similarities between the districts and some notable differences. They had a similar percentage of low income students, and the low achievement rates at the beginning of each reform posed similar challenges. However, in San Diego there were many more Hispanic students and more students with English as a second language. The San Diego district included Years K-12 and was six times larger than District #2 with about 141,000 students, whereas District #2 was K-8. They shared the same goal, to improve student achievement in literacy with a core focus on the effectiveness of instructional practice. In San Diego the reform was centralized, emanating from the district leadership through instructional leaders in schools who made instructional, operational, and professional development decisions. It was comprehensive in that all schools in the district were to be involved and it was fast paced with all the major elements introduced from the first days.

There are differences of opinion about how much effect the reforms in SDCS had. If we apply the criteria of acceleration and a changed distribution, the reform would be seen as having marked but only partial success. Overall, the number of students reading at or above grade level increased by almost 20 per cent from a little under 38,000 in 1998 to a little over 45,000 in 2002, a substantial increase.

But more gains were needed to reach parity with national levels. The whole distribution shifted upwards because the number of students in the lowest quartile decreased and the number in the highest quartile increased by the same amount (about 5,000 students). Differences between ethnic groups in the district reduced in elementary school, but high school students made minimal gains and at least one analysis reported that the reform was not successful with high school students and that ethnic differences remained the same or were mildly exaggerated (Matthew Effects). On other measures, such as drop out rates and course completions to apply for university, there were still large gaps between ethnic groups.

What was clear by 2002 was that the replication had not delivered what was expected and it needed a major overhaul and change of direction. It was apparent that the scaling up had limitations. Hubbard, Mehan, and Stein (2006) painstakingly analysed the San Diego reform at each of the intersecting levels of the district policy and organization, schools and classrooms, and teacher–student interactions. The argument they develop from the data is that the scaling up was undermined by the wholesale adoption of the reform as a template without adopting the reform process as a developmental process.

The reform in New York had a developmental history. When fully implemented after several years the district itself had features of a well-functioning and sustaining community within which new leaders and teachers were socialized into instructional practices that were well understood and well designed. But the roll out of the specific literacy programme actually occurred at a relatively slow pace. It was planned and developed and modified over several years. It was applied to schools in a slow, incremental fashion, putting in place staff development and organizational features to underpin the practices.

In contrast, the San Diego reform process was from the beginning comprehensive and the size and pacing were markedly greater. Changes for the instructional leaders, principals and teachers happened rapidly. The entire school district was saturated with the reform simultaneously and with content that was complex. The 'balanced literacy programme' required new practices that used new knowledge and associated expertise. For example, choosing books for 'read alouds' to students required expert judgements of ability level, interest level, and matching of the books with unit planning. Upper grade teachers found the new practices involving small groups and use of questioning techniques jarred with pre-existing ideas and ways of instructing, which influenced how the reform was enacted. The result according to the researchers was implementation mostly at a surface level with marked deviations from the programme by teachers.

The analysis of this case of limitations in a planned scale up hinges on the distinction I set up earlier. The product, but not the process, was scaled up. The product was important but the process was even more important and the developmental process key to adopting a more effective programme. The case of the San Diego schools is a very powerful example of where the process was not replicated, which the researchers argue compromised the scaling up.

A more successful example: SFA

Success For All (Slavin, & Madden, 2001) is an example of very successful scaling up (Borman, Slavin, Cheung, Chamberlain, Madden, & Chambers, 2007; What Works Clearinghouse, 2009b). It uses a prescriptive approach to school change exponentially implemented school by school. The first step by the researchers occurred in 1986, as a response to policy makers and the Baltimore superintendent's and the school board president's challenge to researchers at John Hopkins University to actually design more effective schools (rather than write about them). An intensive research and development sequence started with the pilot school in 1987 in which procedures for instruction in reading and writing in the early grades were tested, professional development and leadership components were designed at a school level and student outcomes were monitored. The following year the programme expanded to five more Baltimore schools and a school in Philadelphia. A Spanish version of the SFA reading programme was designed in 1990 for bilingual schools and in 1992 maths and science and social studies programmes were added. The growth from 1989 has been 40–100 per cent each year and by the year 2000, SFA was in about 1500 schools in 670 districts in 48 states through the United States, amounting to about 3 per cent of Title 1 elementary schools. The model has been exported to other countries too.

The reading and writing programme is closely specified, based on research and effective practices for beginning reading. As described earlier, it has some elements of a literature based approach within a very strong focus on direct instruction of decoding skills. It includes requirements for grouping of students and the use of cooperative learning techniques. The important point is that the design of the reading programme as it occurs in the classroom is pre-specified, including the sequencing and teacher actions within the sequence. It is described as highly scripted.

The overall SFA programme in a school brings additional resources to ensure an infrastructure. In addition to the classroom teacher there is a tutor who has several key roles including working one-on-one with children having reading difficulties, serving as an additional teacher during the mandatory daily 90 minute reading sessions and carrying out detailed eight week assessments. A preschool and kindergarten programme operate and a family support team builds relationships and adds parenting skills workshops. A programme facilitator works with the principal on schedule planning, classroom organization, and implementation of the curriculum. The teacher and tutors receive manuals scripting in detail the programme and individual lessons and three days of in service training (with two more for tutors). Thereafter, follow up visits and further professional development amount to 25 person days of training in the first full implementation year, 12 in the second and eight in each subsequent year. An advisory committee with the principal, programme facilitator and teachers, parent representatives, and family support staff meet regularly and review the progress of the programme and address problems of implementation. It is a school wide, coordinated, and proactive plan for what the Success For All designers call a "relentless focus on the success of every child" (Slavin, & Madden, 2001, p. 15).

Scaling up involves replicating all of the components. A school is required to adopt the whole package to qualify for the funding and the long-term training and support. Schools opt for the programme, and a secret ballot of at least 80 per cent agreement from the staff is required. But from that choice point they are choosing a particular model of reading instruction, particular use of federal resources, and an already designed model of what a whole school programme should be. A calculation in 2000 of the cost per school for the tutor, facilitator, materials, and professional development for a school with 500 students was $73,000 in the first year. At the head office in 2000 there were 240 full time trainers and a further 16 at another core site. Full implementation schools are certificated for purposes of further access to federal funding.

The major problem facing SFA given its 'prescriptive' model is to expand without compromising any of the rigorousness of the programme. The solution is a tightly knit system of quality controls by a central agency to guarantee fidelity to the programme. Local, regional and national networking through conferences and seminar keep links strong. The headquarters of training and dissemination was at Johns Hopkins University, reflecting the roots of SFA, but is now at a not for profit organization, Success for All Foundation. The developers note that a model of programme development and training with whole schools does not easily fit into university structures. The partnership between the foundation and their schools is long term.

This is a particular model of scaling up. While the overall programme has been modified somewhat from its beginning, it is essentially a one size fits all approach. The authors deliberately contrast this approach with claims that schools should innovate and invent reform, saying the very strength of their approach is that it is an externally designed package.

Describing it as prescriptive draws on the analogy of taking a sick person and prescribing a course of treatment with a resultant efficiency and predictability in curing. This is an obvious solution to changing schools. Take a known remedy (the programme) and apply it (implement in the school), requiring the patient (the school) to adhere to and comply with the course of treatment. The programme has known properties that under known conditions can produce known outcomes. The outcomes can be measured in growth on standardized achievement tests. In this model, all schools or perhaps all Title 1 schools serving poor communities and mostly Black and Hispanic and other culturally diverse communities, have the same problem and the same solution is required.

There are evaluations of SFA, both by the researcher developers and by independent researchers. It is patently one of the best models for school change that has been designed. But it too has limitations. One was noted in previous chapters. The design solves some but not all literacy problems. Notably, it is very effective in the early instructional phase, but less effective at upper grade levels. Developmental sustainability is limited.

The limits on developmental sustainability reflect a more systemic problem. School based capabilities to solve ongoing challenges are limited because the solutions lie with the external agents. Other consequences have been identified too. As I noted earlier, there is a very high turnover of staff in the early implementation phase. Those teachers who are less able to adopt the new programme, and this includes those that find the programme difficult as well as those that resist a highly scripted approach controlling their teaching, leave.

Of charter schools

There is an alternative. It is the second approach, the 'exemplary' approach. In this approach exemplary schools are designed; sometimes under the wing of a university. These are the charter schools. Given the example of the San Diego district approach to scale up it is useful to find examples of this alternative approach also in San Diego. The Preuss middle/high school is located on the University of California San Diego campus at La Jolla (Alvarez, & Mehan, 2006). It is a middle school and high school with Grades 6–12. It opened in 1999 for low income students, the majority of whom are Hispanic and African American, who already have demonstrated high motivation and parent support through attendance and performance in the primary schools. Their parents are not college graduates. The school was established by the university, is run by the university, and is funded by community donors.

The over-arching aim is to meet the requirements of acceleration and changing the distribution of achievement, and surpassing them by being dedicated solely to preparing students for college and increasing access to university. Like other scaled up projects the exemplary model is built on research and best practice in school organization and instruction. Its various elements reflect research based lessons learned about the risks and barriers to being effective identified in previous chapters. The design of the school targets the needs of students and has processes for avoiding the negative effects of differential treatment and Matthew Effects. It deliberately created a set of cultural practices incorporating high expectations around the goal of students going to college and only has one track, students are college bound, which is designed to meet and exceed University of California entry requirements.

Preuss employs highly qualified staff with a college major in teaching subject areas and expertise in their subject to pursue the aim, unlike many teachers described by Ladson-Billings (2006) teaching in schools serving low income communities. These teachers work in a strong professional learning culture with ongoing professional development. The resources of the university enable innovative curricula to be developed; for example in 2006 and 2007 the school won regional competitions in robotics. Drawing on the lessons of summer learning and school effectiveness it has increased the time at school on the one hand and on the other hand built connections with families into the model. It has done this by expanding the school year (198 days versus the traditional 180 days); extending the school day (7 hours versus the traditional 6 hours); making class sizes smaller in all grades (27 students versus 34 district wide); establishing mandatory parental involvement (a minimum of 15 hours); and including parents in the guidance strategy for students. Other resources of the university are brought to bear, including tutoring by UCSD undergraduates, and the senior year is integrated with the UCSD freshman year.

Does it make a difference? As is typical in the area of research, there has been debate about some of the claims, but those that are clear cut are compelling. For three years up until 2007, it had 91 per cent of graduates going to a four year college or university course, and in 2007 it was 96 per cent. Based on measures of college readiness, performance of economically disadvantaged students and performance on Advanced Placement tests, Preuss school was ranked 10th in 2007 by US News out of some 19,000 high schools (JaCoby, 2009). The answer is that it appears to work very well. Exemplary redesign within a well resourced and research based institution can change the achievement patterns markedly, showing that schools can be effective and can meet the criteria set for demonstrating effectiveness.

But the very causes of its success set real barriers to the limits of its scalability. Replicability of the model of charter schools was identified by Mehan (Alvarez, & Mehan, 2006), one of the academics working with Preuss, as an issue from the beginning. Deliberate moves to show that it could be done elsewhere led to the model being adapted to work at Gompers Charter Middle School (Williams, & Bersin, 2006). This was an existing school but one which because of consecutive poor academic results was legally required under the 'No Child Left Behind' legislation to be restructured. In 2004 there had been 1,000 suspensions.

The scaling up didn't involve establishing a school but rather rebuilding an existing school from the ground up. The process has been fraught. One of the problems had been that teacher selection was determined by the contract requirements, which meant the school had no control over staff hiring. The exemplary model requires control over selection and development of staffing to overcome the challenges described by Darling-Hammond (2006). Yet changing status required a majority of the teachers to be supportive. The relationship with the union deteriorated in the establishment phase, and the school board was antagonistic. Teachers had to abandon union membership to support the school.

Change happened and new teachers were selected by the changed school under a regime that provided teacher performance bonuses and salary supplements. Changes have been introduced gradually with the initial focus on the school culture including an extended school day and a longer school year. Suspensions and expulsion dropped in 2004–2005 to 305. Test scores have risen, although they are still markedly below San Diego's average and the California targets.

Obviously, charter schools are very hard to reproduce without considerable expenditure and resourcing. The replication of the Presuss model at Gompers was dependent on the strong backing of the superintendent, and extensive financial support including hundreds of thousands of dollars of government and foundation funding, estimated at $7,000 per student in 2005–2006 in addition to the $5,200 per students from the state (Williams, & Bersin, 2006). In recent months changes in the superintendent and in the support from the district administration has meant that there are stresses on further progress.

A third approach: scaling up the process with a specified programme

Rather than the extreme makeover of charter schools, the third approach is to take an existing site, and try to develop the best practice solution from the ground up, figuring out for each school or set of schools what was needed to become most effective. Having developed and tested this exemplar then the solution would be extended from site to site.

There are a number of versions of this strategy. Our research team's strategy has been to scale up the process of on-the-ground problem solving rather than the content of the solution although there may be commonalities between schools in the instructional programme they need. The intervention with schools relies on this process to solve the enduring gaps in literacy between on the one hand indigenous Māori students and students from Pasifika communities, and on the other students from mainstream communities described in previous chapters. The gaps have been present for a long time and despite New Zealand's deservedly high reputation in literacy this has meant that these students are overly represented in the tail of the achievement distribution and by the middle primary school years in the poorest schools they are about two years behind in average levels of reading comprehension. The acceleration problem and the distributional shift problem are stark and have been for much of the post colonial period for the Māori children and more recently from the 1970s for Pasifika children whose families came in numbers for work and educational aspirations to New Zealand, in waves of immigration.

The scaling up has involved clusters of schools in an area of Auckland that has high numbers of Māori and Pasifika communities and where employment and incomes are at the lowest levels for New Zealand. The scaling up has also been tested in an extension to the cluster of primary schools in the rural and isolated areas of the West Coast of the South Island of New Zealand described earlier (McNaughton, & Lai, 2009).

The critical use of local evidence about teaching and learning is a key component. Rather than import a ready made programme in writing and reading comprehension (the prescription approach), the process starts with systematically gathering local patterns of achievement and learning in the target areas and intensive descriptions of classroom practices. This information is critically examined by the professional communities based on a partnership between lead teachers, the research team, and local administration officials. The critical analysis and testing of hypotheses about more effective teaching against the evidence is followed by targeted professional development that uses the evidence as the starting point. Built into the process are mechanisms to heighten sustainability of the process so that the problem solving and testing of practices can shift to new problems, and can cope with teacher changes and changes in personnel and other vicissitudes of the messy life of schools. Teachers plan together and observe and discuss each other's teaching, and inquiry skills are developed. Clusters plan mini conferences in which teachers' action research projects are shared and added to the evidence. The programme of change through professional development draws on research based practices, using whole school groups and careful attention to the coherence of assessment and management of teaching resources around the changes.

The process is highly specified and is implemented in three phases involving problem solving, professional development, and sustaining the changes. All of which usually takes three years. Although the content at the beginning may start with generic dimensions that feed into inquiry, the process produces a highly specified programme of what to teach. In reading comprehension this has meant specific aspects of instruction in middle and upper grades have been systematically modified, including the manner of strategy instruction, the intensive instruction of vocabulary, and the tailoring of classroom activities to increase reading mileage. In writing, it has meant in some interventions attention to developing more extensive knowledge about the linguistic dimensions in writing and types of writing and changing patterns of feedback.

The treatment integrity of this approach initially is in the process. The process is highly specific (and in this sense also prescriptive). But the outcomes of the process lead to highly specific changes in instruction. The local evidence is necessary to avoid risks of making unwarranted assumptions about needs, as well as to build a community of practice that is capable of and committed to learning from its own practices while using the most up to date research evidence. Developing practices of problem solving and inquiry using local data is also crucial for being able to sustain.

This model of change assumes that teachers can act as adaptable experts rather than needing the discipline of highly scripted lessons. It also assumes that the demonstrably highly effective practices in New Zealand schools can be the basis for change.

Is this approach successful? A replication series of studies has established that acceleration can be achieved in reading comprehension and writing. In two urban clusters described previously, each of seven schools in the poorest areas with almost entirely Māori and Pasifika students, gains over three years amounted to about one year of change in addition to expected change over that period. This meant that on average students were now within the national average bands of achievement. The achievement distribution was close to but not completely matched with national distributions of achievement (there were for example still fewer than expected numbers of students in the highest achievement levels, as explained in Chapter 6). The ubiquitous summer learning effect was present. Not always in the form of a drop but even as a plateau this meant that the rate of gain per calendar year resulted in small cumulative acceleration. It was not just the most advanced readers who gained, so those Matthew Effects were avoided.

The process does not stop after three years, however. The partnerships switched attention to other aspects of literacy instruction in successive cycles. For example, these two clusters have examined instruction for writing and for 'intertextuality,' that is the deliberate fostering of connections between content and processes in reading and writing as well as connections thematic and otherwise between what is being read and written. In the most recent analyses overall reading comprehension (with new groups of students) in Years 4–8 has remained close to average levels and there are schools whose averages and distributions now match national patterns, and in one exceptional case, exceed the nationally expected distribution. I will have more to say about that school in the final chapter.

In terms of concerted problem solving it has taken up to 10 years for these schools to get to national averages. And it has taken a committed long-term partnership between researchers and the other members of the professional communities. It also relies on a degree of local autonomy by schools in organizing their own budgets and commitments, which draws on a 20 year old policy in New Zealand of local self-governing schools.

The process was scaled up to a group of schools unlike the two sets of urban schools. These were schools in the rural and isolated area of New Zealand. They were at average levels in reading and writing in the middle and upper grades of primary school. But in this group of schools comparable rates of gain have occurred; now shifting the distribution away (positively) from national patterns.

Using complex statistical modeling we can produce models of the rates over the school years and drops over summer quite precisely, as shown in Figure 7.1 (page 80). The model for change is plotted over three years for gains in reading comprehension in Years 4–8 at primary school (9 year olds to 13 years olds) and against stanines. Stanines are units based on the normal curve, which has been broken up into nine steps.

The actual gains are approximated by mathematical models. In the initial cluster of schools (Urban 1) the beginning level of achievement was around stanine 3, about two years behind national averages. A like cluster of schools (Urban 2) to which the intervention programme was applied one year after the first was even lower. But in both cases acceleration occurred. Given that stanines are age adjusted year by year, a flat line would represent 'expected' progress and the upward trends in both the original and like clusters are significantly different, going upwards. The unlike cluster (Rural 1 schools), which received the intervention two years after the original, started above national averages but also showed acceleration, although the SLE punctuated the upward trend more and the upward trend was not as steep.

As referred to earlier, the process did not stop after those years. After three years the original cluster was considerably closer to national averages and considered, as a cluster, to be within the average bands (stanines 4 to 6). But the distribution was still not as closely matched to national distribution as it needed to be, the situation described in Chapter 6. The like cluster took longer to get to national averages. But the school described in Chapter 10 that exceeds the national expected distribution came from that cluster.

What are the limitations in this model? This approach is time consuming. It requires a partnership with external research and development partners that is long term. It also requires the capacity of teachers and leaders to act in expert ways. It requires researchers to be able to engage in collective problem solving and testing of solutions in a situation that is open and not able to be controlled experimentally in the usual ways (a means of handling this is discussed in the final chapter).

Our results to date show there is variability in success. But the continuous collection of data at several levels (not just student achievement or teacher instruction but also features of the schools and the communities) means that the variability can be linked to particular aspects of school functioning (Lai, McNaughton, Timperley, & Hsiau, 2009). We know that what makes a difference between schools is how the professional community functions and the role of the leadership in the schools, as well as more prosaic elements such as whether timetabling enables optimal frequencies of reading lessons. But we also know that substantial and educationally significant gains are possible.

Lessons

These examples provide very important evidence about the effectiveness of schools. The less successful example in the San Diego district was by no means a complete failure. But its partial success shows that if the conditions for producing the scaling up are not patterned on the original conditions then the reform is likely to be limited. In that case the need for teachers to develop deep knowledge and the need for the communities of schools to understand and to have time to bed in new practices were not met. The specific programme with its new complex requirements had little time to be either understood or be practised. It was applied in classrooms that contained children who were different from the original children in quite significant ways. In some case they were older and in some cases they had different language identity and status.

The solution to this problem in the more successful example of SFA is to create a programme of change with high fidelity. This has meant specifying in minute detail each component of the programme – how the leaders lead and how the curriculum is sequenced through to the instructional moves of the teachers step by step through each lesson. Each instance of the programme at a site looks like any other and each has been specified very closely so that the degrees of freedom that teachers and leaders and schools might have to modify the programme are limited. This approach guarantees an outcome but at a cost.

The cost is twofold. First it is in the role of teachers as 'adaptive experts,' the description that currently best describes effective teachers (Darling-Hammond, & Bransford, 2005). The second cost is in the vulnerability of the programme. Close prescription is possible at some levels and in some aspects of teaching literacy. This is especially so in early literacy. As I argued, SFA is a very successful programme in the early levels, where teaching constrained skills should be very well structured and deliberate. And can be tightly specified. But at later levels, where sophisticated language and knowledgeable reflection on the multilayered messages and content of texts is needed, and where writing to achieve different and often multiple purposes occurs, the moves of teaching need to be more flexible and reliant on well-developed knowledge. Teaching needs to be based more on deep knowledge of the content and teaching, and even more adaptable to circumstance of student and community. The evidence is that at the later grades this close duplication of the programme is problematic.

Does this mean that specification is not possible and that every time we want to change a school or cluster of schools we have to reinvent the wheel? Or, as in the case of the second approach, we have to expend considerable resources each time to build a new school to create the ideal schools because if we don't the process of fitting any change runs up against obstacles? Clearly being more effective in a school reform exercise demands specification of the process that a school community goes through to becoming evidence based and knowledgeable and capable of changed practices. The resulting practices also need to be highly specified so that new teachers can be inducted, so that accountability and testing of components can occur, and also so that innovation can be derived from a solid base of practices.

The lesson from each approach seems to be that change requires going through the same process. Or at least a qualified process depending on circumstances. The reform in New York took place over 11 years. It was a long and windy road. When literacy became the focus of the district there were two years of internal analysis and widespread consultation within and outside the district before a suitable programme was developed. Components were gradually introduced. The literacy experts from outside worked with the school personnel developing the deep knowledge of the principles and the practicalities of the intervention. More importantly, the programme continued to develop through the intervention. Modifications continued to be a feature through the 1990s, initiated from the educators in the field using evidence from the schools and planned research. As evidence became available and feedback from the educators happened, the leaders could understand the design requirements for modifications.

The process is the message, to paraphrase Marshall McLuhan (McLuhan, & Fiore, 1964). There are two reasons why the process is as important as the resulting programme. One is that the local circumstances are critical. The significance of collecting and analysing data, rather than making assumptions about what children need (and what instruction should look like) without careful analysis, recently was underscored in a study by Buly and Valencia (2002). Policy makers in the State of Washington had mandated programmes without actually analysing profiles of low progress students identified by test scores from 4th Grade National Assessment of Educational Progress (NAEP) scores. The assumption underlying policies and interventions was that poor performance reflected students' difficulties with more basic decoding abilities. Yet, there was little data about this assumption or knowledge about whether focusing on such skills would improve the comprehension at 4th Grade students.

Using a broad band of measures, Buly and Valencia (2002) identified five groups of low progress readers, some of whom did indeed have limited fluency and accuracy in decoding. But mandating phonics instruction for all students who fell below the proficiency levels had missed the needs of the majority of students, whose decoding was strong but who struggled with comprehension or language requirements for the tests.

The indicators of low achievement in literacy for any one school in the middle and upper grades may arise for different reasons. Consider what might be involved in low achievement in reading comprehension. Generally, there is considerable consensus around what students need to learn and what effective teaching looks like. In order to comprehend written text a reader needs to be able to decode accurately and fluently, to have a wide and appropriate vocabulary, have appropriate and expanding topic and world knowledge, active comprehension strategies, and active monitoring and fix up strategies (Block, & Pressley, 2002). So it follows that children who are relatively low progress may have difficulties in one or more of these areas. The consensus around effective teaching identifies attributes of both content (curriculum) and process (Taylor et al., 2005). In the middle grades these attributes include instructional processes in which goals are made clear, and which involve both coaching and inquiry styles that engage students in higher level thinking skills. Effective instruction also provides direct and explicit instruction for skills and strategies for comprehension. Effective teaching actively engages students in a great deal of actual reading and writing and instructs in ways that enable expertise to be generalizable and through which students come to be able to self-regulate independently.

In addition, researchers have also identified the teacher's role in building students' sense of self-efficacy and more generally motivation (Guthrie, & Wigfield, 2000). Quantitative and qualitative aspects of teaching convey expectations about students' ability which affect their levels of engagement and sense of being in control. Culturally and linguistically diverse students seem to be especially likely to encounter teaching that conveys low expectations (Dyson, 1999). There are a number of studies not directly of reading comprehension but in schooling improvement that have shown how these can be changed and how they impact on instruction and learning. In general, both changes to beliefs about students and more evidence based decisions about instruction are implicated, often in the context of school wide or even cluster wide initiatives (Bishop, O'Sullivan, & Berryman, 2010; Phillips, McNaughton, & MacDonald, 2004; Taylor, Pearson, Peterson, & Rodriguez, 2005).

It follows that low achievement by students from different communities could be associated with a variety of teaching and learning needs in one or more of these areas. Out of this array of teaching and learning needs, those for students and teachers in any particular instructional context may therefore have a context specific profile.

So there is a good reason for a process of analysis and checking of the local circumstances – a prescribed programme might be ill matched to local needs. But there is a second reason why matching to local circumstances is important – the process is a core part of developing the school professional communities' practices needed for all the forms of sustainability. The practices need to go beyond the immediate need to duplicate a prescribed programme, such as to deal with developmental sustainability and innovation, and to be able to scale up to new circumstances. Change is a constant in schools so the issue for sustainability is to have a robust process and community in place. The same is true for scaling up. This is what the third approach, the retuning approach, adds to the picture.

What this means is that if a school is already acting as a community that examines its practices, that uses evidence to determine effectiveness and in which the cultural practices of the community are designed to enable members to learn from each other, then half the solution is in place. The other half is the programme itself. I will return to the argument in the final chapter but the issue here is that the idea of school reform needs to accommodate the ongoing role of outside experts who provide technical and content based know how for the programme to help the schools develop new, or innovative, or modified programmes to continue to be successful. And all of that means that schools becoming more effective takes time.

Conclusion

What is common to the 'prescriptive,' the 'exemplary' design, and the 'retuning' approaches to scaling up is the presence of expert partners. The role of the partner is different in each approach. In one it is to prescribe, implement, and monitor. In another it is to take over the design, help manage, and provide a flow of resources. And in the third it is to engage with the school and collaborate in solving problems.

The research process in each of these relationships is different. In one the research and development phase precedes the roll out. In the second, component research is within each exemplary instance. For the third, partners engage in an ongoing process of research and development with the school. What is common is the presence of a partner who is a critical component in the design and hence in the evidence about effectiveness.

The conditions in different countries and districts might dictate which of the approaches is most effective in the longer term using our criteria of acceleration and redistributed achievement, as well as the challenges of sustainability. But the evidence is that schools can not and should not be islands and that research based external partners bringing research capacity and research based expertise are critical to their capacity to change or to continue to be effective.

From these examples of approaches it appears that the commitment to the partnership needs to be long term. This is a lesson in the scaling up examples, particularly from the less successful example. There are no short cuts here and once schools are established the ongoing needs are for expert knowhow that feed into the community of practice. There are policy implications here, which will be addressed in the next chapter. But one is that a substantial research and development infrastructure is needed within countries if enduring partnerships are to be a role for university researchers.

10

UNDERSTANDING THE CONTEXTS FOR EFFECTIVE TEACHING

The evidence presented points to a firm, if qualified, conclusion. It is possible for individual schools to impact effectively on the achievement of children from communities who have traditionally not been well served by schools. If this is true it means that it is possible to work against social and cultural inequalities. But the qualification is that the effectiveness of schools is likely to be limited. Limited in terms of how sustainable, how reproducible and even how much change can really be expected in achievement for those groups of children. The limitations are only partly set by the teachers and schools themselves. The worlds within which they operate also pose limitations.

What do we know about these other influences? In different chapters I have commented on them and they are a challenging array. At one level they include policies that impact on schools directly. The policies of funding, of accountability, of the nature of schools and their autonomy, of resourcing, and of requirements for professional education, are instrumental in reducing or exaggerating differences between schools in their effectiveness. These policies themselves exist in a larger policy setting that impacts on the lives of families and therefore the effectiveness of schools. These are policies that affect such things as levels of and disparities in poverty; access to and affordability of housing; access to and levels of employment; and the overall well-being and recognition of communities including of their languages and identities. These latter are the policies that increase or reduce the barriers that communities face and they constrain what those directly aimed at schools can achieve.

Much of what I have described in previous chapters focuses on the features of the school that can make a considerable difference. These include the degree to which schools collect and use information about practices, and their effectiveness is one such feature. The practices of acting as a community that enable members to be highly aware of and focused on being effective is another. The relationship with the local community and the resources present and needed in that community is another. So too is the leadership in the school to inspire, to inform and to solve ongoing problems related to their effectiveness.

An obviously critical component determining the effectiveness of schools is how teachers teach. School communities and their leaders, and the policies that surround their practices, are ultimately dependent on one teacher in his or her classroom acting in ways that create the most effective conditions possible for learning. The ways in which teachers use resources, their expectations and management of those expectations about children in the classroom, their respect and understanding and care for those children and their sheer pedagogical competence each play a part. On any one day the teacher makes a difference.

In addition to the teacher in his or her classroom's context, the school context itself, and the regional and national policies there is another context. This context concerns the partners that schools can call on. The educational research community, or at least some parts of that community, are critical partners. Through these partnerships their science can contribute relevant, rich and usable knowledge about practices that make teaching and schools more effective.

A model of nested and coherent systems

This conglomeration of contexts means that there isn't one answer to the question of where the problem lies to creating more effective schools. The challenge is to make sense of this complexity so that the promise of individual examples in the opening paragraph is more generally able to be met. In this chapter I want to focus on understanding the complexity to potentially increase schools' effectiveness, particularly in the hard process of sustaining and scaling up tested ways of making a difference to the achievement of children. This means on the one hand developing an integrated and generative model of the levels of influences on effectiveness. On the other hand it also means connecting these levels of influence with a model of teaching that is best suited to meeting the robust criteria of accelerating and shifting distributions.

Underlying much of my analysis in previous chapters is a set of concepts about development, teaching and learning that draws on socio cultural theories. This theoretical approach explains development as being co-constructed through processes of guidance and learning. It has a strong emphasis on tutorial processes and the processes through which what is at root social and cultural come to be personal. The significance of layers of influence on the primary processes of guidance and learning, through patterned interactions, is recognized in these theories. Barbara Rogoff (1995) has a detailed conceptual and methodological approach for analysing these layers. She uses the model of planes of sociocultural activity. In the first plane is a focus on the processes through which the developing child participates in activities and appropriates ways of thinking, knowledge and skills through that participation. A more general layer comprises the forms and functions that guidance takes within the activities. Yet a more general layer is the layer of socialization that occurs through membership in communities and their practices. The practices provide the specific activities within which the guidance and the personal appropriation take place.

This is a layered approach to understanding development, teaching and learning. Given what I have said thus far about such factors as the influence of neighborhoods and the resources that families have access to, as well as the manner in which teachers are selected and prepared and schools are resourced, the understanding of influences needs to encompass very wide and very narrow layers simultaneously. We need to understand how the layers of influence provide constraints on the effectiveness of teaching and learning at school. How school activities are influenced even indirectly by resources and policies needs to be captured in the layering of influences too.

A useful model of influences needs to see teachers and students, and teaching and learning, as nested in and constituted by schools and the professional communities and leadership within the schools. In turn, the school is nested in a wider community setting. The community and its neighborhoods hold cultural, linguistic, and psychological resources. These and the local infrastructure determine how schools, teachers, parents, and students can act together effectively. Finally, classrooms, schools, and communities are in turn nested within a wider regional, state, and national policy context. That wider context is powerful in determining the functioning of each of the previous levels. In essence each layer is constituted by the layers it contains, but it also constitutes them. It does this by creating either directly or indirectly the resources, tools and meanings that channel and direct the activities of children with teachers.

This more nested view of teaching and schooling draws on a model of the ecology of human development by the developmentalist Urie Bronfenbrenner (1979). His original model used the analogy of Russian dolls. Bronfenbrenner (1979) proposed that the immediate unit for child development was the parent and child who constitute a 'microsystem.' The establishment of this microsystem creates the primary developmental vehicle in and through which developmental processes are constructed. For example, the early emotional bond, the attachment between a baby and its caregiver develops from the characteristics of the interactions co-constructed in this microsystem.

Bronfenbrenner's insight when he proposed this in 1979 was to understand that this system exists and is in turn constituted within other systems. This moved thinking away from the dominant models of development that located the locus of development and processes of learning solely within the child as he or she constructed ideas from the immediate physical and social world. This in itself was a radical shift, but he added a further principle. The functioning and well-being of this primary microsystem is dependent on relationships with significant other microsystems with which the child is engaged, including that created by the teacher and the child.

He called the system of microsystems a 'mesosystem' and proposed a set of operating principles about how development is enhanced by the relationships within that system. These include the degree to which information flows between microsystems and the degree to which there is mutual articulation between the activities and features of guidance operating across microsystems.

The mesosystem is in turn embedded in the world of the local neighborhood and the community. This next widest system, the 'exosystem,' contains resources and institutions that impact on the mesosystem and microsystems. The presence of good public transport and accessible community libraries, for example, would make a difference to whether families could access books to read during summer. And the degree to which the selection and use of books and the guidance and forms of reading had similar properties to the activities of school reading would in turn impact on the child's development at school.

Finally, he proposed a wider system embedding the previous systems. This is the system of ideological beliefs about children and families, and the policy and legislative environment, which affects the good functioning of families and more particularly the primary microsystem of caregiver and child. Beliefs about and legislation for equitable outcomes and welfare systems, or about health care and educational funding, are part of this 'macrosystem.' In the Bronfenbrenner model (1979) it matters whether a state has policies that have assumed students will achieve irrespective of background and there are policies in place to reduce inequalities in incomes and resourcing that are associated with those backgrounds.

The ecological model helps answer the question of how we can really make schools more effective. The model suggests that greater effectiveness in meeting the criteria for effectiveness will depend on the degree to which the sets of systems are well articulated and are coherent in supporting the microsystem, which in the case we are considering here is the teacher and child.

Bronfenbrenner's (1979) original formulation was modified over time. Because systems change over time he added another dimension, a chronosystem that captured the sense that the embedded systems are not static but change. The presence of change adds a further layer of impact on the primary unit. Adding this system directs attention to how the microsystem of teacher and child might change over time in response to events in the other systems, as well as in the participants themselves. For example, transitions occur between parts of the school system that can have effects on the child and their interactions with teachers and with caregivers. The issues of sustainability I raised earlier can be applied to an individual child. One sense is in terms of how ongoing development is affected by what has already developed (and what this enables a child to engage with), just as much as how events such as transitions, changes in teachers, or changes in housing impact on ongoing development.

In this chapter several layers of this nested system are examined in greater detail to illustrate the challenges to gaining what I will call coherence between layers. In general, Bronfenbrenner's (1979) model of development leads to the proposal that the effectiveness of teaching will be limited by the degree to which the systems do not cohere to support the quality of teaching and learning.

Finding coherence: state policies

There are clear and present limits to what schools can achieve in the face of state policies that create and sustain divides between its communities. In terms of the Bronfenbrenner (1979) model it makes sense that state policies be in accord with state objectives to have equitable outcomes in achievement for all groups (if these are indeed the goals). Two sorts of policy environments are needed. One is at regional, state, federal, and national levels that affect the well-being of communities whose children find schools risky places for achievement. Policy is needed for the family contexts of childrearing so that practices that are conducive to achievement and development at school are better able to be adopted and added to family repertoires. The second policy context is one specifically directed at schools; policies that will directly enable them be as effective as possible.

These state policies should not rely on raising gross domestic product with the assumption that greater wealth comes trickling down to those who need it most. Indeed, the evidence suggests that trickle down is an unlikely outcome from state pursuit of greater wealth. The 10 years to 2006 had been good economically for many countries but inequalities generally did not reduce. In nearly all of the 18 welfare states surveyed by Howard Glennerster (2009) from the London School of Economics, inequalities in income continued to rise, and in some the inequalities have become a great divide.

The reverse of this is true too. I am writing this book at a time of savage economic downturn world wide, and the evidence suggests a kind of Matthew Effect occurring. The most vulnerable members of society are disproportionately the ones bearing the load. This load can be seen in unemployment and forced sales of houses or forced relocations.

Assuming that becoming wealthier will have equitable flow-on effects ignores the likely Matthew Effects among other matters. The issue is more about distribution and access to the resources that currently exist; and an education system funded for excellence through targeted programmes. The rationales for wealth distribution can be couched in terms of what Gloria Ladson-Billings (2006) called the compounding 'educational debt' which societies owe the communities as well as principles of social justice and equity. Policies aimed at reducing these disparities in resources have a direct effect on academic achievement through access to resources such as libraries and capabilities to interact and engage with children to support their development. There are wider effects, which come to influence academic achievement indirectly too.

Wilkinson and his colleagues have written extensively about the impact of inequality (Wilkinson, 2005; Wilkinson, & Pickett, 2009). He has argued that the relative degree of social, economic and political injustice, the gap between the haves and have nots, has a significant impact on achievement disparities. Wilkinson uses an epidemiological argument for wealth redistribution. He points out that despite the levels of income and lived luxuries that are much higher for black working class people in Harlem in New York or in the South Side of Chicago than for the poorest countries in the world like Bangladesh, some morbidity indices and death rates are higher. The mechanism for the problem lies in the distribution of wealth and services. When gaps are large there are predictable effects on the social and psychological well-being of communities, such as stress and depression, as well as the quality of social relationships, which then find expression in the morbidity picture. As Wilkinson puts it, "Inequality is socially corrosive" (2005, p. 20).

His comparisons between districts in the US and the very poorest countries show that it is the perceived and lived gap that is the determinant. It is not the overall level of wealth. Wilkinson (2005) tracks out this relationship exhaustively across cities, across districts and states and provinces, and across countries. He uses very powerful measures of inequality and deprivation, and well-being and morbidity (including violent death and alcoholism). An ironically robust pattern merges: the larger the differential, the greater the impact. It is this relative gap in income, housing, and health that seems to create the conditions in which families find it harder to raise children and harder to access those practices and tools that will make a difference to achievement at school.

Housing and employment policies make a direct and very obvious difference to schools. The US Department of Education (Compton-Lilly, in press) has identified Reading Recovery as the gold standard of early inventions in literacy in schools. But the effectiveness of the tutoring in Reading Recovery is determined in part by continuity of housing and employment. In the United States it benefits poor black children as much as any other child, and in New Zealand it the same, it benefits Māori and Pasifika children as much as other children. But this is the case only if these children are in the programme for the same duration and receiving at least the same number of tutoring sessions. In the United States Compton-Lilly (in press) showed that low SES African American children were more likely to not receive a complete programme due to a number of factors including high mobility and transience. In New Zealand a similar pattern emerges. Māori and Pasifika children are more likely to not successfully complete the programme and a feature of those children not successfully completing is fewer lessons than others (McDowall, & New Zealand Council for Educational Research, 2005).

Success in Success For All (Slavin, & Madden, 2001) is the same as Reading Recovery; its effectiveness is sensitive to presence. The reason is obvious. These programmes, and schooling generally, are not just incremental. They are sequential and build knowledge and skills through integrated threads of teaching and learning where previous learning is a building block to continued learning. Continuity matters, and no matter how effective an educational programme is, it is vulnerable to policies and practices that jeopardize continuity. So if your family has only intermittent access to jobs and lives in temporary housing it is hard to remain in one place for extended periods of time.

Berliner (2006) made the same plea in his address on the limits of our science to the American Educational Research Association. He quoted Jean Anyon, "Attempting to fix inner city schools without fixing the city in which they are embedded is like trying to clean the air on one side of a screen door" (p. 988). His list of policy and practice changes includes legislation to require large companies to be better employers, providing adequate income, medical insurance and retirement plans to promote healthy families and healthy children. Raising the minimum wage, and gender and ethnic wage equity are also on the list of properties of the macrosystem that would ultimately enable the microsystem of the child with his or her teacher to function more effectively. Wilkinson (2005) the epidemiologist proposes a similar agenda. Short term government strategies to do with progressive taxation, together with more economic democracy in which there is more involvement and ownership by employees, are on his list.

One can extend the list. Higher quality and more equitably provided early childhood education associated with state support for parental leave does make a difference to the well-being of families. There are productivity arguments for this just as there are educational benefit arguments and these can be seen as complementary.

These are policies that affect the inequities in a society, which act to reduce disparities in resources. In addition, policies are needed that directly impact schools, that enable them to function as effectively as possible. In earlier chapters I described Darling-Hammond's (2007) research showing how schools serving 'minority' children are systematically under funded, under resourced, and under supplied with qualified teachers. She too has a policy agenda. The first is equalizing resources at all levels in the US system; state, district, schools, and amongst students placed in classrooms, courses and tracks that provide very different opportunities to learn what matters in schools. The resourcing includes investment in high quality and well-qualified teachers, who are hired and incentivized to teach effectively in those areas that have been under resourced where the Matthew Effect has operated.

She argues that selection, training and employment standards need to be aspirational if not inspirational for teachers. These highly trained teachers need to be recruited and retained where they are needed to ensure students who have been in under resourced schools have access to them. Policy aimed at curriculum and assessment reform is needed to overcome teaching defaulting to component and basic skills teaching, rather than developing higher order and complex thinking. She draws these lessons at least partly out of the international comparisons. Those countries with centralized systems that fund these sorts of policies for teachers are more successful in building high achievement without exaggerating achievement disparities.

The coherent community

The school is both part of the mesosystem for the individual teacher and child and is also part of the neighbourhood and community in which teachers and families function. The way the school functions impacts on the teacher in the classroom. The evidence in previous chapters also suggests features of schools that are critical if they are to be effective at raising achievement levels for children in classrooms.

The features include being able to operate as a community that has a clear focus on critical enquiry and using evidence to inform practices, to become even better at what they do. The practices of the community should be designed so that each member is knowledgeable and able to participate in inquiring about and then honing their teaching. The community shares and actively strives to meet criteria such as acceleration and changing the distribution patterns if there are disparities to make up. But the community is also able to innovate and is open to change.

This is a view of the school as a cultural entity whose practices are shaped by shared goals. Members are deeply immersed and knowledgeable about the practices of the community. And there are transition practices for new members to be inducted, who move from being peripheral to the community to central fully functioning members.

What are the state policies, the elements in the macrosystem that might affect schools' capability to be like this? The elements include policy relating to the autonomy of schools to solve and innovate but balanced with centralized accountability. The existing models for this balance include the system in Finland (OECD, 2006). At a more local level there is the funding that provides the infrastructure to gather, store and interrogate evidence on student achievement. And there is the funding of schools and the employment conditions of teachers that provide space and time to engage in these activities including the professional conversations about that evidence.

The list goes on. There are policies to do with attracting and retaining highly skilled and trained leaders through salaries and promotional gradients; and policies for preparing and supporting teachers through their professional development to act in the ways required by the effective school practices.

Models of teaching

What does all this mean for the individual teacher in his or her classroom? The policy environment is one or more steps removed from the classroom action. The truism is that on any one day it is the teacher in his or her classroom that makes the difference. But it is not just their presence in the classroom, it is what teachers do that matters. There is a further aspect of coherence across the nested systems that needs to be modeled in detail. It is how teachers are viewed. Enacting and deploying the policies that directly affect teaching positively are dependent on how teaching is perceived and appreciated; by all those affected by and hoping to affect teaching including by policy makers. This is more than a question of definition; it is also a question about what our narratives of teaching should be and how the wider community understands the role and work of teachers. Sustaining effectiveness and building innovation requires a new view of teachers and teaching that avoids the risk of creating technicians and sees them as experts in the socialization of our children.

What does teaching in schools with the students from communities traditionally not well served by schools require of teachers? The answer to this can be easily made concrete by thinking about a teacher teaching reading with 10 year olds. These are students assessed in the international studies. What do these internationally agreed programmes of assessment think reading looks like? The PIRLS rubrics (Mullis, Kennedy, Martin, & Sainsbury, 2006) assess two purposes of reading comprehension. Reading for literacy experience and reading to acquire and use information. In each, the assessments target four processes. These are 'focus on and retrieve explicitly stated information' (p. 13), 'make straight-forward inferences' (p. 14), 'interpret and integrate ideas' (p. 15) and 'examine and evaluate content, language and textual elements' (p. 16).

The first of these has the following description:

> The reader must, however, recognize the relevance of the information or idea in relation to the information sought . . . in each case the information is usually contained within a single sentence or phrase.
>
> (Mullis, Kennedy, Martin, & Sainsbury, 2006, p. 13)

The last of these has the following description:

> Readers draw on their interpretations and weigh their understanding of text against their understanding of the world – rejecting, accepting, or remaining neutral to the text's representation . . . they draw upon their knowledge of text genre and structure, as well as their understanding of language conventions. They may also reflect on the author's devices for conveying meaning and judge their adequacy, and question the author's purpose, perspective, or skill.
>
> (Mullis, Kennedy, Martin, & Sainsbury, 2006, p. 16)

Some of the elements of the skills and knowledge required to read in this way can be taught in direct and prescribed ways. But others require a style of learning that is more open ended and inquiry based. Teachers need to be able to design and carry out instructional events in a variety of ways, potentially creating multiple configurations of guidance that range from being didactic and instrumental on the one hand through to discursive and collaborative on the other. Some of these con-figurations are more effective for learning some things; for example, a direct modeling and imitation configuration is very effective for learning constrained items of knowledge such as a template for a particular form of writing, for example a software application, or the American Psychological Association editing style. You just have to learn the stuff and there is no negotiation. And some configurations are more useful for other things; for example, a more discursive scaffold style is appropriate for the close reading of a text, say Orwell's (1945) *Animal Farm*, where the goal is to develop understanding of the author's intent, the roles of personification and metaphor as well as aspects of narrative structure and character development. Political meanings need to be related to the students' background knowledge and instructional bridges designed to enable the core ideas of fascism and dictatorship and the conditions under which these develop to be understood.

Teachers of literacy need to be well versed in particular forms of guidance, how these are associated with the effectiveness of particular instructional tools, and how they are best used in particular settings. The descriptors of literacy provided by the designers of PIRLS not surprisingly reflect a variety of literacy theories. Perhaps the most elegant model of contemporary forms of literacy able to be recognized and promoted by curricula was provided by Allan Luke and Peter Freebody (1999). Their four resources model proposes that in order to engage in reading and writing activities, learners need to be able to do four things. They will break the code of texts, participate in the meanings of text, use texts functionally, and critically analyse and transform texts. The Luke and Freebody model (1999), like the PIRLS rubric, identifies different levels of literacy. Their model highlights more strongly than the PIRLS rubric the area of critical literacy. Despite their differences, the models of literacy carry the implications I noted above. Different aspects require different configurations of guidance. It would be an oxymoron to have critical literacy worksheets. Similarly, it would be at best ineffectual to focus on world views of vowel consonant blends, in order to teach early decoding skills. Teachers need to be very knowledgeable, very strategic and very adaptable in the instructional practices.

These capabilities include the practices of teachers themselves as users and creators of texts. That is, they need to be very practiced in literacy activities; knowledgeable, strategic and adaptable as text users and as authors of texts. Interestingly this aspect of teaching is not as often the focus of our research. We should spend more time considering the significance of what teachers read and write themselves, what media they might study and enjoy, what patterns of communication both professional and non professional they participate in and how each of these might impact on their teaching of literacy. Arguably we should consider this aspect of their expertise given descriptions of effective teachers of language and literacy illustrate how motivated and informed they are by their own knowledge of media and texts (Dyson, Bennett, Brooks, Garcia, Howard-McBride, Malekzadeh, et al.,1997). My sense is that we will find that teachers' personal literacy practices provide a major basis for promoting the literacy knowledge and skills required by contemporary curricula.

Andreas Schleicher (2007) from the PISA programme of studies captured the general view of teachers from the twenty-first century when writing about the countries that are effective in producing high achievement. When the characteristics of teachers in countries performing well are examined, the indicators are that they personalize their learning, making informed professional judgements. Schliecher calls them 'knowledge workers,' who have high expectations for their students, relate very well to their students and who have well-managed and structured classrooms.

The implication of each of these perspectives is that a highly effective teacher could not be like a technician following a largely prescribed set of procedures. Rather, teachers are more like experts, they have a type of expertise the nature of which is to be deeply knowledgeable about what they do, how they do it, and why they do it; and they ply their practices with great adeptness. The general psychological definition of an expert is they are very goal focused and intentional; they are strategic, being able to adapt to circumstances and to modify their tools or even develop new tools and ways of performing. They know the medium within which they act very well. Experts are keenly aware of the effectiveness of their performances in the sense of being in control by being able to monitor, check and modify their actions (McNaughton, 2002). There are other more social aspects of being an expert. An expert is immersed in the traditions and practices of their community including the standards, rules, and procedures (Olson, 2003). The combination of these attributes give experts the twin features of being technically adept as well as innovative and adaptable.

The distinction, between being technically competent and being an expert is echoed in recent foundational statements about the nature of what teaching should be like in the twenty-first century United States. The editors and authors, Darling-Hammond and Bransford (2005) representing the National Academy of Education draw a distinction between 'routine experts' who develop a core set of competencies that they apply with greater and greater efficiency, and 'adaptive experts' who continuously add to their knowledge and skills. They change their core competencies and expand the breadth and depth of their expertise.

A pedagogic oath?

This idea of adaptive expertise is a compelling view of teachers. It captures in the description of practices of instruction one of the two features I highlighted earlier, needed by teachers to avoid Matthew Effects. The feature is teachers needing to be able to innovate and modify to personalize instruction, being adept at using evidence to inform their own practices to avoid channeling children into lower trajectories of learning.

But this adaptation is dependent on a second feature that is critical to avoid Matthew Effects. It is the need to be an effective teacher with those groups of students who have not been well served by schools. It is the need to have beliefs about and understandings of children and their families and communities as resourceful. These ideas and the associated knowledge would provide a basis for a commitment to and expectation of children's fundamental ability to be successful in academic development. We have learned, sometimes very painfully, that it is not possible both to teach effectively and to see the children being taught as deficient.

Delpit (2003) made this point in a commentary on the need to teach intensively the vocabulary required by schools. She was commenting on the classic study of vocabulary development before school I described earlier, carried out by Hart and Risley (1995). The researchers compared the rates of acquisition of children from professional families and those from below the poverty level and how the dramatically different rates of acquisition systematically reflected rates of 'input,' the quantity and quality of language in which the child was involved. The authors of the report calculated how many hours of quality input would be needed in an intervention starting at 4 years to make up the difference. It was a staggering 41 hours of high quality interactions per week. Their book ends on a very pessimistic note, responding to the seeming impossibility of schools being able to do this.

The risk in studies such as Hart and Risley's (1995) is to draw the conclusion that it is the families and the children who are deficient. They are incapable or limited or mistaken in what they have been able to do because of who they are. They need to forsake their usual (limited or wrong) ways and do things like professional families. But the deficiency position gets in the way of innovation and flexibility and, ultimately, optimism. It does so because if one believes children and families are limited one adjusts expectations accordingly or we design a programme to replace the problematic ways of doing things (such as talking with children) to replace them with the 'right' ways with predictable limited outcomes. These expectations that are held in concert with beliefs about deficiencies are one of the drivers for creating Matthew Effects. Replacement programmes that do not acknowledge the skills and knowledge and culturally appropriate ways that already exist are a form of paternalism at best which maintains dependency and reduces transfer and generalization.

Delpit (2003) does not argue against the need for intensive vocabulary programmes at school and does argue that there is sufficient evidence to suggest that schools can have an impact, even in the face of Hart and Risley's (1995) estimates of the staggering differences. But she adds the critical set of beliefs:

> Only a consciously devised, continuous program that develops vocabulary in the context of real experiences, provides rigorous instruction, connects new information to the cultural frameworks that children bring to school, and assumes that the children are brilliant and capable, and teaches accordingly can (accelerate vocabulary acquisition).
>
> (Delpit, 2003, p. 17)

This is not to say we should be naively optimistic. The lines of evidence presented in previous chapters would counsel against that. But we can hold to the position that children living in poor circumstances and families who have limited economic, social and political power nevertheless have psychological resources that they use and on which they can call. The lesson from previous chapters is that it is the circumstances that are deficient.

What are the policy implications of this view of teachers and their teaching? They are in part those of Darling-Hammond (2006), which I have already discussed. The need in a coherent system designed to reduce inequalities is for high levels of education and professional preparation. They include the requirement for salaries and professional recognition that reflect the complex nature of the role. But more than this is the need for teachers to have cultural knowledge and beliefs about the resources children may have access to and how one can add value to their already existing repertoires of practices.

How does one select and prepare teachers for that? Something like a Hippocratic Oath is needed. In New Zealand a statute that land developers need to comply with is called the Resource Management Act (1991). It is designed to balance the needs of preservation and respect for what exists with the need to develop new uses for the land. Something like that is needed for teachers, in which principles direct us to respect the resources that children have, their repertoires or funds of knowledge and keep that respect in balance with the requirements of the curriculum and the need to guarantee high achievement. This would include a set of principles about what it means to have a focus on equitable outcomes.

Some teacher education programmes have tried to develop such views. In the Boston College's programme there is a strong theme of social justice (Cochran-Smith, Shakman, Jong, Terrell, Barnatt, & McQuillan, 2009). That theme together with other recent design changes in their Teachers for a New Era programme is associated with graduates having greater commitment and perceiving they are better prepared to teach cultural diversity. However, these are very recent developments and the designers are keenly aware of the need to research planned effects. They are following cohorts of graduates to examine whether the whole programme, which now has this core commitment, makes a difference to the effectiveness of teaching.

The core idea of social justice is not the only way different states might rationalize the need to have beliefs about and a commitment to teach for equitable outcomes. That is, it is possible that different states could provide different emphases in the rationale for a core commitment to equitable outcomes. In New Zealand one part of the rationale is in the form of a Treaty signed between many of the indigenous tribes and the colonising power in 1840. This Treaty of Waitangi functions in part like a social contract and in part like a founding document. The import of this is that equitable outcomes can be seen as guaranteed in the Treaty articles. If the present day treaty partner (in practice the government of the day and not the Queen of England) does not enable these outcomes then the partner is in breach of the contract. In Singapore the argument for equitable outcomes may also be about needing to have all of its citizens contributing effectively to a dynamic and knowledge based economy, because the state's only resources are its people and there is an ideological commitment to a meritocracy (Luke, Freebody, Shun, & Gopinathan, 2005). In the United Sates a social justice position is understandable given the history of the accumulated "educational debt" (Ladson-Billings, 2006, p. 3).

These are powerful beliefs about the need to have equitable outcomes. They need to be married with equally powerful beliefs about the resources that children and their families can have. Teachers who are experts have ideas and beliefs not just about the medium for their practices and the practices themselves. They also have beliefs and knowledge about the nature of learning and development and the nature of children and families and diversity. Their awareness of these ideas is a fundamental part of their expertise. They need to be able to monitor, check, and modify their ideas and knowledge of diversity as much as their knowledge of the processes of reading.

Concluding comment: policy and research partnerships

To build more effective schools requires challenging one of Oscar Wilde's famous aphorisms. His teasing challenge to be different was that "Consistency is the last refuge of the unimaginative." But we have to build consistency as coherence between levels in an educational system. The present chapter has been concerned with the coherence in terms of state policies and the other systems nested within these. One of the participants in the development of state policies is the research community. How can we as researchers contribute better to more effective state policies?

Researchers cannot contribute to the design of more effective schools without policies being aligned that enable schools and teachers to be as effective as possible. This implies that researchers need to be more direct in their involvement with policy makers. We need to contribute to the development of detailed policies that create conditions that enhance schools effectiveness.

The second argument for why researchers should enter collaborations with policy makers comes from an analysis of policy contexts as setting conditions for effective applied developmental science (Lerner, Fisher, & Weinberg, 2000). The crass point to be made would be that funding that enabled research and development to take place is needed from policy makers. But the argument is much more than this. It is very like the idea of programme coherence, which applies to the school as a system (Newman, Smith, Allensworth, & Bryk, 2001). If we take the broader system of policy, research and practice in a national sense then the issue is coherence or alignment in terms of policy at a national and local level and how that creates a setting for effective research and development with schools.

The effect of creating coherence can be illustrated in the example I have already used from New Zealand. It is the shift in national policy that occurred in New Zealand starting with the implementation of the 'National Literacy and Numeracy Strategy' in 1998 (New Zealand Ministry of Education, 2002). The strategy developed alongside reports by a national Literacy Task Force (1999) and an associated Literacy Experts Group (1999) convened by the New Zealand Government. The participants in the Task Force comprised representatives from a broad cross section of stakeholder groups including teachers, researchers, policy makers, and community members. The Experts Group of researchers was set up to provide advice and recommendations both to that group and the Ministry. The shared focus across the stakeholder groups became literacy achievement in Years 1–4, and especially the achievement of Māori and Pasifika children in low decile schools.

The recommendations from those reports influenced a coherent and concerted policy, which set national guidelines for reporting achievement in schools which was to include mandatory annual reporting of achievement for Māori and Pasifika children. Guidance in how to apply the curriculum in the early years occurred which redirected schools' attention to the core activities of literacy and numeracy. Other developments included new resources for teaching and assessing literacy, which were commissioned and implemented, and funding pools were provided for innovative schools and research with schools. The shared awareness of a national problem to be solved focused on Years 1–4 and the low 'tail' in the achievement distribution.

This policy context increased the conditions for concerted professional development and research-practice collaborations to occur. In the New Zealand case the first of these was research focused on the transition to school I noted earlier. The context enabled funding to be available but for an agreed programme of research and development that would contribute nationally to understanding the shared problem. Funding for professional development costs was given to lead schools in clusters with partner funding coming from the researchers drawing on outside funding agencies. The funding also gave a rationale to schools to commit themselves to high stakes collaboration with high risks. Descriptions of the schools, their achievement and teaching would be highly visible and interventions closely monitored. Public funding required transparent accountability.

The effects of this policy change and concomitant research attention have been described in previous chapters. One additional effect of the policy convergence was to direct research attention to solve real world problems, the most pressing of which were to raise achievement levels in selected schools in ways that met the criteria I have outlined of acceleration and shifting distributions. Innovations have come from this. An example is the solving of methodological debates about appropriate designs in applied contexts. In the New Zealand case the press to solve large-scale applied problems that contributed to the policy direction meant developing quasi experimental design formats. The need was to substantially change whole schools in a research development sequence without severely compromising scientific criteria for validity and believability, and given the messiness and variability of schools for which randomized control group designs are often unsuited (Phillips, McNaughton, & MacDonald, 2004). The acceptability of such designs to academic peers is an important outcome, as is the continuing modification and innovation to meet challenges posed by our peers (Lai, McNaughton, Amitvanai-Toloq, Turner, & Hsiao, 2009).

A second example is that in the New Zealand case research has confronted and uncovered new dimensions of teaching and learning that have arisen through the close contextualized profiling needed to design interventions to suit the specialized contexts of the poorest and most diverse schools and their literacy challenges (Lai, McNaughton, Amitvanai-Toloq, Turner, & Hsiao, 2009). The research uncovered a risk in reading comprehension strategy instruction. The risk was ongoing explicit instruction defaulting to teaching the strategies as ends in themselves. This risk, although noted, had not been systematically examined in the literature and finding it can be directly linked to the need to solve real world problems in the messy contexts of schools.

11

A SCIENCE OF PERFORMANCE

Research and development partnerships

I have made the claim that building more effective schools that continue to be very effective is dependent on ongoing partnerships. The forms and functions of those partnerships vary considerably. In the context of partnerships between professionals and researchers to change schools systematically, they take the form at one extreme of researchers helping to set up and resource a new school. More generally in school reform, external research partners design, implement and monitor a new programme that has been externally designed. More recently, there are partnerships that are collaborative and developmental, in which schools and partners redesign the schools' activities. These latter are what Raphael and her colleagues call second generation models (Raphael, Au, & Goldman, 2009). The most effective of these are focused on processes which design instructional programmes that have fidelity. In each of these cases the partnership draws on research based expertise. This chapter is about what research partners can and should contribute.

Becoming better

In 2007 Atul Gawande wrote a book, the title of which was simply *Better*. The sub title was *A surgeon's notes on performance*. Gawande (2007), the surgeon whose notes these are, asked the question, "What does it take to be good at something in which failure is so easy, so effortless?" The question was directed at how to make medical practice more effective. The question could equally be applied to educational practices and how to make them more effective.

His argument is that three factors make the practice of medicine, or indeed any endeavor that involves risks and responsibilities (and that surely includes schooling) better. The first is diligence. This entails giving the fullest attention to the detail needed to avoid error and to overcome obstacles. His analysis of cases of diligence reveals the complexity behind this idea. In examples such as how to reduce bacterial infection rates in hospitals and controlling new outbreaks of polio in India there are identifiable features where dramatic solutions have occurred. For example, major occurrences of virulent infections can fall from four to six instances per month to that many in an entire year or even zero in hospitals through innovative practices around an everyday solution: hand washing. He describes several components of being diligent. There is looking for evidence for effectiveness, and getting all the steps right. These components are very dependent on each other, using examples of practice out of the ordinary in terms of their effectiveness. In this he draws on the concept of 'positive deviance' (Frerichs, 2010), which is the idea I introduced earlier of searching for variability. In Gawande's (2007) case it is the search for the examples of medical practices associated with being effective. Finally there is building on the capabilities that exist already, and scaling up tried solutions, from one unit or one town to many units and many towns. Like Gawande (2007), I argued earlier that scaling up is a core part of creating more effective schools and scaling up is a major challenge to our solutions.

The second is in his words 'to do right.' This is a concern to be committed to the principles that define the profession, to prevail over human foibles, avarice, arrogance, insecurity, and misunderstanding. Payment for doctors, the role of insurance, and when to give up on a sick patient are uncomfortable topics that push the limits on what is right. He discusses these and presents his own position. His point is not so much what his position might be, but that these need to be discussed and considered where it matters. Doing right by the patient is not always clear, but the wisdom he offers is to err on the side of pushing and not giving up. Be ready to recognize when it is just ego or weakness rather than informed decisions continuing the pushing. This recapitulates another of my arguments. It is the need to have a commitment to children and their families and seeing them as resourceful. The need for a pedagogic oath can be extended to this idea of continuing to push for ways of being more effective.

The third is ingenuity, thinking in new ways. On the one hand this involves recognising error and failure and on the other deliberate reflection on that failure and a searching for new solutions, which he even suggests borders on being obsessive. His examples for this involve such different fields as childbirth and cystic fibrosis. For the former he rehearses Virginia Apgar's 'ridiculously simple idea,' which transformed childbirth and the care of the newborn. She devised a score, the Apgar score, which rated the condition of babies at birth on a scale from zero to ten. Used at one minute after birth and five minutes after birth, it revolutionized practices when it was introduced in 1953. The score enabled doctors to observe, compare and document on the basis of an agreed method. It motivated doctors to find ways to produce better scores and hence better outcomes. It enabled staff to evaluate the effect of interventions such as different types of anesthesia, and helped propel neonatal intensive care units into being because the data showed it was possible to save more babies. In this and other examples, such as those of cystic fibrosis, getting the data is crucial. This is what the Apgar score provided. Through the evidence provided by the score and what that meant for account-ability, plus other advances in early detection and use of ultra sound, the rate of full term deaths dropped from one in 30 in the 1950s to the contempory rate of one in 500.

Others (A template for saving lives, 2007) have made similar observations about medical practices. A recent investigation followed up a 2001 study into critical differences in emergency services across 50 US cities. It identified critical differ-ences between successful cities that had remarkable 'save rates' for heart attack victims, and others. For example, Seattle's save rate was 45 per cent while Atlanta's had been 3 per cent. The study documents how Atlanta has improved its emergency services, replicating the 'positive deviancy' of the few highly successful cities such as Seattle in the 2001 report. The change demonstrated the significance of key ingredients identified by Gawande (2007). They were accountability involving actions based on systematically collected and analysed data on effective-ness. Cities that have improved their services have joined a central database designed to help city leaders see problems and solutions for like cities. City officials can track how services are doing and compare with other cities developing shared solutions.

Other key ingredients are leadership to bed in, extend, and scale up solutions. The report describes how Atlanta, under its Mayor, improved its performance five fold through scaled up solutions such as training ordinary citizens in CPR. The Mayor and all 8,000 city employees took the training and the rate by which bystanders gave help rose from 7 per cent to 17 per cent. Successful cities have ingrained such practices, with CPR training in schools, and in some professions. In some cities the bystander CPR rates now exceed 40 per cent. The leadership extends to forced coordination between departments for a coordinated and coherent approach.

The idea of exploring variability in practices and searching for positive deviance famously occurred to John Snow, a doctor in nineteenth century London (Frerichs, 2010). He was a public health official during a cholera outbreak in the early part of the century, and is credited with discovering its source. He plotted each case of cholera on a map of London and realized that 'the deaths are most numerous near to the pump in Broad Street.' The site of cholera was a water source.

His test of this hypothesis is compelling in its thoroughness. He looked for all of the exceptions to the idea that people using that pump would contract cholera. The list included low incidence in a workhouse very near the pump. He determined that the premises had its own pump well and the workers never used the Broad Street pump. Similarly, despite working at a brewery at the epicentre of the cholera deaths few of the brewery workers died. But this brewery had its own private well. These were the positive deviancies. But other exceptions and variability filled out the picture. Four school children had died who lived some distance from the pump. Investigation showed they drank from the pump on the way to school. Two adults living even further away died. Again, digging deeper it was found that one had temporarily lived in Broad Street, and the other had nursed a dying friend in the street. Finally there were some deaths nearer to another pump in Rupert Street but although being geographically closer to that pump the routes to the pump were circuitous. Despite living nearest to that pump, some residents had found it was easier to go to the Broad Street pump. Snow's systematic analysis is a great example of using exceptions to explain the rule.

Better research on teaching?

Do these insights apply to the focus of this chapter? Do they clarify the nature of partnerships between researchers and educators which lead to designing more effective instruction for students who come from communities not typically well served by schools? Like Gawande's (2007) concern, this is surely an endeavor that involves high responsibility by researchers and teachers and involves considerable risk for the students. Each of Gawande's (2007) three principles apply. But they need to be complemented in ways that are idiosyncratic to educational research.

The first, diligence, is partly about being able to recognize 'better' when you find it and to do this you need to observe and, among other things, systematize, including count, what you observe. This is the real lesson behind being 'evidence based' in education. In order to solve problems we need to be able to see and evaluate a range of outcomes. There are prosaic but powerful outcomes of better learning and achievement, the primary focus of this book. There are also more detailed processes such as the 'engagement' of students (Guthrie, & Wigfield, 2000), which are the core to motivational outcomes. Most importantly there are the deep outcomes of students' cultural well-being.

But as well as these 'outcomes' we need to see and evaluate the processes involved in these outcomes. These are the forms that instruction takes. In the past researchers and educators have tended to concentrate on one-half of the phenomena of concern. Often it has been measures of student performance with which we have been preoccupied, their achievement on tests and standings in various local, national, and international comparisons.

The PIRLS, PISA and TIMSS international studies well illustrate this bias. The bulk of the analyses are about students' achievement. But something equivalent to Gawande's analysis (2007) of the process is needed. The critical processes to know about are the everyday practices that make a difference. For hospital infections this is practices of washing hands in hospitals. Knowing about the process means knowing about how that washing happens, when, and with what rigour or ineptitude. It means knowing the conditions of hospitals including space and timetabling that help or hinder good practices.

In the most effective examples of solving problems in schools, we need to know in detail the processes in schools and classroom processes that substantially accelerated achievement and produced matched distributions of achievement. Conversely, analyses of when solutions have been less than optimal, paying due diligence means examining processes that are not working well. The detailed analyses of both New York's District #2 and the attempted replication in San Diego illustrate this point.

Doing it 'right' also applies. This is in part to do with the commitment I described earlier. It is about the beliefs and expectations we hold about teaching and students. One set of beliefs that teachers have concerns the capabilities and needs of their students. Starting from the classic 'Pygmalion in the classroom' study there is a long but somewhat confusing literature about teacher expectations (Weinstein, 2002). The original study showed that teachers who believed students were to be 'bloomers' in their classrooms, something that they had been led to believe by bogus tests of 'intellectual blooming' given by the researchers, had students who did indeed bloom in achievement. It makes sense because a well-known observation in the educational literature is that the best predictor of success is what a teacher judges your likely achievement to be in school.

But some confusion has reigned because subsequent studies have had mixed success replicating effects of general expectations and identifying the exact mechanisms by which an expectation translates into classroom events have been elusive. It is likely some of that confusion is due to the lack of specificity around what expectations are and relationships between expectations, student perceptions and teachers' actual practices.

However, when we look at how beliefs and dispositions are related to specific aspects of teaching the picture becomes much clearer. For example, grouping for instruction can be associated with differences in properties of instruction, which can exacerbate the very differences between groups. The risk is that through features such as correction of errors, or aspects of feedback, students who are defined as low progress and grouped as such are given more compartmentalized and simplified instruction, more item focused instruction, thus putting in place Matthew Effects. With more focused analyses such as these we now have much better explanations of the processes through which expectations become influential in accumulated experiences over time (Weinstein, 2002). The processes include how the theories children hold about themselves and their learning are influenced by stereotypes about low ability that are evoked in specific situations and reinforced through expectations and then contribute to underperformance (Molden, & Dweck, 2006).

Researchers and teachers do 'right' to the extent that they continually question their assumptions about children, their resources, their potential, and their capacity to learn. Researchers are as culpable as anyone in undervaluing children's learning and teachers' teaching. My own disciplinary background, psychological development, illustrates this. Constructivist theorizing often led to comparisons of children's development using models of development, derived from middle class and mainstream groups that see development along a single sequence. These comparisons contributed to seeing children from communities with limited economic, social, and cultural power as necessarily being 'deficient' or slow (McNaughton, 2002).

Finally there is ingenuity. Researchers and educators need to be ingenious in searching for solutions. For both teachers and researchers this means searching for and learning from variability, from the outliers. But it also means a preparedness to try out new ideas; taking the glimmer of an idea, the hunch of a teacher, a new way of doing things that a teacher has worked out and exploring its potential.

Teachers are wonderful sources of ingenuity. An example from New Zealand's educational history is the invention of 'natural language texts.' The mercurial teacher and educator Sylvia Ashton-Warner (1963) is credited with this idea, although there is some evidence now that several teachers were thinking about this in the 1920s and 1930s and a 'tipping point' occurred, with the idea catching on rapidly. At the beginning of her career she found herself teaching Māori children in a remote rural community. The books from which the children were meant to learn to read in English did not match the experiences of the children, let alone their language. Her brilliant idea was to use the children's own language and the events encoded in their language as the basis for early readers. She wrote texts about fishing for eels in the river, swimming and farm experiences, the everyday worlds of the children and their language, although tidied up somewhat and controlled for complexity of word usage.

Warner (1963) recounts her discovery and its effectiveness in her book simply called *Teacher*. But from that idea grew a national commitment to publishing natural language texts that have been the backbone of New Zealand's early reading programme, which is justifiably internationally famous for its general effectiveness.

A science of performance

How can educational research contribute to successful solutions like those described by Gawande (2007)? He makes some bold claims about what research which contributes to being better looks like, proposing a 'science of performance.' This is the idea of scientists and practitioners needing to understand how to make a difference in the sites where it matters, and that problem solving and evidence based enquiry are central to this.

Like medical professionals, both researchers and educators can do something about making our practices better, engaging in a science of performance. Here are some features of what our science of performance would look like.

Site based

Researchers have been limited in the places we have been looking for how to make schools better. We need to understand the nature of teaching and learning in the schools. Not only this, we need to know how this relates to the other complex features of the school and how the school is itself embedded in other systems. In the previous chapter I provided a model and a rationale for why this is needed.

This concern for understanding just how everyday sites constrain change is behind Olson's (2003) analysis of why large-scale movements such as the child centered education movement in broad terms failed to change teaching practices. He approached the question as a cognitive developmental psychologist. But despite the usual foci of cognitive developmentalists on individual change his explanation is not about the individual teacher and their knowledge in isolation. His explanation was that change agents hadn't understood how schools are cultures. Schools are living systems that have their own internal practices. The assumption from a simplistic model of adult learning unrelated to context is that transmitting new knowledge would be sufficient. But without a focus on embedding new knowledge in changed cultural practices major reforms have failed.

Added to this is a feature of schools I have also discussed in previous chapters. They are open systems and constantly changing; with new students, new teachers, new leaders, new curricula, and new technology. All these and more, including the encompassing systems such as educational and economic policies, have an influence. These twin features of being an open system and being a cultural system have an important implication for research. They mean that testing ideas about instruction in highly controlled laboratory studies may be a necessary step in developing our theories, but they are a very limited part of what we need to know to design better classroom learning.

The science we need is one that is firmly grounded in the practices of schools. Here is a simple school problem with a complex solution. In the schools in South Auckland in New Zealand with whom I work there is large-scale movement of students into and out of the schools in any one year (perhaps not surprisingly, it is true also for the teachers). Up to a third of the students can change in any one year. For any intervention process this has several consequences. There are methodological consequences. In one study we started with over 1,500 students in seven schools in the middle and upper primary years. Over the course of three years as we tracked students over time we ended up with fewer than 300 students for whom we had full records. There are statistical solutions to this methodological problem but the problem facing effective practices are very much more complex.

The challenge of the problem is easily put. In the study with fewer than a fifth of the original students remaining after three years, there was a difference in achievement levels between the students who stayed for three years and new students entering the school at any level. The students who were tracked over three years were on average a full half year more advanced in reading comprehension achievement compared with the students who entered the school.

Much of the student movement is associated with the social conditions that the communities face. There are issues to do with housing and temporary rental accommodation. There are associations between the health related conditions in housing and employment and access to medical services and student mobility or transience. Time off school for these reasons accounts for some of the movement. There are issues to do with changing employment opportunities. Some of the children in South Auckland are sons and daughters of families newly arrived from the different Pacific Islands and movement to where work opportunities exist is common. In addition, there are cultural processes at work where children move within the extended family for a variety of reasons and may shift homes to stay at grandparents or with aunties and uncles. All of these factors illustrate why the nested systems approach to understanding schools' effectiveness is needed.

In the past this pattern of movement would be seen as a problem that is outside of the control of the school, and hence of the researchers' interests and the educators' ambit of influence. It is something that we may have in the past parked outside of the research issues as noise or error variance. These students and the problem might not be included as part of the evaluation of the 'treatment' or an intervention, because these students had not received the full treatment, and hence needed to be excluded from the analysis to preserve our judgements of treatment integrity and treatment effectiveness. Generalizations about the treatment would be compromised because the effects of the treatment would be contaminated by students who only received partial amounts of our intervention.

What if we adopted Gawande's (2007) position and saw this as at least something we need to consider as a performance problem? Even given that there are policy and structural dimensions which are out of our control, is this a problem to which the schools can contribute partial solutions? Understanding of this issue requires appreciating what is possible with teaching and learning and what is possible through the partnerships both between researchers and educators and collectively with local communities.

The schools in South Auckland haven't fully solved this yet but there is evidence that they are making progress. Irrespective of whether students have been present for an extended period of time or they have entered the school recently the overall average achievement is rising. How have they done that? One way is that they make sure that the new students are engaged in the classroom learning as quickly as possible.

An earlier study with these schools into young children making the transition to their schools used the idea of both students and teachers 'picking up the pace' of both teaching and learning in order to meet the acceleration criterion (Phillips, McNaughton, & McDonald, 2004). The schools are now trying to find ways in which new students in the middle and upper primary years can be engaged in the classroom processes as quickly as possible. The problem becomes how can we speed up their apprenticeship, moving them as quickly as possible from peripheral members of the classroom community to fully functioning and engaged. The teachers needed to find ways of assessing quickly and identifying the entry skills and strengths and gaps quickly. Their problem solving includes thinking about how to make the goals and requirements of classroom activities even clearer for the new students. They are also considering the careful balance required in differentiating their instruction, keeping in mind that they teach to meet their needs for acceleration. The professional knowledge and advice for communities to help their decision making is part of this too. Some schools even look to their relationships with local businesses to develop shared understanding about employment needs and how the well-being of both students and their families may be a shared goal.

Similarly, the movement of teachers into and out of the schools could be seen as something beyond the orbit of schools and a research focus on being better. It again has policy dimensions including the recognition and payment for teachers, reflecting the expertise required for working in diverse and poor urban schools. But again, rather than seeing this as a threat to treatment integrity it can be seen as a property of this system and one that needs to be understood and solved. The problem is in principle able to be solved just as the student movement problem. A science of performance identifies this as a problem to be understood and something that with ingenuity we need to be able to solve, or at least contribute to partially solving.

The issue for researchers is to figure out how to cope with this radically different way of looking at our science; that is to see the significant theoretical concerns as well as the pressing educational problems as located in the everyday world of classrooms, schools and their communities in all their messiness. This argument does not exclude laboratory sites or highly controlled classrooms as important sites for our research. But it defines the everyday context of classrooms, schools and communities as sites in their own right requiring basic research. There has been a distinction between basic and applied science in the context of education, which sees the search for principles and explanations in controlled environments as somehow basic science. But this has been very misleading and has led to our limited capability to change things. The assumption has been that we need to establish basic principles in clean, highly controlled circumstances, uncontaminated by the messiness. But it is the very messiness of the everyday contexts that sets the most complex challenges to our explanations and redesign.

The problem of teacher movement into and out of schools is a complex problem to be solved on the ground. Theories of communities of practice developed from everyday examples of such communities provide one means of answering the question of how a school can continue to function effectively despite such movement (Rogoff, Barlett, & Turkanis, 2001). If the school has a well-functioning community then the entry into the practices of the community is key. This means harnessing a process like apprenticeship and having well-targeted induction policies. It means creating opportunities for collegial mentoring and guided experiences in the practices by way of observing in classrooms and debriefing about what has been observed. In addition, advertising for positions at the schools highlights that teachers will expected to be fully functioning members of the community, getting to know and be expert in the practices of the community. That puts part of the responsibility with the new teachers as well with the community into which he or she is moving. Other answers include regional or national policies to attract, retain, and celebrate effective teachers in these schools.

Putting these ideas into practice sounds like a common sense solution. And in some respects that is exactly what it is. But it has a theoretical base that like all good theories, after the solving, gives it the elegance of simplicity. The theoretical base to the first answer is the idea of a community of practice and the function of the rules and roles of members within that community. There are very detailed accounts of everyday communities and their maintenance, from which basic concepts and explanations have been built (Rogoff, Bartlett, & Turkanis, 2001; Wenger, 1998).

The science of performance is for education a science of performance in a complex, messy world, one in which schools and their communities are open cultural systems; and which need to be understood in those terms. Research that does not consider these attributes may have limited generalizability. Bronfenbrenner (1979) made a similar argument 30 years ago for shifting the science of developmental psychology. He called the science of his day the science of strange situations, in strange circumstances with strange people for the briefest possible periods of time. He was describing the canonical approach of science of his day, a lab based approach which was located outside of the worlds in which children actually developed, with people with whom the children had no relationships and where they were required to do tasks that were unlike those they confronted in those everyday worlds.

His critique was of the established practice of studying children, their learning, and development in laboratory settings, mimicking the tools in trade of some of the physical sciences. But he argued and subsequently demonstrated in elegant experiments that even relatively simple developmental phenomena such as children's strategic memorizing is different in different contexts. He didn't argue against laboratory studies, and here I don't want to rule these out. Bronfenbrenners' (1979) argument was one about 'ecological validity.' Know your context and the limits to which results from it can be generalized to other contexts. Some carefully designed studies in labs are critical to further our understanding. Some control group comparisons in the real world are essential. But a science of performance needs to be grounded in everyday settings.

Evidence based

In addition to being site based, an educational science of performance needs to be evidence based. Data is central to any scientific endeavor. The science of performance requires evidence, evidence about the products or outcomes as well as evidence about the process and conditions for being effective.

The general idea of gathering information is not particularly novel. Assessing students both formally and informally to make judgements about progress and learning needs and on which to base instruction, is well known. But what is novel is using this information about students and other evidence to judge effectiveness at a variety of levels of the school's functioning. This requires skills for selecting, gathering and using a range of data, skills that are not very familiar to professionals in schools. Critically, the evidence is not just of students. As I argued earlier, it is essential that the evidence be sought about instruction. And not just about instruction, but also about aspects of the school such as how it is functioning as a professional learning community.

An interesting phenomenon occurs when psychologists systematically study effective instruction in real world contexts. Their research leads almost inexorably to their becoming more like organizational psychologists. Ann Brown (1997) with colleagues developed the method of comprehension instruction called Reciprocal Teaching. As she studied how to put the programme into practice she shifted her focus to how groups function in classrooms and described 'jig saw' arrangements and collective forms of problem solving within which the instructional programme would best work. Clay (1997), the designer of Reading Recovery, became concerned with how the tutoring programme could be contextualized in different countries and how the administrators and academics could develop efficient organizational patterns. The psychologists and literacy specialists working on school interventions have needed to become experts in, or at least have working knowledge of, dynamic properties of schools as communities.

The corollary also applies. That is, researchers concerned with school culture and organization have needed to attend to the psychology of teachers (Fullan, & NetLibrary Inc, 2007; Robinson, & Lai, 2006). The rationale for these shifts can be laid with Bronfnebrenner's (1979) Russian dolls. The parts of the system are inextricably entwined and their relationships create the basis for effective instruction.

Take as an example the evidence that would be needed to understand the workings of the summer learning effect with any school and its community. Different patterns of learning between academic years occur in different schools and their communities. In some the gap between two school years is punctuated by a plateau or a drop in student achievement over the long school break. In Chapter 7 I discussed the explanation for this effect which is related to family social and cultural practices that provide differential exposure to school related literacy activities over the summer. In order to understand the immediate properties of the effect evidence from at least three sources is needed. One source is the families and communities within which they live and would include evidence about the literacy practices of families and their access to and use of resources. A second source is in the classrooms and would include evidence about how instruction did or did not enhance children's literacy activities outside of school. Yet a third source would be the children themselves including their practices, their reading strategies as well as their achievement patterns.

A generically useful source of evidence for researchers and educators to better understand what their role might be would come from examples of 'positive deviance.' Are there teachers like those in Anderson's study (Anderson, Wilson, & Fielding, 1988) whose students were much more likely to gain over summer? In a cluster of like schools it might be whether there is a school that bucks the trend. Gathering some information perhaps in the form of the teacher explaining their practices, perhaps by asking students about what they did over summer or even carrying out more systematic forms of recording such as diaries might take place. It could be that schools also surveyed or had focus groups with parents to examine what current practices were. This would all be prior to doing anything to change circumstances. Can researchers and school communities do this, with the capacity to identify problems in performance and gather evidence to help solve them? The answer is that we have to be able to do it, in order to be effective.

It is perhaps an obvious point to make, but a science of performance requires judicious and efficient use of data. Not just any data or evidence for the sake of evidence. Just as in medicine we need to know what we are looking at, to understand it. This means a constant need to check and refine our theories of the site and its systems and the relationships with effectiveness. A science of performance needs to be more theoretically informed.

Collaboration based

This science of performance requires new forms of partnership between researchers and practitioners. The business community has recognized the need for closer partnerships in order to produce more effective technologies, and the rationales are very similar (The Economist, 2007). Research and development in business used to be two distinct endeavors. The model was of the boffins in the lab making breakthroughs and a relatively independent industry developing the basic findings so they could be marketed. The model of the two distinct activities had some stunning successes. AT&T's Bell Labs gained six Nobel prizes through inventions such as the laser. Similar track records exits for IBM and Xerox.

But analysts now argue that the model needs to be more like a continuum. The old model applied particularly where there were monopolies and vertically organized companies. Innovation is now needed in diffuse networked organizations. Researchers should not be isolated. Innovation is dependent on their working with professional colleagues solving localized needs and with a deliberate focus on innovation and knowledge transfer to develop scaled products. The fusion solves the problem of how to develop ideas into commercial innovation.

The idea of close collaboration requires mutually supportive and mutually influential roles. This sense of collaboration also requires a degree of overlap in expertise as well as complementary forms of expertise. Teachers with adaptive expertise in more effective schools need to be able to 'read' data, to discuss theories and hypotheses about their practices, and to inquire into their practices. The inquiry has features of the research expertise that researchers have. In order to make sense of evidence to identify, discard ineffective practices, or zero in on promising new practices, and to effectively design tests of solutions to problems, researchers need some content and pedagogical knowledge. Their pattern recognition and appreciation of what variability means, as well as their capability to build theory is dependent on a knowledge base that overlaps with teachers'. This is not the same as assuming that teachers are necessarily researchers or that researchers know and act like teachers. But it does assume that each shares some aspects of each other's adaptive expertise.

Each needs to be somewhat more like the other than they might currently be but they need to be able to bring their complementary skills together. The reasons for this are that the solving of school problems in all their nested complexity requires distributed expertise. Researchers have sets of skills and teachers and professional educators have sets of skills. I have argued that teachers need to function as adaptive experts. Teachers need deep pedagogical and content knowledge as part of this expertise. Researchers need a different form of adaptive expertise. They need to have a deep theoretical knowledge of and the explanations for aspects of educational phenomena. For the researchers collaborating with schools the explanations are particularly those relating to teaching and learning in specific domains of development. But not exclusively, because they also need to understand the layers and the nesting of educational systems. They need developed understanding of the set of technical tools in the methods kit. And they need to be able to adapt and modify their thinking and their tools in the light of the evidence and the context, to which their collaborators contribute their knowledge and skills.

In the examples of school change, especially the scaling up part of school change, different forms that this collaboration might take were illustrated. Each of the approaches, the 'prescription,' 'exemplary design,' and 'retuning' approaches require research expertise although perhaps elements of this are required in different measure. Clearly, the first two require less flexibility and adjustment to local circumstance than the third, although in prescribing and in redesigning (as present continuous endeavors) the need to continually adapt and respond to context are still present. But more than this, what these examples illustrate is a set of relatively unrecognized skills that are part of the expertise. These skills are as critical to the collaboration as the academic knowledge. They are a set of interpersonal skills that are needed more in some models than others.

It doesn't take much in the way of skills involved in forming mutually influential relationships if the researcher has primary control over the design and implementation of change. This was the case in the traditional lab based manner of studying instruction or developmental processes, the manner stereotyped by

Bronfenbrenner (1979). The very design of strange tasks, strange situations over brief time periods and in the setting that only the strangers (i.e. the researchers) are familiar with, guarantees control, and reduces the need for collaborative skills. But to develop and maintain a working, mutually informative and trustful collaboration requires interpersonal skills that need to be explicitly recognized and gained directly in our training programmes.

The role of 'basic' science?

I have touched on the obvious tension in this picture of a science of performance. It is the issue of what counts as basic science. There are risks in using parallels with a commercial model of research and development. One risk is an unintended reduction in the potential for innovation by being driven by immediate need. Basic science does exist in the formulation of a science of performance but it is one part of a more seamless continuum where the extremes are capable of influencing each other.

Put crudely for a science of performance located in schools: from where would the breakthroughs in new knowledge come? Wouldn't a science of performance located in schools and sites where the educational phenomena occur in all their messiness take energy and resources away from where the cutting edge of knowledge and theory might be? We could easily get bogged down in the minutiae and the sheer pragmatism of what counts as effective teaching day by day.

This is a very powerful argument. From where have the new ideas – the new ways of thinking about teaching and learning typically come? Is it the case they have come from laboratory studies with unknown or barely glimpsed applications to school? Sometimes, but not always. And probably increasingly less often is the answer.

In the past 70 or so years the breakthroughs in theories of effective teaching have come from a variety of sources. Yes, there have been programmes of research in laboratory sites away from schools, which have made substantial contributions. The instrumental learning psychology of Skinner (1968) is one example. Although often dismissed these days, some of the stock practices we have for motivating students and classroom management came from that tradition but very little in the way of lasting principles for complex learning came from that source.

Often too there have been practitioners who have theorized about their work and have seeded new practices and programmes of research based on their theories in practice. A good example is the innovation in the design of more appropriate textbooks by the educator Sylvia Ashton-Warner (1963). Still other breakthroughs have come from painstaking observation and explaining and testing from educational sites. Reading Recovery is a good example of this.

Powerful theoretical concepts have come from many sources. The idea of using the metaphor of a scaffold for teaching came from a study of maternal tutoring of children with blocks, where the 'mother' wasn't the actual mother but a research team member behaving as if she was a mother (Wood, Bruner, & Ross, 1976).

A science of performance wouldn't discount these sources of new ideas or the need to have all these sources generating good ideas. But the overriding concern is that the ideas need to be developed and tested in practice. And the sites for this must be those where the teaching and learning take place.

Gold standards and fool's gold

There is an obstacle for a science of performance in education that is able to work in the messiness of school sites. It is the naive commitment to what has been termed the 'gold standard' of research design. It turns out to be more like fool's gold unless the pan handlers know the limitations of that method and the strengths of others.

Gawande (2007) has something to say about this too. He argues that modern obstetrical research practice, from which big advances have occurred, has not been very good at adhering to the tenets of approved science. The traditional view is that a profession advances through controlling the evidence in particular ways. Nothing is introduced into practice unless it has been properly tested in research centres; preferably through double blind randomized controlled trials. But obstetrics tends not to do this and largely in his view ignores results of randomized trails. Obstetricians and research practitioners look for the evidence in practice.

There are risks here if we were to ignore experimental designs. The obvious ones from the logic of science point of view are risks to the robustness of our knowledge. The rationale for tight experimental designs is to rule out possible other explanations for any 'effect' and hence increase confidence in establishing causal relationships. To the extent that we don't control we can't rule out the alternatives. But researching in schools forces flexibility on this thinking.

Schools are open and dynamic systems. Day to day events change the properties of teaching and learning and the conditions for teaching and learning effectively. Among those are how teachers come and go, how principals may change, how the formula for funding might be altered, and how new curriculum resources can be created. More directly, and more problematic for experimental control, teachers and schools constantly share ideas, participation in professional conferences and seminars adds to the shared information, and new teachers bring new knowledge and experiences. Such inherent features of schools are compounded when the unit of analysis might be a cluster of schools that deliberately share resources, ideas and practices. There is an evocative term in the methodological literature for this latter phenomenon: 'diffusion of treatment.'

All these sources of messiness pose tensions in a randomized experimental and control group design. On the one hand, the *internal* validity need is to control these sources of influence so that unknown effects do not eventuate which may bias or confound the demonstration of experimental effects. On the other hand, if schools are changed to reduce these influences so that, for example, there is no turnover in teaching staff, *external* validity is severely undermined because these conditions may now not be typical of those schools to which one wants to generalize the findings.

It is of course possible to conceive of selecting sufficiently large numbers of teachers or schools to randomly assign. Then one assumes that the 'messiness' is distributed randomly. If the teachers and the schools in the total set are 'the same,' then we might assume that messiness is distributed evenly across experimental and control classrooms and schools. Leaving aside the challenges which large numbers of schools pose, a problem here is the assumption that we know what makes teachers and schools similar, and hence are able to be sure about the randomization process. This is a questionable assumption to make. For example, the presence of different types of classrooms within some schools, say bilingual classrooms or classrooms for special education purposes in only some schools, create difficulties for random assignment as well as for comparability across teachers, let alone across schools. So what counts as an appropriate control is not necessarily known other than hoping randomization covers everything. There may also be insufficient instances of different types of classrooms or schools even to attempt random assignment.

There is another difficulty: that of withholding treatment from the control group of schools. Just about any well-resourced, planned intervention is likely to have an effect in education (Hattie, 2009). The act of deliberately withholding treatment, as required in control group designs, raises ethical concerns. Some researcher groups in the United States, also concerned for educational enhancement with schools serving poor and diverse communities, have deliberately adopted alternatives to randomized experimental and control group designs because of ethical concerns for those settings not gaining access to the intervention (Pogrow, 1998; Taylor, Pearson, Peterson, & Rodriguez, 2005; Hattie, 1999) proposed that the ethical difficulty could be overcome by comparing different interventions, thus not withholding potential benefits from any group. This is not always a workable solution, for example when the theoretical question is about the effects of a complex multi-component intervention that reformats existing teaching in a curriculum area, such as literacy instruction. Here there is no appropriate alternative intervention other than existing conditions. The American Psychological Association (2002) has detailed guidelines for conditions under which withholding treatment is justified. For example, if an intervention is shown to be effective, then it should be implemented in the control group.

The most damaging problem, however, is the underlying logic of experimental and control group designs. In these designs, the variation within each group (given the simple case of an experimental and a control group) is conceived as 'error variance' and, when substantially present, is seen as problematic. The logic is essentialist. That is, underlying or within the variability is the true picture, the true score. One should try to control all of the messiness so that the truth is revealed.

I argued earlier that there is an alternative logic. It is to view variability as inherent to human behaviour and consequently it is a fundamental feature of applied settings (Risley, & Wolf, 1973). A science of performance needs to understand the variability rather than trying to make it go away by controlling it statistically. Making some sorts of variability disappear might be the long-term goal but to do that we must understand the sources. Moreover, being able to replicate and scale up, essential stages in designing more effective schools, requires close attention to conditions that are local.

Deliberately incorporating variability and the sources of the variability into research designs is called for and there are alternatives to the standard design, not surprisingly called quasi experimental designs. Questions about the characteristics and sources of variability are central to knowing about effective teaching and learning, and can be explored within the design. Such a design is more appropriate to the circumstances of building effectiveness over a period of time (Raudenbush, 2005). These designs enable sources of variability in achievement to be explored and when carried out longitudinally are really the gold standard for a science of performance. Without them the contributions of influences such as levels of implementation of a programme, the establishment of professional learning communities, coherence of programme adherence, and consistency of leadership and programme focus over time cannot be judged (Coburn, 2003).

12

BUILDING MORE EFFECTIVE SCHOOLS

Notes on a cautious optimism

Atul Gawande's (2007) advice for a better science of teaching, learning, and development is to gain knowledge about actual practices which is tested in everyday contexts. Even given that we were better at doing this there is still the central question of this book. It is the question of just how optimistic we can be. Even with the best science in the world how realistic is it that through changes in schools generally equitable outcomes are achievable? This book started with the tension between traditions in educational theorising about schools and their effectiveness. There is a fractured terrain of ideas about the agency of schools in overcoming the abiding gaps in achievement that those children for whom schools have traditionally been risky places have experienced.

On the one hand all that we know about the nature of learning, development, and teaching suggests that we should be able to be more effective than we have been. On the other hand, looking at schools as the major societal institution for socialization other than the family leads to the view that they must inexorably reflect existing power structures. And on balance the evidence is compellingly in favour of the view that schools are hard to change en masse to produce more equitable outcomes that are sustainable. But there is sufficient evidence, sufficient variation to the general picture, to maintain a cautious optimism.

The argument about optimism in this book is a qualified one. Schools can make a difference to the children and communities that are positioned as having lower status with less access to economic and political resources; those minorities discriminated against by structural inequities. There are instances of where the daunting challenges have been shown to be overcome.

The contribution that the science of teaching, learning and development can make is dependent on us becoming more adept in our core activities and more nuanced in our accumulating knowledge base. Echoing Gawande's (2007) argument, the science has been limited to the extent that researchers have prioritized the identification and explanation of properties of teaching, learning and development using settings and circumstances that have questionable relationships with the real worlds of families and schools in all their complexity.

The challenge just at the level of the classroom system is to both know about properties of teaching, learning, and development under different circumstances as well as how their components as a whole operate. An act of teaching and its effectiveness are not just about the properties of feedback or strategy instruction. A child's learning is a co-construction reflecting how they make sense of and what they take from the ongoing activity within which the teaching acts occur. The specific effects of any part of the activity including such factors as the teacher's feedback are not isolatable from who the child is, what its history has been, and what its classroom and life outside of classrooms affords for its learning. Even in a specialist programme in one limited area of learning such as the Reciprocal Teaching programme for reading comprehension (Brown, 1997), the whole is more than the sum of its parts. The researcher who designed the pro-gramme was very explicit in her qualifications around how components worked. As isolated components they were less significant for instruction than how they are melded together and developed over time. Furthermore, the effectiveness of the teaching programme was crucially dependent on how classroom activities were designed including how a class of students functioned as a community and their interpersonal roles and relationships.

The adeptness and nuancing required just at the level of classroom activities, leaving aside how these are embedded in the wider systems that Bronfenbrenner (1979) identified, is in keeping with Stephen Jay Gould's (1989) description of evolutionary palaeontology as an historical science. An historical science develops principles and predictions that recognize and incorporate contingency. Especially in the case of evolution and palaeontology there is a degree of unpredictability and randomness because of uncontrollable and unforeseen events. This means that explanations after events have occurred are necessary. Explanations draw on how events impacted on developmental processes and predictions are based on these contingent relationships.

So too with our analyses of teaching, learning, and development. But unlike Gould's (1989) science we have the capacity to conduct small- and large-scale tests of our hypotheses and try to change 'history.' We can manipulate and change events to more directly test theories. Despite this strength, like Gould (1989) these need to be with the full awareness of the messiness, complexity and contingent nature of what happens in schools and families. The knowledge base we need is one that relates the components of teaching, learning and development to con-texts and contingencies in the immediate and distant systems that Bronfenbrenner (1979) identified.

Making more productive contributions requires balancing types of activities including using descriptive and experimental approaches, and methods that reflect the multifaceted nature of the phenomena with quantitative and qualitative frameworks. This need is recognized in current calls to use mixed methods (Croninger, & Valli, 2009), although the idea of mixing the methods may be misleading. Rather, the challenge is to use methods that are suitable for the questions that need to be asked – again a matter of contingent relationships.

One of the greatest methodological challenges in this respect is to be able to cope with how children's co-constructions are embedded within systems that are layered. There are different approaches to this problem, which reflect the frameworks which disciplines bring to the study of teaching, learning and development. As I noted earlier, Barbara Rogoff (Rogoff, 1995) has a conceptual tool that enables researchers to foreground different layers at different points of an analysis. Elsewhere in this book I have used examples of how statistical modelling can do something similar; that is, to try to understand how interacting parts of a larger whole might put constraints on or add to effects. Raudenbush's (2005) analysis of the multiple and compounding effects of deprivation and movements into and out of such conditions is an example.

What is required is harnessing the best ideas from the psychology of learning, development and instruction as well as from our understandings of how environments impact on these. It is not possible to make substantial and enduring gains without this integrated approach.

The solutions require a policy environment that directs resources into reducing inequities. So housing policies, social support policies and other economic, social, and educational policies are necessary to create an environment where disparities are minimized. The educational policies include funding and having a productive balance between accountability and autonomy for schools so they can be problem solving communities able to demonstrate their effectiveness. The policies include according the less powerful cultural groups and the institutions and practices which serve those groups the status and well-being their children need for teachers to teach effectively.

Educators themselves are limited in what they can do, but they can make a positive difference. Unions and spokespeople can act to influence policies. Researchers in relationships with schools can see themselves as part of a larger community which includes policy makers and can learn new ways of communicating and responding to their colleagues in policy positions.

There are some countries that have more equitable outcomes than others. How do they do it and how might other countries do it? Wilkinson and his colleagues (Wilkinson, & Pickett, 2009) point to examples like Japan immediately post war and there are examples from Scandinavian countries. On the school side there is a combination of factors including a context of high accountability. In addition, schools are enabled to be sites for active relatively autonomous professional learning communities who are responsive to and in partnership with their local communities. Teachers are trained, recognized, and supported to teach as highly talented, respected and knowledgeable 'adaptive experts,' who base their actions on coherent and well developed theoretical and design principles. One final characterisitic would be that there is a coterie of researchers who can develop a science of performance, who have the knowledge, skills, and tools to help solve problems on the ground.

Could there be a developmental relationship here that needs time to play out? Could schools through their increased effectiveness with students change structures over the long haul without policy environments that were overly conducive; and thereby change the structures? That was in part the intention of the initial Head Start project, to break the so called 'poverty cycle.' There is evidence of longer term gains for the children and their families who were served by the interventions and evidence for the continuing and even increased effectiveness of the present generation of facilities. But despite this there is very little evidence for a widespread deeply embedded change, either in new generations of students and their achievement or in their families' and communities' access to political and economic structures. It is very difficult, as different groups of researchers have found for interventions at the school level, to have the power to scale up regionally and nationally and sustain the gains over time. But even more limited is the power to create a quiet revolution from within. Piecemeal change through schools alone is insufficient to change the representation of equity groups.

There are other more radical approaches than the solution offered here. One is the old idea captured in Illich's (1971) proposal of 'deschooling society.' Perhaps the institutions of schooling themselves are so archaic that we do not need them. There are two responses to this. The evidence is that we need places of formal learning and development more than ever. The designers of the PISA assessments have this in mind, anticipating that the learners of the future need to be socially adept, communicative problem solvers. The second problem is the nemesis of well-meaning educational decisions: Matthew Effects. The alternative schools, home schools, and websites for communities of learning are likely to be the optional privilege of the more wealthy and powerful.

Another radical approach is more revolutionary. Let the system self-destruct under its own weight and with the resulting chaos (read for that social dislocation and destruction) new solutions may be born out of necessity. Perhaps the call to improve schools without improving structural and other inequities in the wider society is shoring up an indefensible system and it would be better to have failure and through the engendered crisis solve the problem caused by the wider political and economic causes.

There are two responses to this cynical position too. One response is that schools operate like the ambulance at the top of the cliff, and it is not possible to ignore the need for that service. There are many children who find schools risky and ceilings are placed on their achievement. If we have some, albeit limited, means to make a difference for them we should not wait or withhold. The de facto revolutionary approach would deny children even more access to resources sacrificing short-term need for possible longer term solutions.

The second response is the core argument of this book. It is to say that both societal and educational reform are necessary to adequately reduce the inequities both inside and outside of school.

I have mapped out a framework for a science of performance that could make a difference. Cautious optimism should drive this endeavour. Changing schools, designing and scaling up more effective schools for diverse students are long-term commitments. They require coherence between a system's layers and ongoing collaborations between researchers, practitioners, policy makers and communities. They require giving teachers the education and resources to be knowledgeable problem solvers and capable of being adaptive and flexible. They require researchers to rethink the sites in which they work and the rules of their engagement with communities.

Vignette: a case study of an effective urban multicultural school

Several of the central arguments in this book can be illustrated using a vignette. The vignette provides a picture of one school – School A. Its gains in reading comprehension over the course of 2009 for children aged 9 years to 11 years at the school are shown in Figure 12.1. They started off at the beginning of the

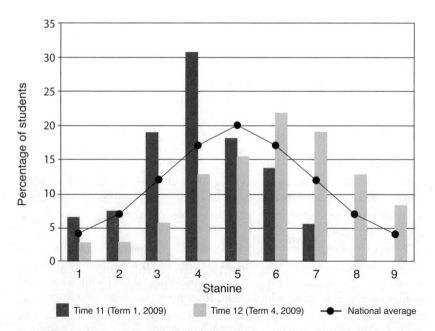

FIGURE 12.1 Achievement distributions at the beginning and end of 2009 for School 'A'.

year, as they often do, with a distribution below a fully matched distribution. This is partly the result of children coming into Year 4–6 (9 year olds to 11 year olds) who are new to the school with below average levels. Students staying at the school tend to not drop as much over summer. By the end of the year the distribution is skewed above national expectations. The achievement levels in 2009 not only show the result of accelerated gains but by the end of the year the distribution of the children at this school went beyond the expected distribution in reading comprehension. It went beyond in writing too.

The vignette illustrates the model of school change described in Chapter 9, which uses a highly specific process to achieve changes in the programme of instruction (McNaughton, & Lai, 2009). It illustrates what an ongoing science of performance in partnership with schools might achieve. It illustrates that understanding what the school has achieved and how it has achieved this requires more than a list of isolated components. The descriptions here draw on several reports that have examined its effectiveness.

The school is a relatively small suburban school of just over 200 students serving a community of Pasifika and Māori families in South Auckland. This local community is in the lowest bracket using New Zealand census descriptors of employment levels and income levels. Three quarters of the children are from Samoan, Cook Islands, Tongan, and other Pasifika families. A quarter are from Māori families. Almost half have English as an additional language. Two thirds of the Pasifika group was born in New Zealand. The staff have been relatively stable over the past 10 years. More than half the staff are themselves Pasifika or Māori. The current staff are well qualified, most having receiving four year degrees at the local university and some are studying for advanced qualifications.

The Principal came to the school over 10 years ago. At that time the school was experiencing 'brown flight.' Families were leaving the school to attend better performing schools in local and other suburbs. The new Principal visited as many of the families as possible in their homes and asked that they reconsider sending their children to his school and he would commit to meeting their goals for the school. Their goals were consistent and have continued to be so 10 years on. They are for the school to enable their children to have high achievement in a culturally safe place.

A coherent and well-functioning inquiry process

A compelling feature is the functioning of the school staff as a professional learning community who have sustained a collective problem solving through which they fine tune their instruction. They have a sustained and coherent focus on student learning and excellence in achievement, with the goal of equitable distributions of achievement for their children. They engage as a staff in ongoing cycles of inquiry using evidence from students' achievement and from classroom teaching.

The school has been through four specific cycles of problem solving since the Principal started. The inquiry and problem solving has been sustained over this time period with new staff and with new foci. The data discussions and planning meeting are well practiced and are very detailed (Lai, McNaughton, Timperley, & Hsaio, 2009).

An initial focus was on raising the pace of learning over the transition to school (Phillips, McNaughton, & MacDonald, 2004). Building developmental sustainability was met through a second focus on reading comprehension (Lai, McNaughton, Amituanai-Toloa, Turner, & Hsiao, 2009). Following this and as a deliberate attempt to achieve a better match to the expected distribution of achievement in the upper bands of achievement, there has been as a complementary focus on writing and interconnectedness with reading. Currently there is a focus on the summer learning effect.

This part of their functioning involves an ongoing partnership with our research group at the University of Auckland. We have been involved in each of the cycles of the problem solving. The partnership is ongoing and mutually supportive as indexed by the achievement outcomes as well as the scholarship outcomes.

The school analyses a variety of classroom and school-wide data to monitor student progress, and identify and target needs. The staff believe that using data to inform teaching has raised the achievement of their students. Additionally, teachers, as part of their professional inquiry, track the progress of specific groups of students in their classrooms using the evidence to identify needs and to determine strategies to put in place for modification of their teaching practice. For example, in the year represented by the achievement data in Figure 12.1 one teacher had deliberately focused on the 11-year-old Tongan boys in his classroom as the lowest achieving group in the classroom. He selected texts for topic study and for reading activities that reflected high interest topics and set shared learning goals with the students who monitored their own performance on assessments over the year.

The school has programmes in place to help socialize new teachers into the school's culture. For example, through an initiative with a cluster of seven similar local schools, an induction programme is provided for new teachers to the area. Lead teachers from the schools spend time explaining how the programmes operate in the school. In this sense there is a clear professional learning community dynamic at play where 'novices' are initiated into the roles and values of the community.

Ongoing instructional design

Observations of classroom instruction reveal very high levels of use of the instructional practices that are shown to be effective with their students but are continuously being fine tuned using the evidence from students and teaching (Amituanai-Toloa, McNaughton, Lai, & Airini, 2009).

Their instruction has general features of what would be considered 'best practice' instruction but the general features have been adapted to fit the local circumstances and the evidence. For example, adaptation of the instruction to be culturally responsive to students is strongly present. In reading comprehension for example this is in part through the selection and use of particular texts and use of culturally familiar artefacts and experiences to activate and build vocabulary, background knowledge, and thematic understandings across writing and reading comprehension. In keeping with cultural values, relationships between teachers and students are close and positive, both respectful and reciprocal. The teachers use humour as one device to express the relationships. Students uniformly report a sense of belonging, that their teachers are warm but they are also challenging, they set high expectations and their instruction is direct and explanatory.

High levels of community engagement

Another compelling feature of the school illustrates the nested systems are well coordinated. This feature is the reciprocal and ongoing relationship with the local communities. The Principal and other members of the leadership team deliberately and strategically plan to include them. It has a deliberate life span approach for family involvement. This includes a home book flood programme, parent tutoring, and community leaders functioning as part of the curriculum and teaching design team. Community initiatives include parents assisting as reading tutors and as language tutors using specific programmes. Parents are seen as key to the success of these initiatives with valued roles within the school.

The involvement of parents and other members of the communities also draws on particular cultural expertise. The school uses the cultural and pedagogical expertise of their teachers and leaders in the local communities to communicate with parents, share the achievement data, and disseminate in their language strategies parents can use to support their children's literacy and numeracy development. The school utilizes key leaders within the various communities to liaise with their community and disseminate information relevant to children's learning. This strategy acknowledges the unique skills that these community members have, and conveys to the communities that their input is both necessary and valued. Finally, parents are involved in what is more traditional for New Zealand schools. For instance, their expertise is recognized and utilized to assist with cultural activities, arts, and school sports. In each of these activities, parents are not added extras or useful adjuncts to core business. Parents are seen as central to their children's achievement gains.

The school's focus on achievement and its strategies is echoed by parent voices. Parents are asked by the school about their views and research into parent views at this school show consistently high aspirations for their children, matched by the desire to provide for their education. They see their role as one that should complement the school's role. They understand the importance of the work the school is doing and support the school in raising achievement for their children.

Final question

Can the science described here contribute to long-term, sustained changes in schools that produce equitable outcomes for communities for whom school has been less than effective? The answer to this question needs to be considered school by school, district by district, region by region, and country by country. The adage is that one instance of a swallow doesn't make a summer. But one instance of a local school making a difference does allow some optimism. In this book I have referred to other examples of both individual schools and of groups of schools where the results support a careful optimism. How much more optimistic we could be if there was consistency in the policies and resources made available to align with schools' work.

REFERENCES

A template for saving lives. (2007). *USA Today, August 24th 2007*.

Administration for Children and Families. (2003). *Head Start (2000): A whole child perspective on program performance – fourth progress report*. Washington, DC: ACF.

Alexander, K. L., Entwisle, D. R., & Olson, L. S. (2007). Lasting consequences of the summer learning gap. *American Sociological Review, 72,* 167–180.

Alvarez, D., & Mehan, H. (2006). Whole school de-tracking: A strategy for equity and excellence. *Theory into Practice, 45*(1), 82–89.

American Psychological Association. (2002). Ethical principles of psychologists and code of conduct. *American Psychologist, 57,* 1060–1073.

Amituanai-Toloa, M., McNaughton, S., Lai, M.K., & Airini with Rolf Turner, Deborah Widdowson, Rachel McClue, Selena Hsiao, & Maryanne Pale (2009). *Ua aoina le manogi o le lolo Pasifika schooling improvement research. Full technical report*. Wellington, New Zealand: Ministry of Education.

Anderson, R. C., Wilson, P. T., & Fielding, L. G. (1988). Growth in reading and how children spend their time outside school. *Reading Research Quarterly, 23*(3), 285–303.

Ashton-Warner, S. (1963). *Teacher*. London, England: Virago.

Baltes, P. B., Reese, H. W., & Lipsitt, L. B. (1980). Life-span development psychology. *Annual Review of Psychology,* (1), 65–110.

Baxter-Jones, A. D. (1995). Growth and the development of young athletes. Should competition levels be age related? *Sports Medicine, 20*(2), 59–64.

Berliner, D. (2006). Our impoverished view of educational research. *Teachers College Record, 108*(6), 949–995.

Bernstein, B. B. (2003). *Class, codes and control*. London, UK: Routledge.

Biemiller, A. (1999). *Language and reading success*. Cambridge, MA: Brookline.

Biemiller, A. (2006). Vocabulary development and instruction: A prerequisite for school learning. In D. K. Dickinson & S. B. Neuman (Eds.), *Handbook of Early Literacy Research* (Vol. 2, pp. 41–51). New York, NY: Guilford Press.

Bishop, R. (2007). *Te kōtahitanga: Improving the educational achievement of Māori students in mainstream education: phase 2: towards a whole school approach*. Wellington, NZ: Ministry of Education.

Bishop, R., O'Sullivan, D., & Berryman, M. (2010). *Scaling up education reform: addressing the politics of disparty*. Wellington, NZ: NZCER Press.

Block, C. C., & Pressley, M. (Eds.). (2002). *Comprehension instruction: Research-based best practice*. New York, NY: Guildford Press.

Borman, G. D. (2005). National efforts to bring reform to scale in high-poverty schools: Outcomes and implications. In L. Parker (Ed.), *Review of Research in Education* (pp. 1–28). Washington, DC: American Educational Research Association.

Borman, G. D., & Dowling, N. M. (2006). Longitudinal achievement effects of multiyear summer school: Evidence from the Teach Baltimore randomized field trial. *Educational Evaluation and Policy Analysis, 28*, 25–48.

Borman, G. D., Slavin, R. E., Cheung, A. C. K., Chamberlain, A. M., Madden, N. A., & Chambers, B. (2007). Final reading outcomes of the national randomized field trial of Success for All. *American Educational Research Journal, 44*(3), 701–731.

Bourdieu, P. (1996). Cultural reproduction and social reproduction. In R. Brown (Ed.), *Knowledge, Education and Cultural Change* (pp. 77–112). London, UK: Routledge.

Bronfenbrenner, U. (1979). *The ecology of human development: Experiments by nature and design*. Cambridge, MA: Harvard University Press.

Brown, A. (1997). Transforming schools into communities of thinking and learning about serious matters. *American Psychologist, 52*(4), 399–413.

Buly, M. R., & Valencia, B. W. (2002). Below the bar: Profiles of students who fail state reading assessments. *Educational Evaluation and Policy Analysis, 24*(3), 219–239.

Cazden, C. (2001). *Classroom discourse: The language of teaching and learning* (2nd ed.). Portsmouth, NH: Heinemann.

Ceci, S. J., & Papierno, P. B. (2005). The rhetoric and reality of gap closing: When the "have nots" gain but the "haves" gain even more. *American Psychologist, 60*(2), 149–160.

Clay, M. (1966). *Emergent reading behaviour*. University of Auckland, Auckland.

Clay, M. (1979). *Reading: The patterning of complex behaviour*. Auckland, NZ: Heinemann Educational.

Clay, M. (1987). Implementing Reading Recovery: Systematic adaptations to an educational innovation. *New Zealand Journal of Educational Studies, 22*(1), 35–58.

Clay, M. (1994). *Reading Recovery: A guidebook for teachers in training*. Portsmouth, NH: Heinemann.

Clay, M. (1997). International perspectives on the Reading Recovery program. In J. Flood, S. B. Heath, & D. Lapp (Eds.), *Handbook of research on teaching literacy through the communicative and visual arts* (pp. 655–667). Old Tappen, NJ: Simon and Schuster.

Clay, M. (2001). *Change over time in children's literacy development*. Portsmouth, NH: Heinemann.

Coburn, C. E. (2003). Rethinking scale: Moving beyond numbers to deep and lasting change. *Educational Researcher, 32*(6), 3–12.

Cochran-Smith, M., Shakman, K., Jong, C., Terrell, D., Barnatt, J., & McQuillan, P. (2009) Good and just teaching: The case for social justice in teacher education. *American Journal of Education, 115*(3), 347–377.

Cohen, D. K. & Ball, D. L. (2007). Educational innovation and the problem of scale. In B. Schneider & S. McDonald (Eds.), *Scale up in education: Ideas and principles* (Vol. 1, pp. 19–36). Lanham, MD: Rowman and Littlefield.

Coleman, J. S., Campbell, E. Q., Hobson, C. J., McPartland, J., Mood, A. M., Weinfeld, F. D., et al. (1966). *Equality of educational opportunity*. Washington, DC: US Government Printing Office.

Compton-Lilly, C. (in press). Counting the uncounted: African American students in Reading Recovery. *Journal of Early Childhood Literacy*.

Consortium of Longitudinal Studies. (1983). *As the twig is bent: Lasting effects of preschool programs*. Hillsdales, NJ: Erlbaum.

Cooper, H., Charlton, K., Valentine, J., & Muhlenbruck, L. (2000). Making the most of summer school: A meta-analytic and narrative review. *Monographs of the Society for Research in Child Development*, *65*(1), 1–118.

Corson, D. (1997). The learning and use of academic English words. *Language Learning*, *47*(4), 671–718.

Croninger, R. G., & Valli, L. (2009). Mixing it up about methods. *Educational Researcher*, *38*(7), 541–545.

Cummins, J. (2001). Empowering minority students: a framework for intervention. In C. Baker & N. H. Hornberger (Eds.), *An introductory reader to the writings of Jim Cummins: Bilingual education and bilingualism* (pp. 175–194). Clevedon, UK: Multilingual Matters.

Cummins, J. (2007). Pedagogies for the poor? Realignning reading instruction for low-income students with scientific based reading research. *Educational Researcher*, *36*(9), 564–572.

Cunningham, P. M. (1976). Teachers' correction responses to black dialect miscues which are non meaning changing. *Reading Research Quarterly 12*(4), 637–653.

Darling-Hammond, L. (2006). Securing the Right to Learn: Policy and Practice for Powerful Teaching and Learning. *Educational Researcher*, *35*(7), 13–24.

Darling-Hammond, L. (2007). The flat earth and education: How America's commitments to equity will determine our future. *Educational Researcher*, *36*(6), 318–334.

Darling-Hammond, L., & Bransford, J. (Eds.). (2005). *Preparing teachers for a changing world: What teachers should learn and be able to do*. San Francisco, CA: Jossey-Bass.

Davis, B., & Sumara, D. (2002). Constructivist discourses and the field of education: Problems and possibilities. *Educational Theory*, *52*(4), 409–428.

Delpit, L. (2003). Educators as "seed people" growing a new future. *Educational Researcher*, *32*(7), 14–21.

Dewey, J. (1915). *The school and society*. Chicago, IL: The University of Chicago Press.

Dickinson, D., & Tabors, P. O. (Eds.). (2001). *Beginning literacy with language: Young children learning at home and at school*. Baltimore, MD: Brookes Publishing.

Dyson, A. H. (1999). Transforming transfer: Unruly students, contrary text and the persistence of pedagogical order. In A. Iran-Nejad & P. D. Pearson (Eds.), *Review of Research in Education* (pp. 141–171). Washington DC: American Educational Research Association.

Dyson, A. H., Bennett, A., Brooks, W., Garcia, J., Howard-McBride, C., Malekzadeh, J., et al. (1997). *What difference does difference make? Teacher reflections on diversity, literacy, and the urban primary school*. Urbana, IL: National Council of Teachers of English.

Economist (2007). Creating tomorrow's technology. Reprinted in *The New Zealand Herald*, March 12, 2007.

Elley, W. B. (1989). Vocabulary acquisition from listening to stories. *Reading Research Quarterly*, *24*(2), 174–187.

Elley, W. B. (1997). *An evaluation of Alan Duff's "Books in Homes" programme: Final report*. Wellington NZ: Ministry of Education.

Entwisle, D. R., Alexander, K. L., & Olson, D. R. (1997). *Children, schools and inequality*. Boulter, CD: Westview Press.

Fisher, R. (1934). *Statistical methods for research workers* (5th ed.). Edinburgh, UK: Oliver and Boyd.

Flockton, L., & Crooks, T. (1996). *Reading and speaking, assessment results 1996 report 6.* Dunedin, NZ: National Education Monitoring Project, Educational Assessment Research Unit, University of Otago.

Flockton, L., & Crooks, T. (2000). *Reading and speaking, assessment results 2000 report 19.* Dunedin, NZ: National Education Monitoring Project, Educational Assessment Research Unit, University of Otago.

Flockton, L., & Crooks, T. (2004). *Reading and speaking, assessment results 2004 report 34.* Dunedin, NZ: National Education Monitoring Project, Educational Assessment Research Unit, University of Otago.

Flockton, L., & Crooks, T. (2008). *Reading and speaking, assessment results 2008 report 49.* Dunedin, NZ: National Education Monitoring Project, Educational Research Unit, University of Otago.

Flynn, J. R. (2007). *What is intelligence? Beyond the Flynn effect.* Cambridge, UK: Cambridge University Press.

Foorman, B. R., Francis, D. J., Fletcher, J. M., Schatschneider, C., & Mehta, P. (1998). The role of instruction in learning to read: Preventing reading failure in at-risk children. *Journal of Educational Psychology, 90*(1), 37–55.

Frerichs, R. (2010). http://www.ph.ucla.edu/epi/snow.html.

Fullan, M., & NetLibrary Inc. (2007). *The new meaning of educational change.* New York, NY: Teachers College Press.

Fuller, B., Wright, J., Gesicki, K., & Kang, E. (2007). Gauging growth: How to judge no child left behind? *Educational Researcher, 36*(5), 268–278.

Gawande, A. (2007). *Better: A surgeon's notes on performance.* London, UK: Profile Books Limited.

Gintis, H., & Bowles, S. (1988). Contradiction and reproduction in education theory. In M. Cole (Ed.), *Bowles and Gintis revisited: Correspondence and contradiction in education theory* (pp. 16–32). London, UK: Falmer Press.

Glennerster, H. (2009). *Understanding the finance of welfare: what welfare costs and how to pay for it.* Bristol, Portland: Policy Press/Social Policy Association.

Glynn, T. (1995). Pause, prompt, praise: Reading tutoring procedures for home and school partnership. In S. Wolfendale & K. Topping (Eds.), *Family involvement in literacy: Effective partnerships in education* (pp. 33–44). London, UK: Cassell.

Gomez-Bellenge, F. X., & Rodgers, E. M. (2007). *Reading Recovery and Descubriendo la Lectura national report 2005–2006.* Columbus, OH: Ohio State University, National Data Evaluation Centre.

Gould, S. J. (1989). *Wonderful life: The Burgess Shale and the nature of history.* New York, NY: W.W. Norton.

Guthrie, J. T. (2004). Teaching for Literacy Engagement. *Journal of Literacy Research, 36*(1), 1–30.

Guthrie, J. T., & Wigfield, A. (2000). Engagement and motivation in reading. In M. L. Kamil, P. B. Mosenthal, P. D. Pearson & R. Barr (Eds.), *Handbook of reading research: Volume III* (pp. 403–422). New York, NY: Erlbaum.

Hannon, P. (2003). Family literacy progammes. In N. Hall, J. Larson & J. Marsh (Eds.), *Handbook of Early Childhood Literacy* (pp. 99–111). London, UK: Sage.

Hart, B., & Risley, T. (1995). *Meaningful differences in everyday experience of young American children.* Baltimore, MD: P.H. Brookes.

Hattie, J. (1999). The relationship between study skills and learning outcomes: A meta analysis. *Australian Journal of Education, 43*(1), 72–86.

Hattie, J. (2003). *New Zealand Snapshot; with specific reference to the yrs 1–13*. Paper presented at the Knowledge Wave 2003, Auckland, February 19–21.

Hattie, J. (2009). *Visible learning: A synthesis of over 800 meta-analyses relating to achievement*. London, UK: Routledge.

Hawley, W. D., & Valli, L. (1999). The essentials of effective professional development. In L. Darling-Hammond & G. Sykes (Eds.), *Teaching as a learning profession* (pp. 127–150). San Francisco CA: Jossey-Bass.

Hewison, J., & Tizard, J. (1980). Parental involvement and reading attainment. *British Journal of Educational Psychology*, *50*(3), 209–215.

Heyns, B. (1978). *Summer learning and the effects of schooling*. New York, NY: Academic Press.

Hobbes, T. (1651/1962). *Leviathan*. London: Fontana.

Hohepa, M., & McNaughton, S. (2002). Indigenous literacies: The case of Maori literacy. In L. Makin & C. Jones-Diaz (Eds.), *Literacies in early childhood: Changing views, challenging practice* (pp. 197–214). Eastgardens, NSW: MacLennan & Petty.

Hubbard, L., Mehan, H., & Stein, M. K. (2006). *Reform as learning: School reform, organizational culture, and community politics in San Diego*. New York, NY: Routledge.

Hume, D. (1739–1740/1969). *A treatise of human nature*. Middlesex: Penguin Books.

Illich, I. D. (1971). *Deschooling society*. New York, NY: Harper & Row.

International Association for the Evaluation of Educational Achievement; New Zealand. Ministry of Education Research Division. (2003). *Reading literacy in New Zealand: Final results from the Progress in International Reading Literacy Study (PIRLS) and the repeat of the 1990–91 Reading Literacy Study (10 Year Trends Study) for Year 5 students*. Wellington, NZ: Ministry of Education. Research Division.

JaCoby, P. (2009). The Preuss School at UC San Diego Makes Newsweek's Top 10 High School Rankings for Third Year in Row. June 11, from http://ucsdnews.ucsd.edu/newsrel/general/06-09Top10.asp.

Jones, A. (1986). *"At school I've got a chance—": Social reproduction in a New Zealand secondary school*. Auckland: University of Auckland.

Juel, C., Griffith, P. L., & Gough, P. (1986). Acquisition of literacy: A longitudinal study of children in first and second grade. *Journal of Educational Psychology*, *78*(4), 243–255.

Kessen, W. (1979). The American child and other cultural inventions. *American Psychologist*, *34*(10), 815–820.

Kim, J. S. (2006). Effects of a voluntary summer reading intervention on reading achivement: Results from a randomized field trial. *Educational Evaluation and Policy Analysis*, *28*(4), 335–355.

Ladson-Billings, G. (2006). From the achievement gap to educational debt: Understanding achievement in U.S. schools. *Educational Researcher*, *35*(7), 3–12.

Lai, M. K., McNaughton, S., Amituanai-Toloa, M., Turner, R., & Hsiao, S. (2009). Sustained acceleration of achievement in reading comprehension: The New Zealand experience. *Reading Research Quarterly*, *44*(1), 30–56.

Lai, M. K., McNaughton, S., Timperley, H., & Hsiao, S. (2009). Sustaining continued acceleration in reading comprehension achievement following an intervention. *Educational Assessment, Evaluation and Accountability*, *21*(1), 81–100.

Lave, J. (1991). Situated learning in communities of practice. In L. B. Resnick, J. M. Levine, & S. D. Teasley (Eds.), *Perspectives on socially shared cognition* (pp. 63–82). Washington DC: American Psychological Association.

Lee, C. (2009). *Culture, literacy, and learning: Taking bloom in the midst of the whirlwind*. New York, NY: Teachers College Press.

Lefstein, A. (2007). *Changing teacher practice through the National Literacy Strategy: A micro-interactional perspective*. Oxford, UK: Department of Educational Studies, Oxford University.

Lerner, R. M., Fisher, C. B., & Weinberg, R. A. (2000). Toward a science for and of the people: Promoting civil society through the application of developmental science. *Child Development, 71*(1), 11–20.

Levin, B. (2008). *How to change 5000 schools: A practical and positive approach for leading change at every level*. Cambridge, MA: Harvard Education Press.

Ludwig, J., & Phillips, D. (2007). The benefits and costs of Head Start. *Social Policy Report, XXI*(3), 3–18.

Luke, A. (1988). *Literacy, textbooks, and ideology: Postwar literacy instruction and the mythology of Dick and Jane*. London, UK: Falmer Press.

Luke, A., & Freebody, P. (1999). A map of possible practices: Further notes on the Four Resources Model. *Practically Primary, 4*(2), 5–8.

Luke, A., Freebody, P., Shun, L., & Gopinathan, S. (2005). Towards research-based innovation and reform: Singapore schooling in transition. *Asia Pacific Journal of Education, 25*(1), 5–28.

McDougall, W. (1912). *Psychology: The study of behaviour*. London: Williams and Norgate.

McDowall, S., & New Zealand Council for Educational Research. (2005). *Reading Recovery in New Zealand: Uptake, implementation, and outcomes, especially in relation to Māori and Pasifika students*. Wellington, NZ: New Zealand Council for Educational Research.

McLuhan, M., & Fiore, Q. (1964). *The medium is the message*. New York, NY: Random House.

McNaughton, S. (1995). *Patterns of emergent literacy: processes of development and transition*. Melbourne, Australia: Oxford University Press.

McNaughton, S. (1998). *Strengthening family and community roles and responsibilities in schools*. Paper presented at the OECD Conference 'Innovations for Effective Schools', Christchurch, New Zealand, February 1–5.

McNaughton, S. (2002). *Meeting of minds*. Wellington, NZ: Learning Media.

McNaughton, S. (2005). Considering culture in research-based interventions to support early literacy. In S. B. Neuman, & D. K. Dickinson (Eds.), *Handbook of early literacy research* (pp. 229–240). New York, NY: Guilford Press.

McNaughton, S., & Lai, M. K. (2009). A model of school change for culturally and linguistically diverse students in New Zealand: A summary and evidence from systematic replication. *Teaching Education, 20*(1), 55–75.

McNaughton, S., MacDonald, S., Amituanai-Toloa, M., Lai, M. K., & Farry, S. (2006). *Enhanced teaching and learning of comprehension in Years 4–9: Mangere Schools*. Auckland: Uniservices Ltd.

McNaughton, S., Amituanai-Toloa, M., & Wolfgramm-Foliaki, E. (2009). Family literacy activities: What is, what ought to be and the role of parents' ideas. In S. Foster-Cohen (Ed.), *Language Acquisition* (pp. 319–336). London, UK: Palgrave Macmillan.

Miller, J. W. (2009). *America's most literate cities*. From http://www.ccsu.edu/page.cfm?p=1917.

Molden, D., & Dweck, C. (2006). Finding 'meaning' in psychology: A lay theories approach to self-regulation, social perception, and social development. *American Psychologist, 61*(3), 192–203.

Mullis, I., Kennedy, A., Martin, M., & Sainsbury, M. (2006). *Assessment framework and specifications (2nd edition). PIRLS 2006.* Chestnut Hill, MA: TIMSS & PIRLS International Study Center, Boston College.

Mullis, I. V. S., Martin, M. O., Kennedy, A., & Foy, P. (2007). *IEA's Progress in International Reading literacy study in primary school in 40 countries.* Chestnut Hill, MA: TIMSS & PIRLS International Study Center, Boston College.

Nagy, W. E. (2007). Metalinguistic awareness and the vocabulary–comprehension connection. In R. K. Wagner, A. E. Muse, & K. R. Tannenbaum (Eds.), *Vocabulary acquisition: Implications for reading comprehension* (pp. 52–77). New York, NY: Guilford Press.

Neuman, S. B. (2006). The knowledge gap: Implications for early education. In D. K. Dickinson & S. B. Neuman (Eds.), *Handbook of Early Literacy Research* (Vol. 2, pp. 29–40). New York, NY: Guilford Press.

Neuman, S. & Celano, D. (2006) The knowledge gap: Implications of leveling the playing field for low-income and middle-income children. *Reading Research Quarterly, 41*(2), 176–201.

Newmann, F. M., Smith, B., Allensworth, E., & Bryk, A. S. (2001). Instructional program coherence: What it is and why it should guide school improvement policy. *Educational Evaluation and Policy Analysis, 23*(4), 297–321.

New Zealand Ministry of Education. (2002). *Curriculum Update.* Issue 50 July 2002. Wellington, NZ: New Zealand Ministry of Education.

New Zealand Ministry of Education Group Maori. (2009). *Ka Hikitia managing for success: Maori education strategy 2008–2012.* Wellington, NZ: Group Maori New Zealand Ministry of Education

New Zealand Ministry of Social Development. (2007). *The social report 2007.* Wellington, NZ: Ministry of Social Development.

OECD. (2006). *Education at a glance 2006: OECD indicators.* Paris, France: OECD Publications.

OECD. (2007). *PISA 2006 science competencies for tomorrow's world.* Paris, France: OECD Publications.

Olson, D. R. (2003). *Psychological theory and educational reform: How school remakes mind and society.* Cambridge, NY: Cambridge University Press.

Olson, D. R., & Bruner, J. S. (1996). Folk psychology and folk pedagogy. In D. R. Olson, & N. Torrance (Eds.), *The handbook of education and human development* (pp. 9–27). Cambridge, MA: Blackwell Publishers.

Paris, S. G. (2005). Reinterpreting the development of reading skills. *Reading Research Quarterly, 40*(2), 187–202.

Penno, J. F., Wilkinson, I. A. G., & Moore, D. W. (2002). Vocabulary acquisition from teacher explanation and repeated listening to stories: Do they overcome the Mathew effect? *Journal of Educational Psychology, 94*(1), 23–33.

Phillips, G., McNaughton, S., & MacDonald, S. (2004). Managing the mismatch: Enhancing early literacy progress for children with diverse and cultural identities in mainstream urban schools in New Zealand. *Journal of Educational Psychology, 96*(2), 309–323.

Pinker, S. (1999). *Words and rules: The ingredients of language.* London, UK: Wiedenfeld and Nicholson.

Plato. (trans. 1974). *The Republic.* Baltimore: Penguin.

Plato. (trans. 1984). Men. In *Dialogues of Plato* (Vol. 1). New Haven, CT: Yale University Press.

Pogrow, S. (1998). What is an exemplary program, and why should anyone care? A reaction to Slavin and Klein. *Educational Researcher, 27*(7), 22–29.

Popper, K. R. (1952). *The open society and its enemies* (Vols. 1 & 2). London, UK: Routledge and Kegan Paul.

Porter, A. C., & Polikoff, M. S. (2007). NCLB: State interpretations, early effects and suggestions for reauthorisation. *Social Policy Report, XXI*(4).

Pressley, M., Raphael, L., Gallagher, J. D., & Di Bella, J. (2004). Providence–St. Mel School: How a school that works for African American students works. *Journal of Educational Psychology, 96*(2), 216–235.

Raikes, H., Pan, B. A., Luze, G., Tamis-LeMonda, C., Brooks-Gunn, J., Constantine, J., et al. (2006). Mother–child book reading in low-income families: Correlates and outcomes during the first three years of life. *Child Development, 77*(4), 924–953.

Ramey, C. T., & Ramey, S. L. (1998). Early intervention and early experience. *American Psychologist, 53*(3), 109–120.

Raphael, T. E., Au, I. K. H., & Goldman, S. R. (2009). Whole school instructional improvement through the standards-based change process. In J. Hoffman & Y. Goodman (Eds.), *Changing literacies for changing times*. London: Routledge.

Raudenbush, S. W. (2005). Learning from attempts to improve schooling: The contribution of methodological diversity. *Educational Researcher, 34*(5), 25–31.

Resource Management Act, 69. New Zealand (1991).

Risley, T., & Wolf, M. (1973). Strategies for analyzing behavioural change over time. In J. Nesselroade & H. Reese (Eds.), *Life-span developmental psychology: Methodology issues* (pp. 177–183). New York, NY: Academic Press.

Robinson, V., & Lai, M. K. (2006). *Practitioner research for educators: a guide to improving classrooms and schools*. Thousand Oaks, CA: Corwin Press.

Rogoff, B. (1995). Observing sociocultural activity on three planes: Participatory appropriation, guided participation, and guided apprenticeship. In J. V. Wertsch, P. del Rio, & A. Alvarez (Eds.), *Sociocultural studies: History, action, and mediation* (pp. 139–164). New York, NY: Cambridge University Press.

Rogoff, B. (2003). *The cultural nature of human development*. Oxford, England: Oxford University Press.

Rogoff, B., Bartlett, L., & Turkanis, C. G. (2001). Lessons about learning as a community. In B. Rogoff, C. G. Turkanis, & L. Bartlett (Eds.), *Learning together: Children and adults in a school community* (pp. 3–17). Oxford: Oxford University Press.

Ross, S. M., & Smith, L. J. (2001). Success for All in Memphis: Raising reading performance in high-poverty schools. In R. E. Slavin, & N. A. Madden (Eds.), *Success for All: Research and reform in elementary education* (pp. 49–78). Mahwah, NJ: Lawrence Erlbaum.

Rowan, B., Correnti, R., Miller, R., & Camburn, E. M. (2009). School improvement by design: Lessons from a study of comprehensive school reform programs. In G. Sykes, B. L. Schnieder, & D. N. Plank (Eds.), *Handbook of education policy research* (pp. 637–651). Washington, DC: American Educational Research Association, Routledge.

Sampson, R. J., Sharkey, P., & Raudenbush, S. W. (2008). Durable effects of concentrated disadvantage on verbal ability among African–American children. *Proceedings of the National Academy of Sciences of the USA, 105*(3), 845–852.

Schleicher, A. (2007). *Is the sky the limit to educational performance?* Paper presented at the CRPP 2007 conference: Redesigning pedagogy: Culture, knowledge and understanding, Singapore, May.

Shapin, S. (1995). *A social history of truth: Civility and science in seventeenth century England.* Chicago, IL: Chicago University Press.

Sidman, M. (1960). *Tactics of scientific research.* New York, NY: Basic Books.

Siegler, R. S. (1986). *Children's thinking.* Englewood Cliffs NJ: Prentice Hall.

Skinner, B. F. (1968). *The technology of teaching.* New York, NY: Appleton-Century-Crofts.

Slavin, R. F., & Madden, N. A. (2001). Summary of research on Success for All and Roots and Wings. In R. F. Slavin & N. A. Madden (Eds.), *Success for All: Research and reform of elementary education* (pp. 17–48). Mahwah NJ: Lawrence Erlbaum.

Slavin, R. F., & Madden, N. A. (Eds.). (2001). *Success For All: Research and reform in elementary education.* Mahwah, NJ: Lawrence Erlbaum.

Snow, C. E., Burns, M. S., & Griffith, P. L. (1998). *Preventing reading difficulties in young children.* Washington DC: Department of Education.

Solzhenitsyn, A. (1976). *Warning to the western world.* London, UK: British Broadcasting Corporation.

Stannard, J., & Huxford, L. (2007). *The literacy game: The story of the National Literacy Strategy.* London, UK: Routledge.

Stanovich, K. E. (1986). Matthew effects in reading: Some consequences of individual differences in the acquisition of literacy. *Reading Research Quarterly, 21*(4), 360–407.

Swanborn, M., & de Glopper, K. (1999). Incidental word learning while reading: A meta-analysis. *Review of Educational Research, 69*(3), 261–285.

Taylor, B. M., Pearson, P. D., Clark, K. F., & Walpole, S. (1999). Effective schools/accomplished teachers. *Reading Teacher, 53*(2), 156–159.

Taylor, B. M., Pearson, P. D., Peterson, D., & Rodriguez, M. C. (2005). The CIERA school change framework: An evidence-based approach to professional development and school reading improvement. *Reading Research Quarterly, 40*(1), 40–69.

Tharp, R. G., Estrada, P., Dalton, S. S., & Yamauchi, L. A. (2000). *Teaching transformed: Achieving excellence, fairness, inclusion and harmony.* Boulder, CO: Westview Press.

Timperley, H., Phillips, G., & Wiseman, J. (2003). *The sustainability of professional development in literacy: Parts one and two.* Wellington, NZ: Auckland Uniservices Ltd for the Ministry of Education.

Timperley, H., Wilson, A., Barrar, H., & Fung, I. (2007). *Teacher professional learning and development: Best Evidence Synthesis (BES).* Wellington, NZ: Ministry of Education.

Valsiner, J. (1994). Culture and human development: A co-constructionist perspective. *Annals of Theoretical Psychology, 10,* 247–298.

Vanneman, A., Hamilton, L., Baldwin Anderson, J., & Rahman, T. (2009). *Achievement gaps: How black and white students in public schools perform in mathematics and reading on the National Assessment of Educational Progress.* Washington, DC: National Centre for Educational Statistics, Institute of Education Sciences, US Department of Education.

Vogt, L. A., & Au, K. H. P. (1994). *The role of teachers' guided reflection in effecting positive program change.* Paper presented at the Annual Meeting of the American Educational Research Association.

Watson, R. I. (1960). The history of psychology: A neglected area. *American Psychologist, 15*(5), 251–255.

Weinstein, R. (2002). *Reaching higher: The power of expectations in schooling.* Cambridge, MA: Harvard University Press.

Wenger, E. (1998). *Communities of practice: Learning, meaning and identity.* Cambridge, UK: Cambridge University Press.

What Works Clearinghouse. (2009a). *Reading Recovery: What Works Clearinghouse intervention report*. Princeton, NJ: What Works Clearinghouse.

What Works Clearinghouse. (2009b). *Success for All: What Works Clearinghouse report*. Princeton, NJ: What Works Clearinghouse.

Whitehurst, G. J., & Lonigan, C. J. (2001). Emergent literacy: Development from prereaders to readers. In S. B. Neuman, & D. Dickinson (Eds.), *Handbook of Early Childhood Literacy* (pp. 11–29). New York, NY: Guilford Press.

Wilkinson, R. G. (2005). *The impact of inequality: How to make sick societies healthier*. London, UK: Routledge.

Wilkinson, R. G., & Pickett, K. (2009). *The spirit level: Why more equal societies almost always do better*. London, UK: Allen Lane.

Williams, J., & Bersin, A. (2006). Extreme makeover: Two failing San Diego schools get new start as charters. November 28, 2010, from http://www.educationsector.org/analysis/analysis_show.htm?doc_id=428171.

Wood, D., Bruner, J. S., & Ross, G. (1976). The role of tutoring in problem solving. *Journal of Child Psychology and Psychiarty, 17*, 89–100.

Wundt, W. (1916). *Elements of folk psychology* (E. L. Schaub, Trans.). New York, NY: Macmillan.

Young, N. (1979). *Rust never sleeps* [Record]. San Francisco: Reprise/WEA.

Zigler, E., & Styfco, S. J. (1994). Head Start: Criticisms in a constructive context. *American Psychologist, 49*(2), 127–132.

INDEX